Routledge Revivals

Local Government Finance

During recent years the financing of local government has become a key issue in developed countries. This book, originally published in 1988 looks at attempts to reform local finance in the UK, the USA, Canada, Australia, France, Norway, Sweden and the Republic of Ireland. Case studies of attempts to bolster or reform local government finance cover a wide range of leading industrialised economies. These are preceded by theoretical chapters on the nature of fiscal federalism and fiscal crises, followed by an international overview of local taxing and spending.

Local Government Finance

International Perspectives

Edited by Ronan Paddison and Stephen Bailey

First published in 1988 by Routledge

This edition first published in 2024 by Routledge
4 Park Square, Milton Park, Abingdon, Oxon, OX14 4RN
and by Routledge
605 Third Avenue, New York, NY 10158.

Routledge is an imprint of the Taylor & Francis Group, an informa business

ISBN 13: 978-1-032-84660-6 (hbk)
ISBN 13: 978-1-003-51436-7 (ebk)
ISBN 13: 978-1-032-84665-1 (pbk)
Book DOI 10.4324/9781003514367

LOCAL GOVERNMENT FINANCE

International Perspectives

Edited by
RONAN PADDISON and STEPHEN BAILEY

ROUTLEDGE
London and New York

First published 1988 by
Routledge
11 New Fetter Lane, London EC4P 4EE
Reprinted 1989

Printed by Antony Rowe Ltd, Chippenham, Wiltshire

British Library Cataloguing in Publication Data

Local government finance: international
perspectives.
1. Local finance
I. Paddison, Ronan. II. Bailey, S.J.
336'.014'1722 HJ9105

ISBN 0-415-00529-9

CONTENTS

Contents

CONTRIBUTORS

STEPHEN BAILEY, Department of Economics, Glasgow College of Technology, Cowcaddens Road, Glasgow, Scotland, UK

NEIL COLLINS, Magee College, University of Ulster, Londonderry, Northern Ireland

TORE HANSEN, FAFO Lilletorget, 1, 0184 Oslo 1, Norway

R.B. HASLAM, County Manager, Limerick County Council, Limerick, Ireland

ERNST JONSSON, Department of Economics, University of Stockholm, Stockholm, Sweden

TERENCE KARRAN, Department of Economics and Public Policy, Leeds Polytechnic, Leeds, UK

MICHAEL KEATING, Department of Politics, University of Strathclyde, Glasgow, Scotland, UK

DAVID KING, Department of Economics, University of Stirling, Stirling, Scotland, UK

DESMOND KING, Department of Politics, University of Edinburgh, Edinburgh, Scotland, UK

DOUGLAS McREADY, Department of Economics, Wilfred Laurier University, Waterloo, Ontario, Canada

RONAN PADDISON, Department of Geography, University of Glasgow, Glasgow, Scotland, UK

KIERON WALSH, INLOGOV, University of Birmingham, Birmingham, UK

1 INTRODUCTION

British readers of this volume, at least, will scarcely need reminding of the reasons why an edited volume on local government finance within the economically advanced nations is timeous. Quite apart from the intrinsic academic value in examining current issues in local finance within such countries, the problem has particular relevance for Britain with the impending introduction of the community charge (or poll tax) and system of assigned revenues, and the abolition of domestic rates. The reform, radical enough in itself, marks an important stage in a long history of debate, centring around dissatisfaction with property rating on the one hand, and the relative merits of alternative local taxes on the other. Contentious as the community charge is, it is unlikely that its implementation - already programmed for Scotland by 1989, and extended to England and Wales in legislation introduced in the third Thatcher administration - will prove to be the last word; local government finance will remain on the political agenda.

It was against the background of the British reform proposals that the germ of the idea for this book, dealing with the international perspective, and its sister volume dealing specifically with the domestic scene, The Reform of Local Government Finance in Britain (Bailey and Paddison, Routledge 1988), emerged. Following a seminar held in 1986 under the auspices of the Centre for Urban and Regional Research, University of Glasgow, at which both the domestic and the international perspectives were discussed through a series of papers, it was decided to broaden the scope of the discussion by inviting further authors to develop specific themes not covered in the seminar and by splitting the analysis into the two volumes.

While the subject of local government finance has particular topicality in Britain, a brief glance at the field shows that the problems which it raises - those of equity, local accountability and autonomy, for example - are recurrent and that in many of the industrial nations, reform, usually incremental rather than radical, provides a continuing source of political debate. The reasons are not hard to find. The system of financing local government, depending mainly on the mix of tax options employed and fiscal transfers, underpins its autonomy. In the liberal democracy one of the chief merits and purposes of local government, it is argued, is the extent to which it caters for diverse local political demands. Local government is a vehicle, then, by which to meet the demands of territorial pluralism, though its ability to do so rests in large part on the strength of its local fiscal base and the degree of local fiscal autonomy.

In analysing local government finance in a number of economically advanced nations the objective of this volume has been to present this not so much as a set of comparative essays in any strict sense or a comprehensive survey of local government finance, but rather, within a broad framework, to highlight the different types of problem within each country and their attempted resolution. To adopt a comparative perspective, however attractive academically, courts the danger of over-simplifying the complex political and administrative milieux in which different national systems of local government operate. States differ too widely in their constitutional make-up, modes of decentralisation and background patterns of economic and cultural development to facilitate ready comparisons. This is not to argue that the comparative method applied to the analysis of local government finance is misplaced: as Karran (Chapter 4) argues from a statistical perspective it is certainly plausible to draw cross-national comparisons. In practice, however, such studies reveal the bewildering complexity of local finance systems, so that the differences are more apparent than the similarities.

At the level of principles, however, the structure of local government finance confronts similar broad issues whatever the state under scrutiny and it is this generalized level of analysis that provides the framework within which this book is structured. David King provides the basic framework within Chapter 2 by discussing four main issues which are raised by fiscal federalism. These are autonomy, accountability, equity and macroeconomic considerations. The question of autonomy lies at the heart of local government, and in fiscal terms this is expressed as to how local taxation should be arranged to promote autonomy. In scrutinizing accountability King examines the difficulties of devising systems of local finance which ensure local governments are able to deliver services efficiently, while equity is examined at both the intra- and inter-authority levels. Finally, by their taxing and spending policies local governments may threaten the effectiveness of the central government's macroeconomic policies, harbouring the possibility that the centre will seek to restrain the localities.

These four facets provide the basic issues to which the country case studies in different ways are addressed. The analyses do not subscribe rigidly to the issues raised by King, but rather use these as a backdrop against which to discuss the main emphases in contemporary local government finance in their respective countries.

While David King develops normative arguments underpinning fiscal federalism, the arguments as to why fiscal stress and crisis have become apparent in local government are developed by Walsh in Chapter 3, extending the basic framework. After examining macro-theories of fiscal crisis, from the Marxist and liberal perspectives, and macro-theories, particularly from the viewpoint of the public choice theorists, Walsh argues that the roots of the crisis in Britain lie within the actions of the state itself, and the interests and institutions which underpin these. In effect, under the Thatcher administrations the fiscal crisis of the state has been translated into a crisis of local government finance, so that the centre has been able to 'pass on' the crisis, exacerbating the conflict in central-local relations. While Walsh confines his argument largely to the British case, some of his arguments are echoed elsewhere. The argument that weakening the institutions of opposition, those of the localities, is essential to the success of cutting back public expenditure is reiterated in the United States, as Des King shows (Chapter 5).

Terence Karran's international statistical overview of local taxing and spending provides a linking chapter both between the preceding largely theoretical discussions and the country case-studies, and also by virtue of scrutinizing the uniqueness of the British reform proposals. Initially, Karran examines the structure of local government and the range of functions which are devolved to it, particularly within Europe. Compared to its European counterparts, Britain is atypical by the lack of a regional tier, and the type of functions for which it is responsible. The reform proposals in Britain highlight its atypicality: indeed in the proposals for assigned revenues and poll taxes being used exclusively as the basis for local tax funding, Britain will be unique. Yet, as Karran shows elsewhere, the justification for such radical reform is hardly based on cogent arguments, concluding in broadly similar vein to the preceding chapter that the problem is deliberately the making of the centre.

The remaining essays are devoted to the country case-studies. The countries selected were chosen to be representative of a broad spectrum of constitutional and political environments in which the status of local government varies from being relatively 'weak', as in Australia, to the functionally much stronger systems of Europe. Local government finance within both federal and unitary states is examined, the first within the 'classic' federations of the United States, Canada and Australia, contrasted with the more homogeneous systems represented by the European unitary states of France, Norway, Sweden, Ireland and Britain. As the analyses of the United States and Australia show, in particular, intergovernmental relations in the federal state, added to their essentially more decentralist nature, introduce a different factor affecting local government finance. Thus by comparison with Britain and other European local government systems, American local governments - though in some states more than others - enjoy a greater measure of autonomy over the types of local taxes which can be used and how they can be used. In Australia federation and federalism has had a different influence: the states are politically strong but fiscally weak, because of a marked vertical fiscal imbalance within the Commonwealth. Local government has traditionally been a weak 'third tier' of government, unrecognised by most State constitutions, and in which it is closely controlled by the States. No equivalent to the Home Rule authorities of states like Ohio or Missouri characterizes the Australian federation.

While the country essays address the issues identified by David King the analyses give varying emphases to these according to their significance within the country under observation. From the British perspective - and the arguments over each of the four issues as they have developed within Britain are discussed by Stephen Bailey in the final case study - the lessons to be learnt from examining the experience of other countries is not so much what kinds of local fiscal options could or could not be improved, but the insights which it provides in helping to understand the present state of flux in Britain. If the British reform proposals are radical, then they are no less so than was the abolition of domestic rating in Ireland in the late 1970's. But radical reform, as Haslam and Collins show in the Irish case, is not only contentious but did not pave the way for the introduction of an alternative method of financing local government which ensured its autonomy and accountability, while at least partly meeting the needs of equity.

Perhaps the basic lesson to be drawn from the case studies, and one which has relevance not only to Britain but to most, if not all, countries is that systems of local government finance are never static, and that their reform owes as much to political expediency and ideology as it does to considerations of economic rationale.

2 FISCAL FEDERALISM

David N. King

INTRODUCTION

There is a fairly extensive theoretical literature on fiscal federalism which covers many aspects of local authority finance. The purpose of this first chapter is to see what the main implications from this literature are for those who are concerned with devising schemes of finance in practice. It is perhaps a little daunting to present such a chapter at the start of a volume which contains analyses of the arrangements in a wide variety of countries, for the practices in the real world tend to depart radically from theoretical prescriptions, and this might be taken to suggest that the theory must be sadly lacking. However, theoreticians could retort that the problem is rather that decisions on local finance are typically taken on the basis of political considerations rather than theoretical niceties. Readers must form their own judgements about the reasons for the discrepancies between theory and practice, taking each case on its merits.

Perhaps one of the political reasons which accounts for some of the discrepancies is that theoretical models tend to explain how an ideal system of subcentral government might be established and financed, while politicians are at best concerned with relatively modest adjustments to an existing set-up. Even the present proposals in the UK for replacing domestic rates with a community charge could be seen as concerned with an adjustment despite being arguably the most radical change in local finance for nearly 500 years. After all, it is essentially just a proposal for modifying the basis on which the percentage of local revenue put up by the domestic taxpayer should be divided between individual taxpayers. There are no government proposals at present for major reforms of the structure of local government - or its functions - despite the support for some form of regional government by the opposition parties.

However, it seems worth exploring what might be done if a country were starting from scratch, even if it were accepted that there was no likelihood of making the major reforms which would be needed for a country to move from its present position to the prescribed one, for such an exploration might at least be useful in indicating the most suitable direction for piecemeal policies to take. With this in mind, the first section of this chapter - headed 'autonomy' - looks at the role of subcentral government. The objective of any system of local finance must be to help local authorities perform the role allotted to them, and it is not possible to devise such a system without considering what that role should be. The first section considers also how local taxation should be arranged to promote autonomy.

The second section - headed 'accountability' - looks at the problems of devising systems of finance which encourage local authorities to provide their services at efficient or optimal levels. It also considers whether there is more of a problem in finding suitable local taxes than in finding suitable central taxes. The third section - headed 'equity' - considers two aspects of equity. One aspect involves equity between people living in the same area; the other concerns equity between people living in different areas. The final section - headed 'macroeconomics' - considers how far local authorities can threaten the effectiveness of the central government's macroeconomic policies, and it also shows that GNP per head tends to be highest in countries with substantial devolution of taxes to states and local authorities.

AUTONOMY

The role of local government

The first question which must arise in devising a scheme of finance for local government is what is the role of the local authorities concerned. Much of the fiscal federalism literature supposes that their role is to provide their allotted services in varying ways and levels in accordance with the varying wishes of people in different parts of the country. As Oates (1972, pp. 11-12) has noted, economic efficiency is attained by providing that mix of output that best reflects the preferences of the individuals who make up society; if all individuals are compelled to provide the same level of output of a publicly provided good or service when variations in consumption among different subsets of the population are possible, then the result is an inefficient allocation of resources, unless, of course, subcentral provision carries with it disadvantages outweighing this gain.

Working on this basis, it is possible to construct a model showing how the optimal size of authority can be found for any publicly-provided service (see King, 1984, ch.2). Assuming that preferences do vary in different parts of the country, there are clearly gains to be derived by devolving the service onto a tier of subcentral authorities, and there is a case for making these authorities very small to enable them to cater as effectively as possible with taste variations. On the other hand, there may be advantages in having large authorities. One possible advantage is that such authorities might be able to exploit economies of scale in the provision of their services. Another is that local services might generate benefits for non-residents, and such external benefits will typically be ignored by local citizens when deciding what types and levels of service to provide; large authorities mean that there are fewer people outside each area and so fewer externalities, and hence the degree to which each area is likely to under-provide will be diminished. Of course, it may be possible to reduce, if not wholly remove, the externality problem if the government gives each area matching specific grants for each service affected, for such grants should result in higher outlays than the citizens would otherwise opt for. It may also be possible to ease the economies of scale problem if small authorities can purchase their services from a large private contractor, but this may not always be a very satisfactory arrangement since the authorities may then find it difficult to purchase quite the type of service they want.

However, taking these factors into account, it is possible to derive an optimum size of authority for each publicly-provided service. Of course, the optimum size is likely to be different for each service, and efficiency in administration could well suggest that a small number of tiers of authorities be established, each tier handling the services for which its size makes it most appropriate. Incidentally, the optimum size for some services may well be the country as a whole, a situation which calls for central government provision. This will tend to occur with services where externalities and/or economies of scale are significant and where local variations in tastes are modest: defence, foreign embassies and consulates, and main road networks would be typical examples. In fact, defence could well be a service where economies of scale are never exhausted, a point which has led to the formation of international defence organisations such as NATO.

Such a view of local government seems eminently plausible, and indeed given that local authorities are run by elected councils which are presumably intended to respond to local wishes, it is a view which might seem to be incontrovertible. However, it is not a view which seems to prevail in all democracies. In Japan, for instance, as noted by Yonehara (1981, p.57), there is detailed central control of local authorities to the extent that, in the case of construction works, even brands of materials and parts are sometimes specified. But there, apparently, it is the government's policy to secure equal local services for all citizens wherever they may live. Yonehara argues that though such equality may not seem desirable, 'differences in preferences appear to be insignificant ... the demand is for services similar in quality to those of neighbouring localities'. As it happens, much the same applies in West Germany. Of course, one obvious question arises in cases like these: if people actually want uniformity, then presumably free local authorities would respond to provide it, so why does the government enforce it?

There is clearly a difference between this view of local government and the orthodox Oates view noted earlier. But is it really a fundamental difference of type or merely one of degree? The key to answering this question lies in deciding whether or not the local authorities in the countries concerned are mere agents of the central government. Presumably they are not, for then there would clearly be no point in having them run by locally elected bodies. More realistically, perhaps, they should be seen more like subcentral authorities elsewhere but subject to greater constraints. There is a spectrum of constraint. States in federal countries, for instance, have very few constraints. But other subcentral authorities may be subject to stringent minimum standards requirements on the one hand - perhaps defended on the grounds that local services have external benefits - and by upper limits on tax or spending levels - perhaps defended on the grounds that control is needed for macroeconomic purposes. The degree of constraint may vary from country to country according to how much need for it there is felt to be. To take a metaphor. Some local authorities may have complete freedom, some may be under house arrest, and others may be tethered on a short lead; but unless thy are bound and gagged there is still room for movement and so still a case for elections to see what movement is required.

The functions of local government

The last section gave a broad overview of the case for local government as providing services where tastes vary from area to area. Does the argument apply to all the functions provided by the public sector? The general consensus seems to be that local government will play a sizeable part in the allocation function, but that it should play no part in the stabilization function and only a modest part in the redistribution function.

There are two separate problems with local government in the context of stabilization. First, local authorities could hardly be given powers to control the money stock and so interest rates, or powers to have their own exchange rates. Thus the authorities would have few instruments at their disposal. Indeed, they would be forced to rely chiefly on fiscal policy, running deficits or surpluses as seemed most appropriate. Second, the effects of a surplus or a deficit run by any one area would have very little effect on demand and so on output, employment or prices in the area itself. For though, for example, a cut in local taxes might well raise spending by local citizens, the high marginal propensity to import likely to apply to most, if not all, local authorities, means that most of the effect of that spending would actually be felt elsewhere.

There is more interest, perhaps, in allowing local authorities a role in regional policy. Indeed, local authorities in the UK do already have some modest powers to attract industry to their areas, but their expenditure is very small compared to the central government's own outlays in terms of tax reliefs and grants. Arguably, the central government should hand the funds it uses over to local authorities to use for the same purpose, in the hope that they, being perhaps even more anxious to attract industry, would spend the funds more effectively. However, such a policy would not increase the tax needs of local authorities and so has little relevance to the current debate on local finance.

The principal problem with local government in the context of redistribution is that it would not be easy for local authorities to pursue different policies, even if tastes varied. The snag is that any area which sought a relatively high degree of redistribution would be liable to drive away the rich, for whom the tax burden would be great, and liable to attract poor immigrants, for whom the area seemed favourable. Such migration of the rich and poor could soon make the redistribution policy untenable. More critically, all local authorities might eventually have to follow the policies set by whichever area operated the least degree of redistribution in order not to lose rich citizens to that area or to gain poor ones from it. Of course, any tax-plus-expenditure combination chosen by a local authority is bound to have some redistribution effects, and Tiebout (1956) has pointed out the advantages of allowing people to vote-with-their-feet for the combination which suits them best. It would seem best, though, for the central government to assume the main redistribution role.

There is, in fact, a further role of government to consider beyond the three discussed so far, and this is what might be termed the legislative role. Local authorities are typically given some powers here, making by-laws concerning matters such as parks and generally having powers over development and effluent discharge. But there is surely a case for considering the devolution to local government of a number of powers currently held at the centre. The opening hours of public houses and the question of opening shops on Sundays are matters that are now handled separately for Scotland and England with no dire consequences, and it is doubtful if there would be a problem if they were handled by regions and counties. Further, the example of Oregon's campaign for a cleaner environment raises the question of whether local authorities should be allowed much wider powers. Of course, states in the United States can even decree whether the death penalty should be used in their states. Few people, perhaps, would argue for this power to be devolved to regions and counties, but how about devolving the power to decide if blood sports be allowed, or pornographic literature be sold or football hooligans be given custodial sentences? There seems scope for at least considering such matters. Such devolution could enable laws to vary according to local preferences and might well be useful in enabling the effects of different approaches to be compared. One incidental advantage of devolving legislative functions is that they create very little extra in the way of local authority revenue requirements.

Fiscal Federalism

Autonomy and taxation

The last section has suggested that local authorities are, typically, concerned primarily with resource allocation. Common functions concern the provision of roads - or at least minor roads - schools, refuse collection and refuse disposal. Local authorities also tend to have a subsidiary role in redistribution and thereby have some housing and personal social service functions. Assuming that these functions are handled subcentrally, so that some account can be taken of variations in tastes, what implications are there for local taxation? There seem to be three chief implications.

First, it is surely necessary that local authorities actually finance a large share of their expenditure needs through their own taxes. The alternative to locally-raised revenue is centrally raised revenue distributed as grants. The problem with this alternative is that the central government is responsible to its own taxpayers for the way in which they are spent. It is unlikely that any central government would, and very debatable whether any such government should, distribute grants without exercising fairly close control over the way in which they are spent. This point suggests that the most pressing need in the UK is to find a new local tax to replace some central government grants, not one to replace domestic rates.

It is possible to counter this argument by saying that the central government should be responsible for providing local authorities with at least the resources needed to provide services at centrally determined minimum standard levels. On this basis, local taxes need serve only to finance any 'topping-up' that local authorities might seek to do. However, it is not <u>necessary</u> for the centre to provide the resources needed through the grant system, for it would be sufficient merely to ensure that each local authority had an adequate taxable capacity. And a decision to provide the resources could be the start of a move along a slippery slope of central control. For instance, a government might decide that schools should meet minimum standards expressed in terms of teacher-pupil ratios, teaching pupils to sit for certain externally set examinations and minimum levels of equipment such as classroom computers. It might settle for this degree of control if local authorities provide their own finance; but if it provides the finance itself through grants, then it might well be tempted to impose further controls over, say, whether selection was permitted, the pay rates for teachers, detailed syllabus requirements, sex education lessons and policies for school meals.

A second implication for local taxation of the need for local autonomy is that local authorities must have some discretion over the tax rates they set. This is necessary so that local authorities can respond to variations in tastes over the desired level of local expenditure. Put another way, it is necessary so that a local authority can respond to a desire for a higher - or lower - level of expenditure on one service without having to make a compensating adjustment in the level of expenditure on another.

It is interesting to look a little further at this point. It can perhaps be argued that for each tax there is an upper rate that would be generally felt acceptable. For instance, there comes a point with taxes on fuel or car licences when it might be felt that an unfair share of the total tax burden was falling on motorists. There comes a point with taxes on income when it is felt that rates are confiscatory, or act as a deterrent to work effort, or simply cause a brain-drain. And there comes a point with regressive taxes such as VAT, or domestic rates, or a community charge, when it is felt that no increase could be allowed for fear of its effect on the poorer payers. Now suppose a government paid lip-service to the ideal of local authorities being able to choose their own budget levels, but actually wanted to keep their budgets close to the level needed to meet minimum standard requirements. A good arrangement would be for it to use grants to finance, say, 75 per cent of the revenue needed to meet such requirements, and to allow local authorities to use a community charge for the rest, carefully devising this balance so that the rate of community charge that had to be set was close to the upper toleration limit. In that case, an area wanting to raise its expenditure by one-quarter would have to double its community charge; this might be deemed unacceptable by its electors so that only much smaller budget increases could be made. Note that most electors might be willing themselves to pay more in local taxes, but might reject a higher community charge for fear of its effect on the poor.

In contrast, suppose the central government financed 75 per cent through grants and allowed local authorities a local income tax at an initial standard rate of 4.5 per cent to finance the rest, while setting a rate of 24.5 per cent itself. In these circumstances, local authorities could double their tax receipts by raising their income tax rate to 9 per cent. This would raise the combined income tax rate in their area from 29 per cent to 33.5 per cent, a rise which might well be thought perfectly acceptable. The upshot of this analysis is simple. If local authorities are to have effective control over their budgets, then they must be able to raise or lower their budgets without having disproportionate effects on the rates at which the taxes they levy are paid. One most straightforward way of arranging this is probably to ensure that local taxes account for a large slice of local authority income. This may well mean ensuring that local authorities have access to two or three different taxes.

ACCOUNTABILITY

The need for accountability

It has been argued that one important attraction of a system of local government is that it makes it possible for the level of public expenditure to vary from area to area in accordance with local wishes. However, if local authorities are to be allowed discretion over their budget levels, then it is clear that they should operate in a financial framework which promotes optimum or efficient budgets. That is, they should be encouraged to provide services up to - but not beyond - the point where the costs of an extra unit of service equal the benefits from that unit. This, in turn, means devising a financial framework where local electors are fully aware of the costs of increases in local services - or, to put it another way, where local authorities are fully accountable to their citizens for such increases.

In practice, it is very easy to devise a financial framework which may encourage overspending. This can be done either by choosing unsuitable taxes or by operating an unsatisfactory grant scheme. Consider taxes first. One danger with local taxes is the possibility of tax exporting. This arises if the incidence of local taxes is borne in part by non-residents, for then outsiders effectively subsidise services and encourage overspending. To see this, consider the extreme case where the whole incidence of a local tax was shifted on to outsiders. In such circumstances, the local authority setting the tax would satisfy its own citizens best by raising expenditure until the benefit from the last unit provided was zero. It needs a detailed analysis of possible local taxes and their incidence to explain just how they fare on this score, but the most promising are doubtless a community charge, a personal income tax and a domestic property tax (King, 1984, pp.274-9). In large areas, though, where inter-area shopping expeditions were rare and costly, taxes such as VAT or alcohol and tobacco duties could also be satisfactory.

Even if taxes were not exported at all, there could still be problems of promoting efficient budgets. One possibility is that the incidence of the tax may not be well spread out among the citizens of a local authority. For instance, a poll tax levied on all citizens who were left-handed would not be exported, but it would be paid by only a minority of citizens. The right-handed majority might well respond to such a tax by seeking to expand the local budget until the marginal benefit to them of local services was zero, well below the marginal cost. If a community charge, a domestic property tax and a local income tax are compared, then there can be no doubt that a local income tax does least well on this criterion, for many low-income households pay no income tax at all. On the other hand, all households will be liable for a domestic property tax or a community charge; at least they will be unless tax rebates are paid to them that meet the whole cost of their tax payments. Incidentally, the domestic property tax will clearly fall on the occupiers of dwellings which are owner-occupied, and it will fall - at least in large part - on the occupants of tenanted property, irrespective of whether the landlord or tenant is formally responsible for payments. It is sometimes argued, though, that not all electors pay the domestic property tax; indeed roughly half do not, mostly because they are spouses or adult children of householders who do (HMSO, 1986, p.6). However, it is likely that the incidence will always be spread on to the spouses, if not always to the adult children.

Another possibility that can arise with local taxes is that people might be unaware of how much of them they are paying and hence might be unaware of the cost of local services. This could easily happen if local authorities relied on a corporation tax or on indirect taxes such as VAT on alcohol and tobacco duties. It is possible, too, that taxpayers have a less clear idea of how much they pay in income tax than in domestic property taxes or community charges, particularly if income taxes are deducted at source by their employers.

A further problem for accountability can arise from the way in which grants are paid. Essentially, grants can be divided into lump-sum grants and matching grants; with the latter, payments to a local authority depend on its expenditure or tax levels. Generally, matching grants rise when a local authority raises its spending. This means that local authorities which seek to raise their service levels will in fact have part of the cost met out of extra grants. In other words, matching grants act as a sort of subsidy and can thereby encourage overspending. The only complete solution to this problem is to replace all matching grants by lump-sum ones, but this leads to inequity between people in different areas. The reason for this and a way of mitigating the problem are noted later in the discussion of equity.

Accountability and central government

It is not difficult to follow the arguments for devising a system of local government finance which - by making local authorities clearly accountable to their electors - promotes optimum or efficient local budgets. This may mean eschewing taxes on spending (other than domestic rates) along with corporation tax on the grounds that the burden is not spread out sufficiently widely. But why, then, are these taxes acceptable at central government level? Does not the use of such taxes encourage people to vote for excessive central government budgets?

It certainly seems clear that there is a danger of excessive central budgets if such taxes are used. A major reason why the UK government is concerned to abolish domestic rates is that they are unpopular, and it is probable that a major reason for their unpopularity is their very clear perceptibility. The corollary of this point is that the relative tolerance shown to central taxes could be taken to mean that they are, typically, less perceptible. If this is so, then this seems to be an argument against them.

Perhaps the only real difference between the local authority situation and the central government one is that local authorities usually have access to just one or two taxes whereas the central government has access to a wide range. Suppose, for instance, that local authorities rely on either a domestic property tax or a local income tax. With the property tax, young adults living at home could be tempted to vote for local extravagances in the belief that they would escape the tax cost; with the income tax, retired people on low pensions might vote for extravagances in the belief that they would escape the cost. However, people will be much less willing to vote for central extravagance, for they know the central government could raise the finance needed through a whole range of taxes and thus ensure that no one wholly escapes the cost.

This line of argument seems to lead to two conclusions. First, there is a case for preferring taxes which are clearly perceptible and well spread out to those which are not. This might be an argument against reducing income taxes too far in favour of taxes on spending, at least in the eyes of a government concerned to reduce the demand for public expenditure. Secondly, there is a case for giving some of the most perceptible and well spread out taxes to each tier of government. This might be an argument for saying that if a community charge were introduced, then separate sums should be exacted by both the central government and by local authorities.

EQUITY

Equity within areas

Suppose that a local authority's services are largely financed through taxes. How should the tax burden be apportioned among the authority's citizens? This is an important question because its answer may indicate that some taxes would be more suitable than others. It is a question which can be approached in a variety of ways.

Suppose, to begin with, that the authority's services had the characteristics of a pure public good in that they yielded benefits which were equal for all its citizens. In such circumstances, a poll tax which exacted equal amounts from all its citizens might seem to be the fairest and most equitable possibility. Such a tax could be seen as a charge: all would pay equal amounts for equal benefits, just as all citizens visiting, say, a zoo would pay equal amounts. However, it is possible to construct a counter argument. If the local authority provides 'normal' goods or services, for which demand rises with income, then the marginal valuation curves for its output will be higher for rich citizens than for poor ones. In turn, the rich will place a higher total valuation than the poor on their access to the same level of benefits. Under such circumstances, it would be arguable that local taxes should take more from the rich than the poor and so pay heed to the ability-to-pay principle.

It seems, then, that there would be room for

debate about the merits of a poll tax or community charge vis-à-vis less regressive taxes if local authorities provided pure public goods. In fact, they do not provide pure public goods. Perhaps the police service comes closest. In so far as the police promote law and order, it could be argued that their services confer equal benefits. On the other hand, in so far as their effect is to deter crime, and in so far as the overwhelming majority of crimes are ones of theft, it could be argued that the rich benefit more than the poor; however, this latter argument is weakened by the existence of insurance which means that the main effect of theft is distress rather than financial loss.

The case for an equal payment from all citizens is weaker for most - if not all - other services. In the UK, for instance, the largest item of expenditure is school education which, it might be supposed, mostly benefits school children. The tax finance must come from adults. A case might be made for levying a tax on parents only, but since education can be seen as a redistributive service benefiting people (children) on currently zero incomes, there would seem to be a strong case for using ability-to-pay finance. Again, it could be argued that the rich make more use of roads, that they generate more refuse, that their houses are spread out further and result in more costly street lighting per unit and so on.

This analysis suggests that it would be inappropriate for local authorities to rely wholly on a poll tax, whether levied on all citizens or confined to adults alone. However, it would not necessarily infringe equity for them to use such a tax to finance a share of their total revenue if the rest came from, say, government grants financed out of less regressive (or progressive) central taxes.

Equity between areas

The main purpose of considering equity between areas is to see if there is a case for equalization grants. In principle, such grants could be paid by

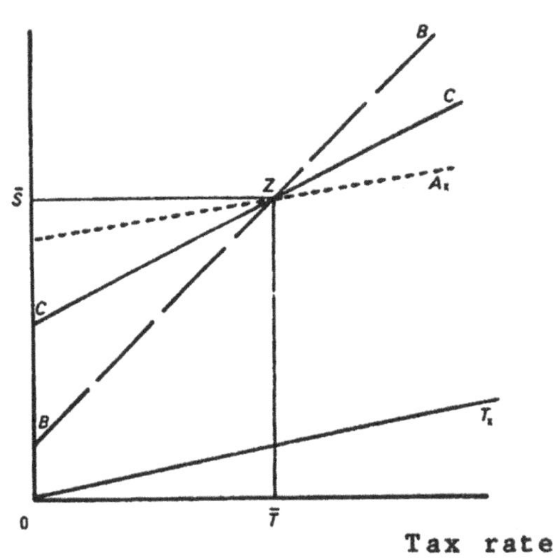

Figure 2.1: Area X

richer areas to poorer ones. In practice they are usually paid to most, if not all, areas by the central (or state) government with more going to poorer areas; this arrangement is used because the grants are generally intended to ease the pressure on local taxes in general as well as to help poor areas in particular. The ways in which a suitable scheme can be devised are illustrated in Figures 2.1 and 2.2 which relate respectively to two hypothetical areas, X and Y, which are reckoned to have access to a single local tax.

The horizontal axes show the possible rates at which the local tax could be set. The vertical axes show the possible service levels which the areas could achieve. The lines T_x and T_y show the service levels X and Y could achieve if they had to rely on the tax alone. The level at any common tax rate would be higher in Y than X. This might be because Y has a higher tax base per head or because it has lower needs - say fewer criminals to catch in relation to population.

The lines T_x and T_y show there is a prima

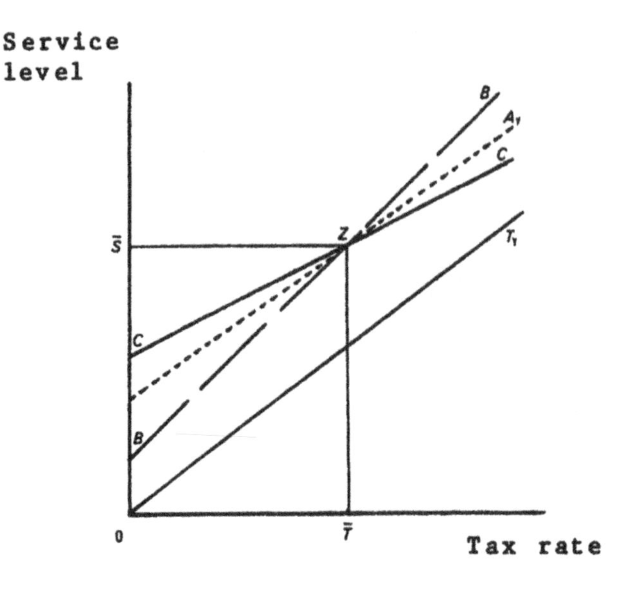

Figure 2.2: Area Y

facie case for equalization. If X and Y set the same tax rate and so take equal sums from people with equal individual tax bases - perhaps equal incomes, or equal domestic property values, depending on what the tax is - then those people will receive unequal benefits. The inequality can be removed by paying grants to X. Now it is sometimes suggested that such grants are not needed and that adjustments in property values will take care of the problem. Suppose the areas seek equal service levels so that X sets the higher tax rate. It is likely that property values will then be lower in X than in Y since X is otherwise, now, a less attractive area in which to live. The result is that potential migrants may be indifferent between cheap housing /high tax X and expensive housing/low tax Y; they may feel there is no need for grants. However, each time X and Y decide on equal rises in service levels, X's tax rate will rise more and so its property values will fall in relation to those in Y. It is difficult to see that X's existing citizens would regard their capital loss as offsetting their greater tax rise. They would argue that it would be more acceptable to give them grants to make the relationship between tax rates and service levels comparable to the relationship elsewhere.

For this reason, equalization schemes are often used. Most schemes start by specifying a standard tax rate $\bar{T}$ and a standard service level $\bar{S}$. Each area is told that if it set the rate $\bar{T}$, then it would be given enough grant to enable it to provide $\bar{S}$. Thus each area *could* opt for the point Z. Schemes differ in deciding what to do to areas which do not set $\bar{T}$. One option is to give them the same grant that they would have if they did set $\bar{T}$. In effect, this would put X and Y on the final schedules Ax and Ay, which are respectively parallel to T_x and T_y and thus show that the effects of the grants on services are the same at each tax rate. The trouble with such a scheme is that inequity can still occur. If X and Y set a common low rate below $\bar{T}$, then services would be higher in X: if they set a common high tax rate above $\bar{T}$, then services would be higher in Y.

This possible inequity can be removed by putting each area on to a common schedule, say BB, so that service levels can be similar at any common tax rate. The trouble with these BB schedules is that they are much steeper than T_x and T_y. Thus each area gets more grant as its tax rate rises. As noted earlier, this can encourage overspending. The scheme shown by the common schedules labelled CC is arguably better. Here, poor and more needy areas like X get grants which rise with tax increases while rich and less needy areas like Y get grants which fall with tax increases. Why is this better? First, because the effect of the scheme on aggregate local spending could be broadly neutral in that its tendency to cause overspending by some areas could be offset by its tendency to cause underspending elsewhere. Second, because it encourages poor and more needy areas to spend more while encouraging rich and less needy areas to spend less. This might well mean that it promotes greater equality of actual provision, for in the absence of such encouragement, poor/more needy areas would probably settle for lower service levels than rich/less needy areas.

One final point about grant schemes deserves to be made. An individual area's actual receipts are likely to be very sensitive to its assessed needs. Now needs have to be assessed on complicated formulae. If these are developed by central government departments, then there will always be a suspicion that formulae are used that favour the sorts of areas which the government wants to favour. There is much to be said for having the formulae developed by a non-political body, such as the Commonwealth Grants Commission in Australia.

MACROECONOMICS

The macroeconomic threat of local government

Central governments sometimes seek to exert some control over the activities of subcentral authorities on the grounds that it is necessary to do so in pursuit of their macroeconomic policies. The control may take various forms. On current account, for instance, upper limits may be set on subcentral authority tax rates, or subcentral authorities may be given little discretion over tax rates, or subcentral authorities may be given no discretion at all; and even where there is some discretion, local taxes may contribute such small amounts that large tax rate changes have little effect on expenditure. On capital account, subcentral authorities may find their borrowing powers severely regulated. Is there really a macroeconomic case for such controls?

The main macroeconomic concern must presumably arise in a situation where there was a widespread change in local spending, say a rise, and the implications of this rise would depend on how this rise was financed. If it was financed out of tax revenue, then any increase in subcentral spending might be largely - if not quite wholly - directly offset by a fall in private spending, so the net effects on aggregate demand could be very small. If it was financed by borrowing, then there would not be any direct fall in other spending so the effects could be more significant.

It seems, then, that an initial rise in local spending may be largely offset by falls in private spending if tax finance is used, but not if loan finance is used. Suppose there is a rise in local spending that is not wholly offset by a fall in private spending. What would the results be? In a closed economy, there would probably be some rise in interest rates, and so some 'crowding-out' of other spending, perhaps chiefly private investment, but also some rise in output and the price level.

In an open economy, the effects would depend on whether there was a fixed or floating exchange rate. With a fixed exchange rate, the interest rate would no doubt start to rise, as in a closed economy; but this would attract capital flows from abroad and so increase the money stock. In turn, interest rates might fall to their initial level. Consequently, there might be little or no offsetting fall in investment, so any effects on output or prices would be more marked than in the closed economy case. With floating exchange rates, there would again be an initial tendency for interest rates to rise and so cause foreign capital to flow in, but this flow would be checked by a rise in the exchange rate. The rise in the exchange rate would cause a fall in the output of export industries and import substitute industries. It can be seen that the balance of payments current account will move towards a (greater) deficit while the capital account will move towards a (greater) surplus. As in the closed economy case, there might be little overall effect on output or prices, but this time the local spending rise is offset by lower output for export and import substitute industries, not by lower output for investment good industries.

In principle, the central government is right to have some concern. If it operates a fixed exchange rate, then its main concern will be over the repercussions on output and the price level. If it operates a floating exchange rate, then its main concerns will be with the output of tradeable goods industries and with the problem that increased borrowing from abroad poses in the way of future interest obligations to foreigners.

How serious is the macroeconomic threat?

The last section has shown that, in principle, increases in local spending could have consequences that impinged on the central government's macroeconomic policies. However, it is worth asking if there is likely to be any serious effect in practice.

An important point to make in answering this question is that the consequences of a rise in local spending financed from higher local taxes are likely to be very small because of the direct offsetting effects on private spending. Suppose, for instance, that local spending initially amounts to 10 per cent of output. Then a rise in such spending by one tenth - a very sizeable rise - will of itself generate extra spending equal to 1 per cent of output; but if the rise is financed by an equal rise in taxes then there is likely to be a cut in private spending of perhaps 0.9 per cent of output. So the net effect would be a rise in spending of 0.1 per cent of output. This is unlikely to lead to serious rises in the output or price level (if the exchange rate is fixed) or on the output of tradeable goods, industries (if it floats).

In contrast, the effects of a rise in local spending financed by borrowing could be much more serious. In the case of the previous example, if the rise in local spending had been financed by borrowing, then there would have been no direct offset. Thus the net effect would be a rise in spending of 1 per cent of output, a much more significant rise than 0.1 per cent.

It follows from the last two points that there is much greater need to control local borrowing than local taxation. Most countries do indeed adopt some control over local borrowing, but it has to be asked whether there is really any need at all to control local taxation. It is true that local authorities might use their tax power to raise local spending and so have some - albeit small - macroeconomic effect. But there is no evidence that the economies of countries with substantial tax power for subcentral authorities have performed badly. Indeed, there is strong evidence to the contrary as can be seen in

Table 2.1.

This table lists the 21 members of the OECD for which relevant data were available. Column (1) shows Gross National Product per head in 1983 (all figures converted to dollars on the basis of exchange rates) while column (2) shows the ranking of these figures. It will be seen that the countries are listed in order of GNP per head. The column (3) figures show the percentage of total tax revenue accounted for by subcentral (that is state and local) authorities in each country, while column (4) shows the ranking of these figures. Column (5) shows the share of gross domestic product accounted for by subcentral taxes, while column (6) shows the ranking of these figures.

It is clear that there is a high correlation between the figures in columns (2), (4) and (6). In fact, the rank correlation coefficient between the figures in columns (2) and (4) is 0.80 while the corresponding coefficient for the figures in columns (2) and (6) is 0.83. The (linear) correlation coefficients between the figures in column (1) and those in columns (3) and (5) are, as it happens, smaller than the corresponding rank correlation coefficients, but they are still high. Thus the correlation coefficient between GNP per head and the share of taxes accounted for by subcentral authorities is 0.69 while the coefficient between GNP per head and the share of GDP accounted for by subcentral taxes is 0.74; in each case the standard error of the correlation coefficient is 0.22, so each coefficient is highly significant. There is clearly evidence to suggest that having a high GNP per head is assisted by - not hindered by - a high level of subcentral taxation.

Of course, these correlations could be explored much further than there is space to do here. For instance, it needs to be asked which way the causation runs. It can hardly be the case that a high GNP per head leads to a devolution of fiscal power since there was much fiscal devolution in many of the higher countries in the table years ago, when their GNP's per head were low. So does a high degree of fiscal devolution promote a high GNP per head, or is there another factor at work, perhaps some sort of national characteristic, which explains both a desire

Table 2.1: GNP per head and figures on subcentral tax yields for 21 OECD countries, 1983

Country	GNP(a) per head (US $000s) (1)	Ranking of column (1) (2)	Subcentral tax yields as % of total tax yield (3)	Ranking of column (3) (4)	Subcentral tax yields as % of GDP (a) (5)	Ranking of column (5) (6)
Switzerland	16.3	1	40.27	2	8.75	4
United States	14.1	2	30.74	4	6.36	8
Norway	14.0	3	18.63	11	6.79	7
Sweden	12.5	4	31.51	3	11.63	3
Canada	12.3	5	45.75	1	13.13	2
Denmark	11.6	6	30.67	5	13.62	1
Australia	11.5	7	20.53	10	6.15	9
West Germany	11.4	8	30.65	6	7.37	6
Finland	10.7	9	26.57	7	8.63	5
France	10.5	10	7.33	14	1.83	14
Japan	10.1	11	25.74	8	5.00	11
Netherlands	9.9	12	2.22	19	0.58	20
Austria	9.3	13	21.28	9	5.94	10
United Kingdom	9.2	14	11.05	12	3.44	12
Belgium	9.2	15	4.74	17	1.49	15
New Zealand	7.7	16	6.79	15	2.21	13
Italy	6.4	17	1.02	21	0.27	21
Ireland	5.0	18	2.04	20	0.68	19
Spain	4.8	19	9.55	13	1.43	16
Portugal	2.2	20	3.27	18	0.80	18
Turkey	1.2	21	5.68	16	1.01	17

Note (a): At market prices

Sources: Column (1) from World Development Report 1985, The World Bank, Oxford University Press, Oxford, 1985, pp.174-5
Columns (3) and (5) from Revenue Statistics of OECD Member Countries 1965-1984, OECD, Paris, 1985, pp.204 and 82

for fiscal devolution _and_ a high GNP per head? Another point to note is that it can be argued that both figures in the table and the coefficients derived from them should be qualified in a number of ways. For instance, subcentral authorities in some countries, including Austria, West Germany, Japan and Norway, have relatively little control over the _rates_ at which they can levy their taxes.

At the very least, though, it seems reasonable to argue that those who seek to curtail the level of local tax power should take a long hard look at this table. It is hardly a good omen for the UK that the level of tax power given to its local authorities will decline when non-domestic rates effectively become a centrally imposed tax.

REFERENCES

HMSO (1986)
Paying for Local Government, Green Paper, London, HMSO, Cmnd 9714

King, David N. (1984)
Fiscal Tiers: the Economics of Multi-Level Government, George Allen & Unwin, London

Oates, Wallace E. (1972)
Fiscal Federalism, Harcourt Brace Jovanovich, New York

Tiebout, Charles M. (1956)
'A pure theory of local expenditures', _Journal of Political Economy_, vol. 64, no. 5 (October), pp.416-24

Yonehara, J. (1981)
Local Public Finance in Japan, Centre for Research on Federal Financial Relations, Research Monograph 36, Australian National University, Canberra

3 FISCAL CRISIS AND STRESS: ORIGINS AND IMPLICATIONS

Kieron Walsh

Metaphors of stress and crisis have been widely used to describe the problems that have affected the state in the 1970s and 1980s. The most common has been the concept of fiscal stress or fiscal crisis. The simplest expression of this thesis is that the state is living beyond its means. The expanding range of state action, it is argued, has resulted from the fact that, from the 1930s onwards, and particularly in the post-war years, the state was seen as the arena for the solution of social and economic problems. The state became 'overloaded' as these problems became politicised and society becomes 'ungovernable'. The overload, in turn, expressed itself as a fiscal crisis because the state found it increasingly difficult to raise the money to finance its expanding activity. Rose and Peters (1978) argue that the result of an overloaded state trying to raise the money to finance its bloated programme will be political bankruptcy, as citizens lose faith in it. Fiscal stress and crisis have been particularly apparent in local government, with tax revolts such as Proposition 13 in California, near bankruptcy in cities such as New York, Cleveland and Detroit, and the financial traumas of Liverpool and other British local authorities. The metaphors clearly point to a reality. Governments, and particularly local governments, in many countries have faced severe financial problems as Newton's work has shown (Newton, 1980).

Fiscal stress and crisis arguments illustrate the need for a more sophisticated theory of the state than was available in the early 1970s. In particular we need a theory that takes account of internal differentiation within the state, for I shall argue that the crisis is as much within the state, as in its relation with the economy and civil society. An adequate theory will need to include an understanding of institutional structures. An important limitation of early theories of fiscal crisis was their apocalyptic tone. In fact, the state has not collapsed under the impact of stress and crisis. What has happened is a transformation of the nature and form of the crises. Mrs Thatcher and President Reagan have been able to change the terms of the debate. The fiscal crisis of the 1970s was the result of the social democratic welfare state, based on economic growth, running into the buffers of economic recession. In the 1980s the ideology of the welfare state itself has come to be questioned. Fiscal crisis has become ideological and rationality crisis.

In this chapter I will examine the theoretical roots of the concept of fiscal crisis, which lie both in micro and macroeconomic theory. At the macroeconomic level both Marxist and Liberal theorists argue that the Keynesian state - the mixed economy - is fatally flawed. Micro-theories, based in liberal political economy, argue that the behaviour of politicians, bureaucrats and state employees will generate fundamental financial problems. The understanding of fiscal crisis has also been developed through historical studies of, normally, American cities. Having examined these various theoretical developments of the concept of fiscal crisis, I shall turn to questions of institutions and interests. In particular I shall consider Peter Saunders' development of the 'dual' theory of the state. Finally I shall set the concepts of fiscal crisis within a wider context of the state, its limitations and the way that one form of crisis may be transformed into another.

THE ORIGINS OF FISCAL CRISIS: MARXISM AND LIBERALISM

Marxism and Liberalism, the fundamental political theories of the nineteenth and twentieth centuries, both provide theoretical grounding for the fiscal crisis of the state. The forms of the arguments are mirror images of one another; for the Marxist the crisis of the state is caused by social and economic crisis, for the Liberal the activities of the state generate crisis. For Marxists the problem lies in the tendency of the capitalist economy to crisis. The state must act to support the capital accumulation process if capital is not to succumb to its own contradictions. The process of capital accumulation leads to an increasing ratio of constant to variable costs and unless the rate of exploitation of labour can be increased, a consequent tendency for the rate of profit to fall. The state must step in to enable capital to solve its problems either directly, for example through restructuring, or through grants to industry, or indirectly through training labour or funding research and development in the universities. The organisation of labour will prevent capital from increasing the rate of exploitation and changing methods of production, so the state can also help capital by weakening labour through restrictive industrial relations law. Some Marxists, for example Gough (1979), argue that the role of the state is determined by the class struggle, rather than the dynamics of production. The scale of state activities then results from the balance of class forces. But, whether because of the nature of production or the dynamics of class struggle, the development of the capitalist economy and the development of the capitalist state go together.

The state must provide the conditions in which capitalist accumulation is maintained. But, in doing so, it is involved in a self-contradictory process. The resources that the state uses to support capital must be deducted from the surplus, which is itself the justification for capitalism. The logic of the state is opposed to the logic of the market, and its actions contribute to the crisis that it is intended to avoid. As Castells (1980, p.57) puts it:

> in order to expand and avoid the barriers existing in the process of accumulation, capital grows by generating in an increasing proportion, a sector of activities, rules and apparatuses that denies its own logic.

Fiscal Crisis and Stress

The fiscal crisis of the state is an expression of the contradiction by which capital will resist the release of the surplus that the state needs to support capital. It is a particular transformation of the general crisis that results from the tendency of the rate of profit to fall.

The mechanism of crisis is made more explicit in James O'Connor's Fiscal Crisis of the State (1973). Using a distinction extensively developed in the work of Offe (1984), O'Connor argues that the state must fulfil two basic functions if the capitalist system is to survive; it must maintain the conditions for both accumulation and legitimation. The conditions for capital accumulation are maintained through public spending on social investment and social consumption. Both these forms of spending are indirectly productive, the first through increasing the productivity of labour, the second through lowering the reproduction costs of labour. Legitimation and security are ensured by spending on the forces of ideology and repression and through social support for the poor and the dispossessed. Both functions are necessary for capital, but it will not be in the interest of individual capitalists to fund them. Capital will wish to socialize cost and privatize profit, and its long-term security can only be secured at its short-term disadvantage. O'Connor argues that fiscal crisis is inevitable because of the structural gap between the state's need to spend and its income. However much capital may, objectively, have need of the state it will not want to supply the money for it to function.

The argument from the right is the mirror image of the Marxist argument. Where O'Connor and others see the crisis of capital as leading to state action (which in turn contributes to the crisis), liberal theorists see the action of the state as the cause of crisis. State spending is unproductive and not technologically progressive and detracts from the ability of the market sector to produce profitably. Economic growth is not possible without the production of material goods that can be re-invested. Unproductive expenditure on state services reduces the growth potential of the economy. Liberal theorists argue that a growth in state activity leads to a misallocation of resources. There is allocative inefficiency because the state has no market mechanism to provide signals about what is and is not wanted. The crisis becomes a fiscal crisis as the activities of the state destroy the economy upon which it is dependent. This is an explanation used to explain the crisis in American cities which were seen as having destroyed the conditions for economic growth and, therefore, their own tax base (for a discussion see Friedland, 1982).

Liberal theorists also emphasize the debilitating effects of the way that the state raises income. If the state raises taxes then it will reduce incentives. If it borrows money in the market then it will 'crowd out' private borrowing and consequently productive investment. It will also raise interest rates by making funds scarcer. Printing money will cause inflation. The liberal critique emphasizes not the difficulty that the state will have in raising finance, but the implications of state appropriation of finance. The theory is most explicit in monetarism and supply-side economics. Though different, both theories emphasize the stability and potential of the market, left to its own devices. Monetarists argue that government cannot have any long-term effects on the level of demand or output. Everybody, according to the theory of 'rational expectations' that underpins monetarism, possesses an efficiently functioning economic model, which allows them to compensate for government attempts to influence the economy. Macroeconomic attempts to influence the economy will, therefore, be ineffective. Supply-side theorists argue that growth can be obtained without pain, by removing obstacles to the operation of the free market, such as strong trade unions, and cutting taxes, which will stimulate growth, and generate higher tax revenue at the lower rate. These theories have been espoused by Mrs Thatcher and President Reagan, but it is difficult to see that either Britain or the United States provide real tests. Monetarism has played little real part in Mrs Thatcher's economic policy and President Reagan has run large federal deficits.

The macro-theories of the fiscal crisis of the

state, Marxism and Liberalism, both have strong metaphysical components. It is not only difficult to test them, but even to know what a valid test would be. Any attempt to test the theory of the rate of profit to fall is bedevilled by the difficulty of transforming values into prices. Monetarism has found it difficult to state what money is. Both argue the difference of short and long-term effects, but with little guide to real time. What Marxism and Liberalism, as general theories, do is give us broad frameworks within which more detailed micro-theories can be developed.

MICRO-THEORIES OF FISCAL CRISIS

Micro-theories of fiscal crisis are based in neo-classical economics. I shall consider three such theories: Baumol's thesis of unbalanced growth; the 'public choice' perspective; and Olsen's argument in The Rise and Decline of Nations. Each of these theories is powerful in generating wide-ranging explanations from a few basic assumptions. Baumol concentrates on the nature of the product; public choice on the power of those active with the public service, as politicians or bureaucrats; Olsen on interest groups, and their impact on the polity. These theories may be incorporated into macro-theories; O'Connor, for example, makes use of Baumol's work in his explanation of fiscal crisis. The historical case-studies, considered below, also make use of the arguments proposed in these theories.

Baumol (1967) examines the implications of different levels of technological productivity in different sectors for economic growth, and uses his results to argue that a larger public sector will lead to unbalanced growth. He develops a model of an economy with two sectors; one in which there is technological progress and one in which there is none.

Given a small number of basic assumptions, for example that wages in the two sectors will rise together, and that there is a constant labour force, he is able to show, using simple mathematics, that the costs of output in the non-progressive sector will rise without limit, that all labour will be drawn into that sector, and that economic growth will be slowed. He uses this argument to claim that the increasing size of the public service sector, which is technologically non-progressive, will retard economic growth. Baumol's argument has been used to argue that there is a 'relative price effect' in the public sector; since wages advance along with those in the private, productive sector, the cost of public services rises and an increasing proportion of the national product is absorbed in public spending.

Baumol's thesis raises fundamental questions about the nature of technological advance, for as Bell (1968, p.883) observes, much of what the public sector produces are services, not manufactured goods, and

> the essential characteristic of services is not that their technology is backward, but that there is an intimate relationship between their production and consumption.

For much of what the public sector produces, for example teaching or social services, measures of productivity are extremely difficult to make. Quality may change while apparent units of input remain the same. Margaret Thatcher's government has argued that privatization is a key means of increasing productivity in the public services. Even in the case of monopoly services, such as gas, operation in the private sector is thought to provide managerial incentive. But it is notable that the services that have been privatized or contracted out are the more tangible and measurable ones. Privatization and contracting out will not cure Baumol's disease - consider for example the private-sector school system, where pupil-teacher ratios are much lower than in state schools. If services are non-progressive, they are equally so in public or private sectors. Baumol's argument focuses upon what is produced rather than how it is produced, and developments in new technology have shown how even basic service industries can change.

Baumol concentrates on the misallocation of resources between sectors of the economy. Others have argued that public sector managers, because they lack incentive, will not use those resources that they have efficiently. The public sector will, in Liebenstein's (1976) terms, exhibit X-inefficiency. This is a commonly asserted thesis (see Breton and Wintrobe, 1982, for a recent variation), for which there is little evidence. Certainly examples of inefficiency can be found in the public sector, but systematic comparative evidence is scarce. The recent debate over whether or not contracting out has improved efficiency in local government and the National Health Service has largely been conducted in terms of claim and counter-claim rather than evidence. Certainly Margaret Thatcher's government has taken the view that X-inefficiency means that more resources are used in the public service than are necessary, and that a key to public sector efficiency is managerial incentive, hence decentralized financial control, such as the Financial Management Initiative, strong management control, as in Griffiths management in the NHS, and performance-based incentives for senior civil servants.

A more generalized set of arguments, having both allocative and X-inefficiency implications, is 'public choice' theory, which attempts to develop economic theories of politics and bureaucracy. Public choice theory is based on the premises that politicians and bureaucrats pursue their self-interest. Crisis and stress will tend to result from the fact that both politicians and bureaucrats will see it as being in their interest to over-expand the public sector. Politicians will tend to generate an electorally based trade cycle as they expand the economy to buy popularity and votes at election time. Bureaucrats at the head of organizations and departments will have incentives to expand their staff, their budgets or the size of their offices. Moreover what public bureaucracies do produce they produce inefficiently. There is no market to give a clear relationship between cost and output. Politicians and bureaucrats, therefore, operate with distorted and inadequate information. The lack of relationship between performance and reward means that bureaucrats are likely to take their reward through leisure on the job and lack of commitment.

Marcus Olsen's (1982) study of the rise and

decline of nations is a particularly interesting example of an attempt to apply 'public choice'-type thinking. He argues that, over time, nations will accumulate organized interests. Such narrow interest groups will strive to maximize their members' share of the national product. They will have little incentive to work to increase the size of the national product, since their own share of any increase would be very small. They will press the state to distribute the national product in their own interest. The implication of Olsen's theory is that older states will have accumulated more distributional interest groups, which will work to reduce the rate of growth of the national product, and increase the proportion controlled and distributed by the state. Olsen is led to emphasize the importance of institutions at the microeconomic level, as they impact upon the supply side of the economy, rather than the state's ability to influence the level of demand. For Olsen (1982, p. 145), society faces:

> not the contradiction that Marx claimed to have found, but rather an inherent conflict between the colossal economic and political advantage of peace and stability and the longer-term losses that come from the accumulating networks of distributional coalitions that can only survive in stable environments.

Olsen, therefore, sees the activity of the state, and ultimately of interest groups themselves, being undermined by the impact of the distributional compulsion on production.

At their worst, public choice theories are naive assertions of the invigorating effects of the market. The roles of altruism, ideology, socialization and commitment are underestimated. The efficiency of markets is overestimated and role of 'hierarchy' (Williamson, 1975) underestimated. Perhaps most importantly they tend to operate with a limited concept of interests. Dunleavy (1985) has recently argued that a more sophisticated concept of bureaucrats' self-interest and institutional form are necessary if we are to explain bureaucratic attitudes to expansion of staff and budgets. Clearly the interests of civil servants in the Treasury and those in the DES and the DHSS are different.

The argument of Baumol and the public choice theorists is that there will be a disproportionate price to be paid for publicly produced goods, especially public services. There will be a 'relative price effect'. Attempts to assess the size of the relative price effect have not found it to be very great. A recent OECD (1985, p.27) study found that it is:

> in general small, and that it would have made little difference to the broad description of social expenditure growth ..... if it has been in terms of expenditure, expenditure shares and income elasticities defined in real rather than deflated terms...

But these theories, however limited the empirical evidence, are valuable in beginning to provide explanations of the mechanisms by which fiscal crisis might occur. Macro-theories, whether Marxist or Liberal, provide general frameworks within which crisis might occur. Micro-theories have had more influence in practice, as can be seen in historical case-studies to which we now turn.

HISTORICAL EXPLANATIONS

Though they are predominantly based on Marxist thinking, historical explanations of particular crises tend to draw on a range of explanation of fiscal crisis, embodying many of the micro-mechanisms discussed above.

For writers such as Piven (1978), Friedland (1982), Hill (1977) and others, fiscal crisis did not result simply from excess spending by profligate cities such as New York. Rather it followed from the nature of post-war urban development and the nature of the American economy. It reflected the move from the productive factory-based city to the corporate city. The city was to be the centre of industrial and commercial command and control. The basic process is mapped by Mollenkopf (1978). Following World War II there was a crisis in central city land values, as the spatial structure of the economy began to change. This led to an alliance of central city bureaucrats, large corporations, real estate interests and the construction industry, pushing for urban renewal and highway programmes. Cities with strong mayors were able to deliver such programmes. The richer moved to the suburbs, and indigenous industry was destroyed, reducing the tax-base of the city. At the same time development destroyed the jobs that had been filled by the working class in the inner city. Federal aid contributed to the crisis by subsidizing the costs of urban renewal and, from the mid-1960s, through President Johnson's Great Society programme, the costs of social support in the city. The process was enhanced from the mid-1950s by the development of interest groups pressing for more from the public purse. The public service unions were first, but they were followed in the 1960s by community groups. As machine politics became less dominant, both groups were able to increase their influence on the budgets of cities. As Hill (1977, p.21) says:

> 'Pork barrel' politics, unreflective incrementalism, and the expansion of bureaucratic, professional and union systems, unresponsive and impervious to change, have resulted in a political system increasingly impervious to the requisites of professional monopoly sector accumulation as well as the social needs of local residents.

This sort of argument would fit well with some of the theories of the public choice school as much as more radical theories.

The detailed historical explanations of particular fiscal crises in work of writers such as Hill and Friedland lays emphasis on the role of class conflict and struggle in the generation of fiscal crisis. It is not simply a reflection of the failing of the accumulation process. The socialization of consumption, as Pahl (1977, p.155) emphasizes, has led to more overt conflict than would follow from market-based services:

> politicisation and conflict seem to arise from the socialisation of consumption and the substitution of the plan and bureaucratic principles and criteria for the market as basic principles of allocation. Decisions on the spatial and social allocation of resources become increasingly political when allocation is determined according to need.

This sort of perspective is helpful in explaining why it is that left-wing, higher spending local authorities in Britain are precisely those that seem to face most public and union antagonism. Crises of need, as cities were re-fashioned, became transformed into crises of demand, especially when demand orientated groups are recognized.

INSTITUTIONS AND INTERESTS

The historical studies of the fiscal crisis of particular cities and local governments illustrates the need for a multidimensional theory, and that fiscal crisis can take more than one form, as the work of Friedland shows. Macro-theories emphasize the origins of crisis in the relationship between state and economy and society. Micro-theories illustrate the need for an understanding of the way that interests and institutions determine the form that crisis takes, and particularly why crisis is manifested at the local government level. In Britain the crisis has been manifested in the relations between central and local government.

Local governments may be more or less subordinate to the central state. In Britain, for example, Ministers have used the assertion that we are a unitary state to increase central dominance, rather than joint subordination to Parliament and the law. The Rate Support Grant has been used not only as a means of distributing central funds, but as a means of controlling local expenditure. Over the long term local government has been left with a very visible, non-buoyant, property tax - the rates - while central government retains income tax to itself. Central government, unlike that in many countries, includes local spending in public expenditure plans, allowing Ministers to have a scapegoat for failures to reduce public spending. The particular British institutional structure has led to a long-running crisis in local government finance. Since the mid-1970s central government has been attempting to cut local authority spending by a combination of cuts in the total level of grant support, grant penalties and targets and, finally, rate-capping.

The tortuous development of the crisis in British local government finance, and the fact that even the extreme measure of rate-capping has failed to control expenditure levels, illustrates the need for detailed institutional understanding if the form of the crisis is to be explained. We need a theory of the state that explains the crisis within the state, as well as in its relations with the economy and society.

One of the most important contributions to the fiscal crisis literature is the development of the 'dual state' thesis to attempt to explain the nature of the relation between central and local government. Saunders (1985), the major exponent of the theory, argues that Cockburn (1977) and others are wrong to equate the local state with the national capitalist state. In his early work Saunders tended to argue that the local state was the sphere of consumption and the central state that of production. The nature of decision-making differed at the two levels, with local decision-making being open and democratic and the centre being closed.

Saunders has developed this thinking in a number of articles. He argues that class interests dominate production politics at the centre, whereas local government is the focus of consumption sector interests. The mode of decision-making depends upon the nature of the interests involved: in production-related matters it is corporatist, on matters of consumption it is competitive. For production interests the state is an instrument for pursuing their interests, for consumption interests a field of bargaining, lobbying and conflict. In production politics the rights of property are emphasized, in consumption politics the rights of citizenship. Saunders (1986, p.750) uses these analytical distinctions to develop the following hypotheses:

> that Marxist-inspired class theories of politics will be more applicable the more political processes relating to questions of production are concentrated at the central level, take a corporatist rather than a democratic form, and are addressed to values of private property and profitability; and second, that pluralist-inspired interest group theories of politics will be more appropriate in explaining political processes relating to questions of consumption, to local levels of state activity, to competitive sectors of the political system and to values stressing rights of citizenship and the alleviation of social need.

The work of Saunders and others is important in emphasizing the internal differentiation of the state. Marxist and Liberal theorising has tended to emphasize the global conflict of objectives of a state needing to spend to support capital, but reducing surplus in order to do so. But the internal differentiation of the state illustrates other conflicts and contradictions that can arise. There is, first, likely to be conflict between the general need to control spending and the specific desire to spend. In part the segregation of the institutions of control and of spending allows the central government to speak out of both sides of its mouth at once. The recent history of British central-local relations has illustrated this thesis, where overall spending targets have been set with little regard to specific spending requirements. One officer, in a study of the impact of grant systems, said:

> this volume target, based upon 1978-79 actual expenditure is a very crude thing, and says nothing about individual services at all, and so we do an analysis of our services to find out where we differ from it and the one service where we are miles over is the police, yet all we have been doing is working within the Home office

limits. (Davis et al; 1983.)

Such conflicts of purpose illustrate not only the divide between the centre controlling and the locality spending, but also that between spending and controlling departments within levels of government. The Treasury and the DHSS do not take the same view about spending.

The contradictions and conflicts of state spending have led to changes in its institutional structure over the last 20 years. There has been a growth of appointed bodies, not constrained by the requirements of democratic accountability. The most important of these are the Manpower Services Commission and the urban Development Corporations. Policy planning systems, such as Housing Investment Programmes and Transport Policies and Programmes, have been established. Bodies to link the planning of central and local government have been set up, such as the Consultative Council on Local Government Finance and the National Advisory Body on Public Sector Higher Education. Surveillance has been increased with the establishment of the Audit Commission and the Social Services Inspectorate. The major impact of fiscal crisis is that there has been an increasing dominance of central-orientated institutions and processes, expressing the dominance of central government.

THE TRANSFORMATION OF CRISIS

The understanding of fiscal crisis as just one, among many, possible manifestations of fundamental social, economic and political problems, helps us understand how one form of crisis may be transformed into another. Fiscal crisis was largely the result of the structures and institutions of the welfare state, essentially social democratic in nature, being faced with the end of the long post-war period of growth. It was relatively simple, though painful for many involved, to solve that fiscal crisis. Sharp cutbacks in expenditure and large-scale redundancies were possible. By the 1980s Peterson (1986, p.29) finds American cities to be in 'a better financial position' than in the 1970s. But solving the fiscal crisis does not mean that the problem is dissolved. Peterson's study finds that cities were able to solve their problems at the expense of those who received services:

> The fact that city budgets escaped relatively unscathed from the first term of federal policy reform reflects, to a significant degree, the ability of city governments to pass on the effects of programme reductions directly to programme beneficiaries. (Peterson, 1986, p.35).

In Britain it has been possible for central government to be able to pass on fiscal difficulties to the local state, so that the crisis is then manifest as a crisis of central-local relations.

The ability of the state to cut back on expenditure has depended upon its ability to weaken the oppositional institutions. The present Government has given a good deal of attention to weakening the trade unions and local authorities, both directly, through reducing their powers, and indirectly, through enhancing the role of the market. The repressive side of the maintenance of legitimacy has been enhanced through strengthening the police force, to cope with the more explosive forms of protest, such as the urban disturbances of 1981 and 1985. The limitation of the fiscal crisis literature of the 1970s was that it mistook the particular for the general. The crisis of the 1970s resulted from having to live without the assumption of growth. It was not a questioning of purpose but of means.

In the 1980s some have come to question the ends of the state themselves. At the extreme we have the 'anarcho-capitalists' (Friedman, 1973) arguing for the private sector provision of law, money and defence. More generally the 'new right' has been able to undermine the ideology of the post-war welfare state. The fiscal crisis of the 1970s was, essentially, a crisis in the growth of the state. The present crisis that faces the public services is one of confidence, rationality and motivation. The public sector cannot justify itself, as it did in the

1950s and 1960s, by asserting the self-evident rightness of the state distributing the national product. The public sector's defence of itself may well be to improve its managerial efficiency. But it will then face the argument that it could just as easy be provided in the private sector. Technique does not provide moral justification.

The new crisis that faces the state, therefore, is the argument for a radical decline in state activities. The consequences are likely to be particularly great for local authorities in Britain. Local authority expenditure is included in total public expenditure planning. It is natural, then, that Ministers will attempt to cut the local government expenditure for which they are indirectly responsible and maintain that expenditure for which they are directly responsible. The structure of interest and institution is such as to allow and encourage the centre to transform the fiscal crisis of the state into a crisis of local government finance. A more extreme scenario is possible. Local government might be greatly weakened in significance - by a fourfold distribution of functions - to the centre, to the voluntary sector, to appointed bodies like the MSC and to the market. Clearly this process is already partly under way with the growth of Urban Development Corporations, the MSC's powers over work-related non-advanced further education, the sale of council houses, contracting out and abolition of the Greater London Council and the Metropolitan County Councils.

The fiscal crisis of the social democratic state has been transformed into a crisis of the rationality of the state itself. The way that the crisis expresses itself depends upon the structure of interests and institutions. In the United Kingdom this structure is such as to make the crisis one of local government and of central-local relations.

FISCAL CRISIS AND THE CRISIS OF THE SOCIAL ORDER

Fiscal crisis may be seen as one manifestation of a more basic problem that confronts modern capitalist society. Habermas (1976) has argued there is a multiple crisis of legitimation, rationality, motivation and the economy. The development of a more complex social and economic system has involved the repoliticization of social and economic affairs that, in classic Liberal theory, were the concern of civil society and not the state. The acceptability of state intervention depends upon its effectiveness in solving problems, for it is not justified in the Liberal ideology that underlies capitalism. It must actually be able to solve the problems that confront society, and, more particularly, the economy. In the 1950s it was thought that we had attained that ideology-free effectiveness: in the 1980s it is apparent that we have not.

Hirsch (1977) and Habermas (1976), amongst others, have added to this argument about the efficiency of the state a moral argument. For Hirsch the fundamental problem faced by the 'mixed economy' is that the moral legacy, upon which the stability of capitalism is based, has been depleted. Capitalism is founded upon individual rights to property and the pursuit of self-interest. Hirsch argues that the unequal results of the capitalist process are only accepted because of the persistence of pre-capitalist 'status' morality. As that morality is eroded so the state must step in to impose the necessary control and guidance. But this involved:

> the progressive extension of explicit social organization without the support of a matching social morality - more rules for the common good, having to be prescribed and adhered to in a culture orientated increasingly to the private good. (Hirsch, 1977, p.120).

But the collective solution lacked a moral base. It was acceptable as long as it worked.

At another level the problems of the capitalist state lie in the fundamental logical structure of the social order and social interaction. Much of Hirsch's argument is based on the thesis that there are social limits to the process of growth which cannot be eliminated by the expansion of production. A good deal of the post-war development of the welfare state was based upon the fundamentally mistaken notion that access to goods, whose value depended upon their relative scarcity, could be satisfactorily delivered by increasing their absolute levels of provision. 'Positional' goods cannot be so delivered. The expansion of educational provision, for example, had the implicit justification that upward social mobility was available to all. Such logical impossibilities have been the focus of increasing attention. Boudon (1982) has written of the perverse consequences of social action. Elster (1978, 1979, 1983) has written a series of books on logical problems of social action.

As the social order becomes more complex and interlinked, so it is likely that the actions of one will impinge upon those of others. Sub-optimisation is likely with individuals pursuing their own best interest, resulting in collective disadvantage. The Marxist and Liberal perspectives both face difficulties in coping with collective and individual rationality and questions of long-term versus short-term rationality. The problem is not one of technical management, an ideal much searched for in the development of the post-war welfare state, but the development of normative agreement in the face of limits to the possibilities of social action.

CONCLUSION

The fiscal crisis of the state, and particularly of the local state, is a phenomenon of the transition from the politics of growth to the politics of decline. Immediate fiscal crises themselves may be solved. It is, for example, relatively easy to see how the financial problems that confront some British local authorities could be dealt with. But the cause of the crisis would not thereby be removed. The crisis of central-local government relations in Britain results from more fundamental constitutional problems about the nature of citizenship and democracy. Mrs Thatcher's government is concerned that the state should be less involved in society and the economy, but has equally asserted its power and authority in pursuit of that end. The Liberal state is not extensive, but nor is it weak. Local government, premised on notions of participation, citizenship and democracy, will be threatened by the development of such a state. The fiscal problems that local authorities have experienced are less significant than this threat to its existence.

In respect of local government, concentration on any one of the macro or micro-theories outlined above may be inappropriate. The fiscal problems are multi dimensional and originate within the state as much (or more than) out with it. If the interpretation is that it is through the structure of interests and institutions that central government has been allowed to 'create' the fiscal crisis at the local government level, the corollary is that crisis is not inevitable. Nor is it accepted that there is no solution. But a durable solution to the current problems of local government will require a reappraisal and reaffirmation of the nature of citizenship and local democracy.

REFERENCES

Baumol, W.J. (1967)
'The Macroeconomics of Unbalanced Growth', American Economic Review, vol. 57, pp. 415-26

Bell, C. (1968)
'Comment on Baumol', American Economic Review, vol.58, pp.877-84

Boudon, R. (1982)
The Unintended Consequences of Social Action, Macmillan, London

Breton, A. and Wintrobe, R. (1982)
The Logic of Bureaucratic Conduct, Cambridge University Press, Cambridge

Castells, M. (1980)
The Economic Crisis in American Society, Blackwell, Oxford

Cockburn, C. (1977)
The Local State: Management of Cities and People,

Pluto Press, London

Davis, E.M., Gibson, J.G., Game, C.H. and Stewart, J.D. (1983)
Grant Characteristics and Central-Local Relations, Report to the Social Science Research Council, INLOGOV, University of Birmingham

Dunleavy, P. (1985)
'Bureaucrats, Budgets and the Growth of the State', British Journal of Political Science, vol. 15, part 3, pp.299-328

Elster, J. (1978)
Logic and Society, Wiley, Chichester

-- (1979)
Ulysses and the Sirens, Cambridge University Press, Cambridge

-- (1983)
Sour Grapes, Cambridge University Press, Cambridge

Friedland, R. (1982)
Power and Crisis in the City, Macmillan, London

Freidman, D. (1973)
The Machinery of Freedom, Harper and Row, New York

Gough, I. (1979)
The Political Economy of the Welfare State, Macmillan, London

Habermas, J. (1976)
Legitimation Crisis, Heinemann, London

Hill, R. C. (1977)
'State Capitalism and the Urban Fiscal Crisis in the United States', International Journal of Urban and Regional Research, vol. 1, no. 1

Hirsch, F. (1977)
The Social Limits to Growth, Routledge and Kegan

Paul, London

Liebenstein, H. (1976)
Beyond Economic Man, Harvard University Press, Cambridge, Mass.

Mollenkopf, J.H. (1978)
'The Post-war Politics of Urban Development', in Tabb, W.K. and Sawers, L. Marxism and the Metropolis: New Perspectives in Urban Political Economy, Oxford University Press, New York

Newton, K. (1980)
Balancing the Books, Sage, London

O'Connor, J. (1973)
The Fiscal Crisis of the State, St Martins Press, New York

Offe, C. (1984)
The Contradictions of the Welfare State, Hutchinson, London

Olsen, M. (1982)
The Rise and Decline of Nations, Yale University Press, London

Organisation for Economic Co-operation and Development (1985)
Social Expenditure, 1960 - 1990 , OECD , Paris

Pahl, R. (1977)
'Collective Consumption and the State in Capitalist and State Socialist Societies', in r. Scase (ed.), Industrial Society: Aspects of Class, Clearage and Control, George, Allen and Unwin, London
Peterson, G.E. (1986)
'Urban Policy and the Cyclical Behaviour of Cities', in G.E. Peterson and C.W. Lewis, Reagan and the Cities, Urban Institute Press, Washington

Piven, F.F. (1978)
'The Urban Crisis: Who Got What and Why', in F. Piven and R. Cloward, The Politics of Turmoil,

Pantheon, New York

Rose, R. and Peters, G. (1978)
Can Government Go Bankrupt?, Macmillan, London

Saunders, P. (1985)
'Corporatism and Urban Service Provision', in W. Grant, The Political Economy of Corporatism, Macmillan, London

Williamson, O.E. (1975)
Markets and Hierarchies, Free Press, New York

4 LOCAL TAXING AND LOCAL SPENDING: INTERNATIONAL COMPARISONS

Terence Karran

INTRODUCTION

Local taxation systems are neither discrete nor static, but are inexorably bound up within the changing local government systems which they are evolving to serve. The rating system in Britain, for example, dates from medieval times when the duties of local authorities were neither numerous nor onerous. As the activities of local authorities have altered so the system of raising funds, to which rates are central, has changed to meet these new demands.

Hence changes in the mode of local taxation do not occur in isolation from the local government structure which enmeshes it, but in response to changes in this structure. The current proposals for the introduction of a community charge in Britain (HMSO, 1986) are no exception. The policy initiative has been taken both at a time of radical changes in the structure of local authorities (with the abolition of the English Metropolitan Counties and Greater London Council), and in response to alterations in the entire rationale of the system. The well established idea of indirect financial accountability via representative local government has been supplanted in favour of more direct financial accountability which relates the benefits of local services more specifically to the willingness of residents to pay for them. What makes the outlined reform unique and worthy of detailed consideration, is that it constitutes a fundamental shift in the system of local fiscs, crucially different from the incremental size and dilatory pace of previous evolutionary changes.

Cross-national comparisons provide a valuable frame of reference for an appraisal of the new scheme mooted for Britain, and this analysis is ordered in three parts to that end. Given that local taxation systems relate directly to the particular local government systems they fund, cross-national variations in local government structures and functions are examined first. Establishing the study's dominant theme, this section examines whether the British system of subnational government and its functions are typical of comparable nations, or differ so markedly as to need a modified taxing method. Following from this, the pattern of local spending and funding is analysed in accordance with the recurrent theme - is the British situation typical or does it vary sufficiently to warrant a different funding scheme? The concluding section uses the outlined mosaic of functions and funding methods as a context for assessing both the viability and durability of the new system and the possible need for reform, by raising three related questions. First, are there any subnational governments with taxation systems like those suggested for British local authorities, or will the British system be unique? More importantly, if the British system will not be unique, have the subnational governments in other countries with a taxation system comprising a poll tax and assigned revenues coped any better than British local authorities in the climate of fiscal stress and retrenchment which has occurred with varying degrees of severity in most Western nations since the mid-1970s? Lastly, if the proposed British system is not used elsewhere, can experience in other nations suggest whether another tax system would best suit the existing structure and functions of British local authorities or if a more radical reform, comprising structure and function as well as finance, is needed?

LOCAL AUTHORITIES' STRUCTURES AND FUNCTIONS

Within most nation states a division of responsibilities and functions between different levels of government is the norm rather than the exception. Nevertheless, considerable heterogeneity exists between nations in both the size of subnational governments (relative to that of the nation state) and the structure of their systems. Such lower-tier authorities range from a limited number of geographically extensive provincial or regional units of government, eclipsed only in area, population, and power by the nation state, to numerous very small polities offering local democracy for individual village and town communities. There is further variation in the structure of systems, with some countries having multiple units at provincial, regional and local level, while others are characterised by simple non-differentiated systems.

In attempting to determine the extent of variety of systems and by extension their degree of comparability, confusion arises from defining exactly what constitutes local government. Within federal systems of government, such as the United States, sovereignty is vested in both the national government (which embraces the geographical nation in its entirety) and the provincial or state legislatures (which are responsible for discrete areal units within this entirety). Sovereign powers defining and controlling local government units are invariably but not exclusively exercised at state or provincial level. Hence local governments are infra sovereign areal administrations, the membership of which is usually but not necessarily chosen by some form of electoral process, the processes used in electoral selection being as varied and diverse as the local government systems which they serve. This broad definition of local government would embrace basic units - municipalities and townships in urban centres and districts in rural areas - as well as intermediate administrations lying above the basic units - such as counties or regions - but would exclude sovereign or quasi sovereign provinces or states. Nevertheless the wealth of variety of local government systems imposes strains even on this very broad definition. The most comprehensive international survey of local authorities (Humes and Martin, 1969) concluded that local government institutions cannot always be distinguished from those of central government, as in practice many institutions are both.

Table 4.1: Structures of Subnational governments

	National			Intermediate				Local		
	Area (000 sq.km)	Population (000)	Pop. Dens.	Type	Number	Mean size	Mean population	Number	Mean size	Mean population
Australia	7,687	14,727	2	S	6	1,281,167	2,454,500	960	8,007	15,340
				C	34	226,058	433,147			
Austria	84	7,507	89	R	9	9,333	834,111	2,301	36	3,262
				D	99	848	75,828			
Belgium	31	9,859	318	P	9	3,444	1,095,444	2,586	12	3,812
				D	44	705	224,068			
Bulgaria	111	8,862	80	P	27	4,111	328,222	1,152	96	7,693
Canada	9,976	23,343	2	P	10	997,600	2,334,300	4,017	2,483	5,811
				C	114	87,509	204,763			
Denmark	43	5,124	119	C	15	2,867	341,600	276	156	18,565
Finland	337	4,788	14	P	12	28,083	399,000	548	615	8,737
France	547	53,788	98	R	22	24,865	2,444,909	36,394	15	1,478
				DP	101	5,416	532,554			
Germany	249	61,658	248	L	11	22,636	5,605,273	8,514	29	7,242
				D	260	958	237,146			
Greece	132	9,599	73	P	52	2,538	184,596	6,049	22	1,587
				D	146	904	65,747			
Iceland	103	228	2	D	21	4,905	10,857	229	450	996
Ireland	70	3,440	49					31	2,258	110,968
Italy	301	57,401	190	R	20	15,050	2,870,050	7,810	39	7,350
				P	91	3,308	630,780			
Japan	372	117,057	315	PR	47	7,915	2,490,574	3,255	114	35,962
Luxemburg	3	364	140					126	24	2,889
Netherlands	41	14,220	347	P	11	3,727	1,292,727	944	43	15,064
New Zealand	269	3,176	12	CL	22	12,227	144,364	223	1,206	14,242

Norway	324	4,092	13	P	20	16,200	204,600	744	435	5,500
Poland	313	35,815	114	P	22	14,227	1,628,091	5,623	56	6,370
				D	391	801	91,606			
Portugal	92	9,933	108	R	2	46,000	4,966,500	305	302	32,567
				D	18	5,111	551,833			
South Africa	1,221	29,285	24	P	4	305,250	7,321,250	456	2,678	64,221
Spain	505	37,430	74	R	17	29,706	2,201,765	9,212	56	4,063
				P	50	10,100	748,600			
Sweden	450	8,320	18	C	24	18,750	346,667	279	1,613	29,821
Switzerland	41	6,329	154	CT	26	1,577	243,423	3,000	14	2,110
Turkey	781	45,218	58	P	67	11,657	674,896	1,400	558	32,299
UK (i) Scotland	79	5,131	66	RI	12	6,565	427,561	53	1,356	95,330
(ii) England /Wales	150	49,155	327	C	47	3,477	663,853	401	382	122,580
USSR	22,402	265,542	12	P	141	158,879	1,883,277	48,641	461	5,459
				D	3,274	6,842	8,102			
USA	9,363	229,804	25	S	50	187,260	4,596,100	35,692	262	6,439
				C	3,042	3,077	75,544			
Mean	1,934	38,662	107		210	89,291	1,296,706	6,249	820	23,026

Notes: (1) Dates of national censuses vary, figures cited are for 1981 ± 3 years.
(2) Key to Intermediate tiers

C = County		P = Province	
CL = Council		PR = Prefecture	
CT = Canton		R = Region	
D = District		RI = Regions and Islands	
DP = Departments		S = State	
L = Lander			

Sources: S. Humes and E. M. Martin, The structure of Local Government Throughout the World (The Hague: Martinus Nijhoff and IULA 1961), 1st edition, p.13 and 2nd edition (1969).
OECD Taxes on Immovable Property (Paris: OECD 1983), p.76.
World Atlas (London: George Philip, 1985), p.v.
Plus some updating.

Accepting definitional difficulties and limitations, and the fact that in Britain as elsewhere the local government structure is often evolving in the long term rather than static, Table 4.1 is an attempt to demonstrate the absence of cross-national homogeneity among substantial governments As can be seen there is extensive variety in terms of the number of tiers of government, the number of units within each tier, and the average population and area of the units. Scrutiny of the data in Table 4.1 reveals no underlying rationale for the establishment of both tiers and units in terms of their number, size or population. Among the more obvious factors influencing structure are the geographical extensiveness of the nation state, the extent of centralisation and the number of basic units. Centralisation of public policy determination within national capitals necessitates greater administration at intermediate government level to ensure that central government political initiatives are implemented locally. Similarly, the level of economic development and urbanisation within a nation state may have a pervasive effect on the number of tiers and units of subnational government within it. The uneven distribution of population and fiscal resources which occurs in rural areas often leads to their having a more differentiated structure than would occur in urban areas. Analysis of the data in Table 4.1 reveals absolute population size to have a stronger statistical impact than geographical area on the number of both local and intermediate units, especially the latter. Comparisons of the local government system within Britain as against those elsewhere show that the lower ier units in both England and Wales, and Scotland, have much higher average populations than those in other countries. English and Welsh lower tier units have over 100,000 more people than their nearest non-British rival and, with a mean population of 122,000, are five times larger than the average population of 23,000 for local governments in all countries. Of greater relevance when considering the possibility of reform, England and Wales are remarkable in not having an elected tier of government at regional level, more especially when compared with their European counterparts of similar size or population, and bearing in mind that a large sector of the British nation state (Scotland) already has regional units.

The system, size and structure of local authorities are clearly interdependent both with the allocation of service functions and by extension the fiscal powers used to fund them. Hence the mode of local funding cannot be considered in isolation from the other features of local authorities. For example the size of the nation state and its structure of national government (federal or unitary) will be instrumental in determining the degree of differentiation within local government units. A highly differentiated system necessarily limits the functions each tier can fulfil and the financial resources it requires. As a result the heterogeneity of system and size (shown in Table 4.1) is mirrored by variety and service functions and, by extension, fiscal powers.

Cross-national variation in the number and type of functions allocated to subnational units and in the distribution of functions among these units generates different levels of both total and individual service spending. Table 4.2 indicates how 31 different functions are allocated between different tiers of government in 15 European nations including the UK. In spite of the large number of local government systems and structures, the dearth of blank cells within the national functional matrix reveals a substantial degree of unanimity about which functions are assigned to subnational administrations. Every function listed is undertaken by at least two countries at local level (with the obvious exception of financial assistance to local authorities which can only be undertaken by superior subnational units). Using this table it is possible first to assess which functions might more usually be designated 'local' or 'regional' and secondly to analyse the pattern of responsibilities in Britain compared with elsewhere.

Across the range of services, each is provided at local level by an average of 10 of the 15 nations, and at regional level by an average of four. Using these mean values as minimum criteria for

Table 4.2: Allocation of functions to subnational

	Austria	Belgium	Denmark	France	Germany	Ireland
Refuse collection & disposal	L	L	L	L	L	L
Slaughterhouse	L	L	L	L	L	L
Theatres, concerts	R,L	L	R	L	R,L	
Museums, art galleries, libraries	L	R,L	R,L	L,D	R,L	L
Parks & open spaces	L	R,L	L	L,R	L	L
Sports & leisure pursuits	L	R,L	L	L	R,L	L
Roads	R,L	R,L	R,L	L,D	R,L	L
Urban road transport	L		L	L,D	R,L	
Ports		L			R,L	
Airports					R	
Disrict heating	L	L	L	L	L	
Water supply	L	L	L	L	L	L
Agriculture, forestry fishing, hunting	R	R,L		L,D	R,L	
Electricity		R,L			L	
Commerce	R,L	L		L	R,L	
Tourism	R,L	R,L		L,D	R,L	

governments

Italy	Luxemburg	Nether-lands	Norway	Portugal	Sweden	Switzer-land	Turkey	United Kingdom	Usual Service Provider
L	L	L	L	L	L	R,L	L	L	L
L	L	L	L		L	L	L	L	L
R,L	L	L	L	L	L	L	L	L	L
R,L	L	L	L	L	R,L	L	R,L	L	L
R,L	L	R,L	L	L	L	L	R,L	L	R,L
R,L	L	R,L	L	L	L	L	L	L	L
R,P,L	L	R,L	R,L	L	L	R,L	R,L	L	R,L
P,L	L	L	L	L	R,L	L		L	L
L		L	L	L	R	L			
L		L	L		R,L	R		L	
L		L			L	R,L	L		L
R,L	L	R,L	L	L	L	L	R,L	L	L
R,P,L		L	R,L	L	L	R,L	R,L	L	R,L
L		R,L	L	L	L	R,L	L		L
R,L		R,L		L	L	R,L	R,L		R,L
R		L	L	L	R,L	R,L	R,L	L	R,L

	Austria	Belgium	Denmark	France	Germany	Ireland
Financial assistance to local authorities	R	R		R,D	R	
Security, police disposal	L	L		L	R,L	
Fire Protection	L	L	L	L,D	L	L
Justice					R	
Pre-school education	R,L	L	L	L	L	
Primary & Secondary education	R,L	R,L	R,L	L	R,L	
Vocational & technical training	R	R,L		R,L		
Higher education		R,L			R	
Adult education	L	L	L	L	R,L	
Hospitals & Conva	R,L	R,L	R	L,D	R,L	
Personal health	R,L	L	R,L	L	R,L	
Family welfare services	R,L	R,L	L	L,D	R,L	
Welfare homes	R,L	L	L	L	L	
Housing	R,L	L		L	R,L	L
Town Planning	L	L	L	L	L	L

R = State, regional government
L = Local government
D = Departments in France
P = Provinces in Italy

Source: Department of Environment, Paying for Local

Italy	Luxemburg	Nether-lands	Norway	Portugal	Sweden	Switzer-land	Turkey	United Kingdom	Usual Service Provider
R		R				R	R		R
L	L	R,L		L		R,L	L	L	L
	L	L		L	L	L	L	L	L
R,L								L	
R,L	L	L	L		L	R,L		L	L
R,L	L	L	R,L	L	L	R,L	R	L	R,L
R,L		L	L,L		R,L	R,L		L	R
R,L						R		L	R
R		L	R,L		R,L	R,L		L	R,L
R,P,L	L	R,L	R,L		R	R,L	R,L		R,L
R,P,L	L	L	L	L	R	R	R		R,L
R,L		L	L	L	L	R,L	L	L	R,L
R,L	L	L	L		L	R,L	R,L	L	L
R,L	L	R,L	L	L	L	L	L	L	L
R,L	L	R,L	L	L	L	R,L	L	L	L
R,L		R,L		L	L	R,L	R,L		R,L

Government, Cmnd. 9714 (London: HMSO, 1986), 131

categorisation, the final column in the table indicates which service can be considered 'local' and which 'regional'. When analysed in this way the national conformity of local government functions is revealed. All but a minority (five) of the functions are in the 'local' category, which not surprisingly includes services which typify municipal provision, viz. refuse collection, parks, police, fire protection, etc. About half of the services provided locally are also provided at regional level, and typically include the more important functions for which larger units may be preferable on grounds of strategic or economic efficiency grounds, such as roads, health, welfare. Of the functions designated regional, only three are specific to this upper tier of subnational government - vocational and technical training, higher education and financial assistance to other local authorities, though the last by definition cannot be undertaken at local level.

How do the service responsibilities of subnational governments in Britain compare with those in other countries? Of the nations listed only four - the Republic of Ireland, Luxembourg, Portugal and the UK - atypically do not allocate any functions to a regional tier of government. However, the average area (55,000 sq. km.) and population (4,579,000) of the other three are much lower than those of Britain (229,000 sq. km. and 54,286,000 people), and are probably not large enough to need or justify a regional tier of government. Of the four, Britain differs from other European counterparts in not making local authorities responsible for district heating, electricity, commerce, hospitals and health. Indeed, Britain is virtually unique in not using a lower-tier elected body to administer these latter two functions. In essence the table demonstrates that British local authorities are typical with respect to the number of functions they undertake, but are aberrant both in the type of functions undertaken at local level, and in not sharing a wide range of functional responsibilities with other subnational governments.

LOCAL AUTHORITY SPENDING AND FUNDING

At an aggregate level variations exist in the degree to which nations are willing to allocate part of their national product to public expenditure on government goods and services. Moreover within these differing public sector portions of the national cake, variation exists in the share of local as against central government spending. However, difficulties are encountered in attempting cross-national comparisons of government spending in total, and local spending in particular. One major problem is that definitions of public sector spending vary between countries. Many national accounting schemes would exclude nationalised industries spending from government spending, for example. By contrast in Britain spending under this heading was listed in the national accounts in the government rather than the non-government sector until 1976. Similarly inclusion of transfer payments between different tiers of government may overstate the size of the public sector. Accepting that any choice of figures may be something of a compromise, the data in Table 4.3 is drawn from OECD sources to try to maximise cross-national comparability. The illustrative statistics for general government expenditure in the table exclude nationalised industries' outgoings but includes transfers, as this shows the total size of the public sector consistent with the common use of the term. (Brown and Jackson, 1982)

As Table 4.3 shows there is extreme diversity in the demands made on the national product by spending in both central and local government. The government slice of GDP varies from 60 per cent in Sweden to less than half that amount in Japan, with the mean value virtually midway between them. Similarly the local government portion of public expenditure itself exhibits variability ranging from 43 per cent of all public spending in Australia to less than 4 per cent in Portugal. Moreover the variety in local spending does not correspond with that of total spending by government - the level of the former seems largely unaffected by the level of the latter, with the correlation between the size of the local government

Table 4.3: General government and local/state spending as % GDP 1984

	General gov't spending as % GDP	Local/state spending as % GDP		Local/state spending as % GDP	
Sweden	59.8	24.3		40.6	
Netherlands	56.5	18.3		32.5	
Belgium	52.9	5.7		10.8	
Italy	51.9	13.0		25.0	
Ireland	51.1	13.8		27.0	
France	49.4	6.3		12.8	
Luxemburg	48.7	5.8		11.9	
UK	44.9	11.8		26.2	
Norway	44.8	15.5		34.5	
Austria	44.8	5.7	(12.0)	12.7	(26.8)
Germany	44.2	5.0	(16.4)	11.4	(37.2)
Canada	44.0	10.3	(30.5)	23.3	(69.4)
Portugal	37.5	1.5		3.9	
USA	36.9	12.9		34.8	
Finland	36.2	15.2		42.0	
Australia	33.4	14.3		42.9	
Spain	31.8	3.8		11.8	
Switzerland	31.2	6.5	(16.1)	20.9	(51.5)
Japan	27.1	10.6		39.0	
Mean Value	43.5	10.5		24.4	

Note: Figures in brackets are for state and local spending

Source: OECD National Accounts Statistics 1972-84, Vol II, (OECD, Paris, 1986).

share and the total government share of GDP only 0.39. Hence countries devoting a large fraction of national output to public spending do not necessarily spend at a high level locally.

Given the currently contentious debate over the size of the public sector in Britain, the need to cut local spending, and the desire for reform of local fiscs, the position of the UK is of especial interest. The UK figures are very close to the average for the 19 nations in the table. The UK lies just above the mid-point in the international table for government expenditure as a percentage of GDP, ranking eighth and below comparable Western European nations such as Sweden, Netherlands, Ireland, France, Italy, and Belguim. Looking at the percentage share of both national product and total government spending devoted to the local level, Britain's position is within 1.5 per cent of the average value for all nations. In the last decade there has been a strong policy commitment to reduce the local government share of GDP in the United Kingdom. The resultant decline was at first confined largely to capital spending with current spending continuing to rise unabated. Further pressure from central government accelerated the reduction in local spending, but this was offset by the economy declining at a faster rate, with the net outcome of increasing the share of the national product going to subnational government (Jackman, 1985). However, in spite of these recent trends, aggregate local spending in the UK is not so untypical of comparable urban industrial nations to warrant a new and specialised system of garnering local revenues.

Local authorities in the UK do not stand out as abnormally high spenders among comparable advanced industrial countries, in relation to either national output or total public expenditure. Essentially the UK is average with respect to aggregate local spending. However, given the different spread of functions of UK local government and their confinement to purely local units, disaggregated service expenditure data should demonstrate discontinuities rather than similarities between the UK and other nations. In order to test this Gould and Zarkesh (1986) disaggregated the total spending of subnational governments in 14 nations on a percentage basis, by different service groups. Coming from different national data sources the figures shown in Table 4.4 are not strictly definitive, but nevertheless provide an illustrative comparison of the UK and other nations.

From the figures in the table spending on services provided at subnational level seems to be concentrated in education, followed by health and social security. Three services are funded only at local level (housing, general public services, and recreation and culture) but between them they make up only 30 per cent of local budgets on average. The high spending services - education, health and social service - are usually supplied at both state and local level, making up on average 61 per cent of the spending of the former and 52 per cent of the latter. The UK is unique in the four services it funds at local level - education, housing, public order and transport (though funding of the last has declined rapidly since the deregulation of municipal transport in September 1986). Additionally the apportionment of local spending between these services in the UK is untypical. The country closest is Ireland, which unlike the UK spends heavily on health (42 per cent of local spending) and does not allocate local expenditure to public order services. Compared with the cross-national average, UK local authorities allocate more than half as much again of their budgets to education, but allot nothing to health or social services, which on average account for 15 per cent and 17 per cent respectively, of local budgets elsewhere. Both housing and transport are funded at local level in the UK, but at half the average budget ration of other countries. Table 4.4 confirms that the asymmetric pattern of functions of UK subnational government is accompanied by an asymmetric budget allocation of funds if this somewhat abnormal pattern of spending is paralleled by a particular taxation mode.

The diversity of local authority funding methods among nations is as great as that of their structure and functions. There are two common elements found in most local fiscal systems, but cross nationally their respective contributions to funding may vary markedly, as may those of additional revenue sources. The first common element is some form or forms of taxation, indirect, direct, or both; the second is assistance in the shape of grants or other transfers from other superior tiers of government. Cross-national surveys (Bennett, 1980) have shown the size and system of such transfers to be important to intergovernmental fiscal relations, while more

Table 4.4: Service expenditures as a percentage of total expenditures of state and local governments

	Education		Health		Social services		Housing		Transport		General public services		Recreation and culture		Public order and safety	
	State	Local	State	Local	State	Local	State	Local	State	Local	State	Local	State	Local	State	Local
Australia	33		19					15	11	27		20		16		
Belgium		28				12		8		10						
Canada	22	42	24		15	8			7	12						8
Finland		25		12		15										
France		14				18		16				12				13
Germany	25	12	7	12	18	19		17		10					9	
Ireland		7		42				9		10						
Italy		9				42				9		7				
Japan		25		6		11						9				
Netherlands	11					27		14		9				7		
Sweden		19				24		12		9				7		
Switzerland	27	23	18	13	11	8		10		10		9		9		
UK		32						5		5						7
USA	16	44	36	8	16	7			10	7						8
Mean value	24.6	19.3	21.3	15.5	15.0	17.4	-	11.8	9.3	10.7	-	11.4	-	9.7	9.0	9.0

Source: F. Gould and F. Zarkesh, Local Government Expenditures and Revenues in Western Democracies: 1960-1982 , Local Government Studies, January/February, 1986, p.40.

detailed analysis (Bennett, 1982) has revealed these features of grant aid to be absolutely crucial in the case of the UK.

Obviously the size of transfer payments will have important ramifications for the existing (and proposed) taxation systems in both Britain and elsewhere. Clearly a large grant element will make the tax contribution to local fiscs less important. However, this may reduce the financial discretion of subnational administrations as it may allow national or other superior governments to vary grant levels with the aim of influencing local expenditure levels. Conversely where taxation is the main source of local funding, subnational governments may exercise greater control over their own budgets, but this has to be weighed against the possibility of additional opprobium associated with raising the tax rate. Possession of a plurality of fiscs may permit local authorities to dissipate the political cost of an increased aggregate cess burden by spreading it between taxes. Furthermore, historical circumstances may bequeath high discretion over local taxing and spending even with high grant levels and singularity of taxes, allowing subnational units to pursue policies diametrically opposed to the retrenchment public expenditure policy objectives of central governments in the 1980s. Consequently central governments may seek to reform the system of local spending and taxing to increase their control over it. Recent experience in the UK and the current proposals for alteration of local property taxes are clear examples of this. Hence it is appropriate to ask whether the level of grant assistance and the local taxation system in the UK are so different from other countries as to justify the reform of local fiscs now under consideration by central government.

The patterns of local funding in the UK and other Western nations are given in Table 4.5. Using the mean values of the contributions of funds from different sources as a yardstick for comparison, the anomalous position of UK subnational governments is readily apparent. Most noticeably the UK is the only nation having no income from direct taxation, with the exception of Ireland. By contrast the other 17 nations all use direct taxes at state or local level,

Table 4.5: Sources of local and state funding, 1984

	Property income as % total		Indirect tax as % total		Direct tax as % total		Social security as % total		Others as % total		Transfers as % total	
	State	Local	State	Local	State	Local	State	Local	State	Local	State	Local
Australia		8.1		38.0						3.4		50.5
Austria	2.0	2.9	25.9	45.4	35.7	29.6	1.6	1.6	0.4	0.7	34.4	19.7
Belgium		12.3		6.0		34.1						47.6
Canada	17.5	1.7	24.0	34.3	29.1	-	4.7	-	2.7	0.6	21.9	63.4
Finland		2.8		0.01		53.3				0.3		43.7
France		2.9		30.9		24.8				0.7		40.8
Germany	1.4	4.9	28.3	31.7	48.9	24.2			2.5	4.2	18.9	35.0
Ireland		7.1		6.1				4.7				82.1
Italy		2.9		4.1		6.9		0.2				85.9
Japan		2.4		32.7		24.7				0.4		39.8
Luxembourg		10.8		47.5		33.6						8.1
Netherlands		9.7		4.0		1.6				1.4		83.3
Norway		9.3		1.4		47.9						41.4
Portugal		3.7		5.7		28.0						62.6
Spain		3.3		42.9		39.8						14.0
Sweden		5.3		1.3		56.3						37.1
Switzerland	2.9	4.9	8.7	2.8	60.7	68.0			2.9	4.9	24.8	19.4
UK		5.7		35.4								58.9
USA		6.4		52.8		18.9				1.8		20.1
Mean	5.95	5.64	21.72	22.26	43.60	32.78	3.15	2.17	2.12	1.84	25.0	44.92

Note: Figures are percentages of total funds.

Source: OECD National Accounts of OECD Countries 1972-84, Vol.II (OECD Paris, 1986).

with local authorities getting nearly a third of their income from this source. Social security payments are levied at local level in only a minority of nations, and only provide a small portion of local revenues. In about half of the nations shown in Table 4.5 subnational governments obtain revenue from other unspecified sources but, as with social security, the contribution to total local taxes from this source is minor. The inability to levy direct taxation naturally leads to greater reliance on other financial resources, namely non-tax income from municipal enterprises, intergovernmental transfers and indirect taxation.

However, local administrations in the UK are averagely reliant on municipal trading and property income to fund their activities, obtaining 5.7 per cent of total receipts in this way, compared with an average of 5.6 per cent in other nations. The share of income which local authorities in the UK obtain from this source has radically declined. Increasing sales of state housing to sitting tenants in recent years have severely depressed rent incomes accruing to local authorities, which declined by 14 per cent between 1981 and 1984. As a result both of having no local system of direct taxation and of declining municipal revenues, the level of transfers between national and subnational governments in the UK is relatively high, ranking sixth out of 19 nations, and at a level 14 per cent above the average. The UK is one of seven nations in which local government units obtain more than 50 per cent of their receipts from grants, in contrast to European counterparts such as France, Germany, and more especially Norway and Sweden, all of which obtain the majority of local funds from non-grant sources. However, the greatest difference between UK funding structures and those elsewhere relate to indirect taxation. Absence of a source of direct taxation leads the indirect taxation contribution of subnational budgets to be more than half as much again in the UK, compared with the cross-national average. In the UK more than a third of local revenues come from indirect taxes, in comparable Western nations the figure is just over a fifth. This overwhelming reliance on indirect taxation prompts more detailed examination of UK

Table 4.6: Individual local taxes as % total local taxes, 1984

	Income tax		Payroll tax		Property tax		General consumption tax		Specified goods tax		Taxes on use of goods		Other	
	State	Local	State	Local	State	Local	State	Local	State	Local	State	Local	State	Local
Australia			35.2		25.9	95.9			13.7		25.3	4.1		
Austria	44.8	37.2		11.0	1.6	11.2	38.5	23.4	6.6	11.1	5.1	1.5	3.5	4.6
Belgium		67.3										14.1		18.6
Canada	44.1				4.1	85.3	19.3		15.4		17.2	1.1		13.6
Denmark		90.7				6.4				0.1		0.1		2.7
Finland		90.4				0.8						0.1		8.7
France		16.1				29.9				3.1		6.6		44.4
Germany	60.8	78.7			6.1	20.3	26.1		2.1	0.3	5.0	0.5		0.2
Ireland						100								
Italy		16.6								9.0		0.3		74.0
Japan		28.8				23.6				12.9		5.0		29.6
Luxembourg		36.4				4.5		8.0				0.9		50.0
Netherlands						73.4				1.2		25.4		
New Zealand						92.6				2.3		5.0		
Norway		84.2				5.9						0.4		9.5
Portugal						1.3		10.1		20.1		5.3		63.2
Spain		35.4				13.4		26.0		13.9				11.3
Switzerland	76.7	87.0			15.3	12.7			1.4	0.2	6.6	0.1		
Sweden		92.9								0.2		0.1		6.8
UK						100								
USA	37.7	5.8			3.7	75.0	31.7	10.2	17.1	4.6	9.7	4.3		
Mean Value	52.8	54.8	35.2	11.0	9.4	41.8	28.9	15.5	9.4	6.1	11.5	4.2	3.5	24.1

Source: OECD, Revenue Statistics of OECD Member Countries 1965-85 (Paris: OECD , 1986), Tables 123, 124.

local taxes to assess the need for further reform.

To obtain a clearer perspective of subnational fiscs in the UK in relation to other countries, Table 4.6 shows the contribution of different levies to total local taxes. Diversity in the number of taxes used is evident; on average local tiers of government use four different levies for municipal funding, though some use as many as seven, with local income tax, property tax, and tax on the use of goods being the most common, while payroll and general consumption taxes are rarely utilised. The UK position is remarkable for its abnormality rather than typicality. Subnational governments in the UK (along with those in the Irish Republic) get all their tax revenue from one fisc, the property tax. A local tax on property is used in many nations, but local government units in other countries are not solely dependent on it, unlike those in the UK. On average property taxes constituted 40 per cent of local taxes cross-nationally in the 18 countries in which they were used. However, the average contribution which this levy makes outside of those countries which are wholly dependent on it (the Irish Republic and the UK) is somewhat lower, at 34 per cent. The other main tax contributor, local income tax, provides about 55 per cent of total local revenue in those 14 nations in which it is levied,while the other commonly used tax on the use of goods generates only a minor contribution, averaging 4 per cent, in the 18 nations which make use of it. Hence with respect to local taxes the UK is exceptional in relying exclusively on the property tax for funding, and in not making use of local income tax.

Given the unusual position of sole reliance on property tax, it is worth examining the features of the levy in the UK compared with elsewhere to attest the case for reform. Systems of taxing immovable property will vary in intricacy between nations: however Table 4.7 summarises the more salient points. Although not conclusive, the table suggests that property taxes in the UK are somewhat different from those elsewhere. First the base of the tax is revalued less frequently in Britain (nominally every five years) than the average for other countries (3-4

Table 4.7: Features of local property taxes 1983

Nation	Tax	Revaluation frequency	Last revaluation	Basis of revaluation	Discretion of beneficiary government over	
					base	rate
Australia	Land tax	2 - 3	1979 - 81	Capital	Unlimited	Unlimited
	Rates	2 - 3	1979 - 81	Capital	Limited	Limited
Denmark	Land tax	4	1981	Capital	None	Limited
	Service tax		1981	Capital	None	Unlimited
France	Land & Land & Building tax	2	1970 - 73	Rental	None	Limited
	Property tax			Rental	None	Limited
Germany	Grundstuer	6	1964	Capital	None	Limited
Ireland	Rates	Nil	1850's	Rental	None	Limited
Japan	Fixed assets Tax					
	- Land	3	1982	Capital	None	Very Limited
	- Business	Yearly		Capital	None	Very Limited
	City planning tax	3	1982	Capital	None	Limited
	Special land holding tax	N.A.		Capital	None	None
Netherlands	Municipal tax	5 or less	1979 - 81	Capital	Limited	Limited
New Zealand	Rates	5 or less	1977 - 81	Cap./Ren	Limited	Limited
Spain	Rural land tax	5	1981	Rental	None	None
	Urban land tax	3	1981	Rental	None	None
Sweden	Municipal guarantee tax	5	1981	Capital	None	Unlimited
UK	Rates	5	1973	Rental	None	Unlimited
USA	Property Tax	1 - 4	1977 - 81	Capital	Variable	Unlimited

Source: OECD, Taxes on Immovable Property (Paris, OECD, 1983).

years). In fact recent legislation has removed the five-year term and placed the timing of revaluations completely at the discretion of central government. In addition British local authorities are among those which have not undergone a recent revaluation (although the Scottish properties were revalued in 1985). Like property taxes in most countries, the discretion for revaluation of the base lies not with the beneficiary local government in the UK but with central government. However, unlike most countries, the valuation base for the property tax in the UK is the rental value which is markedly less buoyant than the system of capital valuations used elsewhere. Finally unlike many other countries, local authorities in Britain have until recently had complete freedom over the setting of the property tax levy. Legislation recently passed in the UK, in spite of fierce opposition from local authorities, has substantially curbed their taxing powers and given central government greater discretion to affect the level of local taxation of property.

NEW LOCAL FISCS IN BRITAIN - VIABILITY OR REFORM?

The mosaic of structure and functions, spending and funding outlined above provides a context for assessing the new system of local taxes in Britain, in which functional allocation and structure are unaltered but funding is shifted from property taxes to assigned revenues and a flat rate capitation fee. Under the new scheme non-domestic hereditaments will have a uniform rate poundage levied at national level. The tax will be collected by local authorities who will retain sufficient such that the rate of local domestic tax per adult will be lowered by the same amount nationally. The tax base of the new levy will be either index linked to the inflation rate or undergo more frequent revaluations than at present. Domestic rates will be replaced by a 'Community Charge' scheme under which a register of all residents will be maintained by local authorities who would levy a flat rate charge on each. Each head of household will be under a legal obligation to supply information on residents, allowing local authorities to compile and update the register.

Three questions are particularly pertinent in evaluating the viability and durability of this system. First are there any subnational governments with a system of fiscs akin to those proposed for British local authorities, or will the British system be unique, post reform? More importantly, if there are any other subnational governments elsewhere utilising poll tax and assigned revenues, either individually or in tandem, to what extent have they coped better than their British counterparts in the period of fiscal stress and retrenchment since the early 1970s? Lastly, if the British system is not used elsewhere, can experience in other nations indicate whether another system of taxation might be more appropriate for Britain, given its current functions and structure or if a more radical solution of structural, functional and financial reform is needed?

Looking first at the use of assigned revenues and poll taxes in other countries. In essence the differences between grants from central government to subnational tiers and assigned revenues are minimal, more especially where the discretion over deciding on the apportionment level lies absolutely with central government. Revenue sharing of this kind does occur between central and local governments in Western nations, but cannot be considered common, although it is used in Germany, Switzerland and Sweden. In fact assigned revenues were a source of funding for local authorities in England and Wales where they were set up by the Local Government Act of 1888 (Ashford, 1980). Under this legislation certain national taxes were assigned to a Treasury Local Account Fund, administered by central government who distributed them among the rural county and city county borough authorities through their Exchequer Contribution Accounts. Assigned revenues in Britain were finally abolished under the 1929 Local Government Act.

Similarly an assigned revenue system had been tried in Italy and abandoned (Martinotti, 1981). Under the system established in 1974 the commune authorities took a share of the income tax collected by the national government. This local share was set by the national government at the rate of the family tax it replaced, plus a 10 per cent allowance for inflation. The failure of the national government to constrain inflation caused the value of the tax to decline, causing the local authorities to seek the right to set their own income tax rates, which they achieved in 1978.

Turning to the poll tax (or 'Community Charge') as a source of local funding, such fiscs have been levied in many countries. However, today this tax is usually confined to undeveloped economies, where its simplicity obviates the problems with administering taxes which can lead to serious shortfalls in expected revenue in such nations (Radian, 1980). The process of industrialisation and the consequent growth of the state necessitates a more sophisticated taxation system, and so poll taxes are rarely favoured in developed Western nations. Poll taxes were first used in Britain in 1377, but were so unpopular as to precipitate the Peasants' Revolt three years later. Levied only intermittently thereafter as a result of their continued unpopularity, the poll tax of 1698 was the last time a general tax of this type was imposed in Britain, though evasion was widespread (Dowell, 1888). In the United States poll taxes at a flat rate of $1 or $2 per head were charged after the Civil War to aid reconstruction. Though some states continued to levy them in the south (Ogden, 1958), most had abolished them by 1920. More recently poll taxes have been levied in African countries such as Kenya and Uganda but have largely been abandoned.

The case for poll taxes in modern conditions, Pepper (1969) considers, is based on the grounds that all citizens 'ought' to contribute at least something to revenue however small their means. More particularly, he suggests, the feeling exists that the privileges of welfare coverage and universal suffrage accruing to the citizen in the modern state warrant some form of universal direct taxation. Such reasoning seems to underpin the outlined proposals for the 'community charge', which both attempts to link the enjoyment of service benefits resulting from local taxation directly to those who pay the levies and calls for some kind of minimum levy to be charged to all irrespective of financial circumstance.

Table 4.8: 'Other' local taxes as % total taxes 1984

Nation	Tax description	'Other' taxes as % total local taxes
Austria	Other (not specified)	0.48
Canada	Misc. (poll tax till 1970)	4.00
Denmark	Other (not specified)	0.01
France	Divers (collective locales)	0.09
Germany	Other (not specified)	0.25
Japan	Taxes not in local tax law	0.11
Norway	Other (not specified)	3.01
Portugal	Tax militaire - divers	1.15
Mean Value		1.13

Source: OECD Revenue Statistics of OECD Member Countries 1965-85 (Paris, OECD, 1986).

Assessing the contribution of poll taxes today is difficult as inadequate information on the fine details of subnational funding elsewhere precludes definitive examination of its use. However, such data as is available suggests that utilisation of the poll tax is very much a freakish occurrence rather than a regular and persisting feature of subnational government fiscal systems. A recent and comprehensive survey of tax systems in Western Europe (OECD, 1983) covering over 23 countries failed to elicit any details of such taxes at local level. Similarly the OECD classifies taxes into six basic categories depending on the tax base, namely income and profits tax, social security contributions, payroll and workforce taxes, property taxes, taxes on goods and services, and other taxes, with poll taxes coming under the last. However, examination of current OECD revenue statistics reveals seven nations in which taxes in the 'other' category are levied at subnational level on individual citizens.

Two points are worthy of note with respect to these fiscs, shown in Table 4.8. The first is that in only one instance, that of Canada, is the tax necessarily a poll tax and then only until 1970. The second is that the contribution to local fundings from these taxes is very low - the highest being 4.0 per cent in Canada and the lowest 0.1 per cent in Japan. In general the poll tax is shown to be an infrequently used tax, utilised only at a very low level.

The low incidence of usage of both assigned revenues and poll taxes indicates that the proposed system of local funding in the United Kingdom will be unique. No subnational units of government elsewhere use these two taxes jointly and none rely exclusively on them for total tax funding. The uniqueness of the British system, post reform, begs the second question posed, namely how well have other nations using assigned revenues and poll taxes in tandem fared. Hence there will be no concrete indication of the viability of the new tax system prior to its installation, although the unwillingness of subnational governments elsewhere to adopt such a funding structure does not augur well for its success.

Given the unique position of the United Kingdom local authority fiscal arrangements under the new proposals, it is worth considering which features of subnational taxing used elsewhere might be appropriate to Britain. First most other systems have a plurality of taxes which can be levied at local level, four being the norm. In addition countries possessing a plurality of taxes tend on average to utilise property taxes as a supplementary rather than a major fisc, with local income tax occupying a predominant role in many subnational government systems. Adoption of such a system in Britain, oft mooted (e.g. Jones and Stewart, 1983) but never implemented, would provide a considerable boost to local authority funding. Hence a movement away from the absolute reliance on a single tax towards a plurality of taxes might strengthen the finances of subnational units in the United Kingdom. Nevertheless, Auld (1986) judges that in terms of efficiency criteria, the existing system of local revenue raising in Britain is superior to that of comparable nations with a plurality of fiscs including local income tax. However, if the property tax is to be retained, albeit as a minor contributor to local taxes, a shift from using rental values as the basis for the tax (as occurs in the United Kingdom), towards the more usual method of capital value rating would do much to strengthen this revenue source.

However, it is impossible to consider reform of the mode of funding in isolation from the totality of the subnational government system. The appropriateness of a fisc is dependent more on considerations of the role of the authority it is to fund. More powerful and geographically extensive authorities clearly require different funding schemes from smaller authorities with limited functions. Small authority size may rule out the levying of certain taxes, while larger authorities may use the same levy readily and economically.

As suggested initially there is a strong link between the structure and functions of subnational units and the system of finances to fund them. Reviewing the United Kingdom subnational government in terms of structure and functions within the perspective of systems elsewhere, specific features are apparent. First the United Kingdom lacks an intermediate tier of government (consisting of regions or provinces), in consequence of which the local government units tend to be on average higher in population than those elsewhere. The average population of some of the British local authorities exceeds those of intermediate tiers in other countries such as Australia, Canada, Denmark, Germany, etc. If population size was the chosen criterion for the granting of regional status many of the English counties would qualify.

Allied to this, the absence of a regional tier of government necessitates that all subnational functions are designated as local. Services that in other nations are performed at intermediate level are either undertaken by local authorities (e.g. higher education) or central government (e.g. electricity generation), or have been passed to non-elected regional bodies (e.g. health and water). Introduction of an intermediate tier, and dispersion of the services between the different tiers as occurs in other countries, would clarify the existing confusing morass of responsibilities and functions.

Moreover, intermediate tier units based on a

regional framework with increased powers and duties would justify the need for additional or alternative tax sources such as are levied by other intermediate subnational governments elsewhere. The taxation systems of local authorities are a reflection of the role ascribed to them by national governments. The proposed system of assigned revenues and poll taxes, and the reduction in local discretion over taxing it represents, provide the clearest indication that central government are seeking to undermine rather than augment the power and status of subnational governments in the United Kingdom. Clearly the viability of any new mode of local funding will depend on the importance central government attaches to having a durable and flourishing system of government at subnational level in Britain.

REFERENCES

Ashford, D. (1980)
Financing Urban Government in the Welfare State, Croom Helm, London

Auld, D. (1986)
'The Efficiency Criteria For Local Government Revenue: An International Comparison'. Occasional Paper 37, Canberra Centre for Research on Federal Financial Relations, ANU

Bennett, R.J. (1980)
The Geography of Public Finance: Welfare under fiscal federalism and local government finance, Methuen, London

-- (1982) Central Grants to Local Governments, CUP, Cambridge

Brown, C.V. and Jackson, P. (1982)
Public Sector Economics, Martin Robertson, Oxford

Dowell, S. (1888)
History of Taxation and Taxes in England vol. III, Longmans Green, London

Local Taxing and Local Spending

Gould, F. and Zarkesh, F. (1986)
'Local Government Expenditures and Revenues in Western Democracies: 1960-1982', Local Government Studies, vol.12, no.1

HMSO (1986)
Green Paper, Paying for Local Government, London, HMSO, Cmnd. 6813

Humes, S. and Martin, E. (1969)
The Structure of Local Government Throughout the World, Martinus Nijhoff, The Hague

Jackman, R. (1985)
'Local Government Finance', in Loughlin M., Gelfand, M.D. and Young, K. (eds.), Half a Century of Municipal Decline, George Allen & Unwin, London

Jones, G. and Stewart, J. (1983), The Case for Local Government, George Allen & Unwin, London

Martinotti, G. (1981)
'The Illusive Autonomy: Central Control and Decentralisation in the Italian Local Financial System', in Sharpe, L.J. (ed.), The Local Fiscal Crisis in Western Europe, Sage, London

OECD (1983)
Taxes on Immovable Property, OECD, Paris

Ogden, F.D. (1958)
The Poll Tax in the South, University of Alabama Press, Alabama

Pepper, H.W.T. (1969)
'Poll Taxes, Payroll Taxation and Social Security', Bulletin for International Fiscal Documentation, vol.23, no.1

Radian, A. (1980)
Resource Mobilisation in Poor Countries: Implementing Tax Policies, Transaction Books, New Brunswick, N.J.

5 SOURCES OF LOCAL FINANCE IN THE UNITED STATES

Desmond King

INTRODUCTION

This chapter presents an account of the sources of local finance in the American political system. 'Local' refers to local governments, but principally municipalities, rather than school districts, townships or other special districts. Altogether there are over 80,000 units of local government in the United States. The purpose of this review is to contrast the situation in Britain with that of the United States against the capacity of local authorities to raise and control their finances. The central argument is that the differences between the two countries in this regard hinge critically upon the degree of local autonomy found in each political system. Local autonomy is fundamentally a political issue deriving from the nature of central-local relations in each country and the political assumptions informing these respective relationships influenced by the political culture. The United States is a federal polity imbued throughout with the culture of decentralization and local autonomy: local governments remain creatures of their regional states (see below), though they exercise some autonomy within those constraints. By contrast, British local authorities are tightly constrained by Parliamentary legislation as to what they can and cannot do. But there is an important tradition of local authorities determining their own revenue needs and allocation of their funds in Britain: it is this tradition which has been eroded since the 1970s by the central government, manifested most forcibly in the realm of central-local financial relations. This erosion of local autonomy is a political process motivated and shaped by political interests and concerns.

Economic, and other, rationales may well be produced for particular arrangements but these must be analysed in their political context.

While the primary concern of this chapter is with the processes of local revenue raising in the United States, this is a comparative exercise intended to illuminate the current British system and the consequences of proposed reforms. In consequence, discussion of American local fiscal practice concentrates upon municipalities since these are the most comparable units of government to British local authorities.

REVENUE RAISING AND LOCAL AUTONOMY

To analyse effectively the conditions of local revenue sources, it is necessary to identify the major constraints upon municipalities, local governments and local authorities. These are of two fundamental kinds, paralleling the sources of local revenue (external and internal). Elsewhere (King and Gurr, 1985; Gurr and King, 1987), I have developed a general theoretical argument about the nature of local autonomy in Britain and the United States distinguishing between (1) local autonomy from local economic conditions and (2) local autonomy from external governmental agencies or levels. Regarding revenue, local governments or municipalities seek to maximize their autonomy over local revenue raising (that is, seek to raise revenues to the extent they want and within as diversified a form as they want); and to maximize their autonomy over central government grants (that is, to have as few restrictions and stipulations attached to central grants as possible).

Clearly, no municipality will enjoy as much autonomy as it would like: for instance, there are local political constraints upon the level of local taxes, be they property or sales or income. Similarly, some central government grants are allocated to local governments to meet specific public policy objectives and cannot be diverted into other areas. But while these maximum levels of local autonomy cannot be achieved there remains potential for local authorities to have some control and discretion over their revenue-raising powers. And while the consequences for local autonomy of increased external funding in both countries has been the focus of analysis until recently, the new British proposals and the character of post-1979 central-local fiscal relations has extended the controls upon local autonomy: that is, local authorities are not only receiving less from central government and have less discretion about its allocation but their control of local or internal revenue raising has been diminished also. These issues will be considered further after examining the revenue raising practices of the United States in detail.

LOCAL GOVERNMENT AND FINANCES IN THE UNITED STATES

The Structure of Local Government

American subnational government is highly fragmented: apart from the 50 regional states, there are 82,290 units of local government (as of 1982, see US Department of Commerce, 1986, table no. 440), of five main types. First, there are county governments (3,041) which have administrative responsibility for a designated geographic area, larger than any of the other units of government. Second, there are municipalities (19,076), which are responsible for specific urban areas and the provision of services within these jurisdictions (see below). Third, there are 16,734 townships and town local governments, responsible for smaller jurisdictions than municipal local governments. Fourth, the 14,851 school district local governments are responsible for the provision of education independently of local politicians. And, finally, there are 28,588 special district local governments responsible for one specific service to a delineated group of citizens; examples include special district governments for natural resources, fire protection and housing/community development. The discussion in this chapter is concerned with municipal local governments, since these are most relevant to a comparative focus upon British local authorities. However, many of the points advanced here apply equally to the other units of local government. Further, while overlapping tiers of local government result in multiple taxation for citizens and sometimes uncertainty about where responsibility lies for particular services, this is less true of the large cities with strong political traditions epitomized by the urban political machine 'boss'. More generally, this fragmented governmental system reflects the American commitment to federalism, which determines in part the status of local governments, to which we turn.

The Status of American Local Governments

As one scholar has observed, 'federalism is the central characteristic of the American political system, its principles animating the greater part of the nation's political process' (Elazar, 1972, p.3). American federalism has always been closely aligned with ideas about democratic decentralization: that is, the federalist ideology has been embraced by Americans partly to maximize local democracy or decentralized control by citizens: 'as put into practice, the expression of individual rights through the community plays an important function in representative government: local governments are the protectors against the potential centralization of democratic individualism in a national government' (Thomas,1986, p.55; see also Magnusson, 1986).

For the 50 regional states, their independence of the federal government is guaranteed by the Constitution: the tenth amendment states that, 'the powers not delegated to the United States by the Constitution, nor prohibited by it to the States, are reserved to the States respectively, or to the people'. This article has been construed as a safeguard against the excessive encroachment of the federal government or its agencies into the affairs of the states. In contrast, the status of local government enjoys no such Constitutional guarantee but is a function of the powers granted by the states of which each local government is a component part. This status was codified by Judge John F. Dillon in Atkins v. Kansas (1903), 191 US 182, who stated that cities 'are the creatures, mere political subdivisions, of the state for the purpose of exercising a part of its powers. They may exert only such powers as are expressly granted to them or such as may be necessarily implied from those granted' (cited in Wolman, 1982, p.172; see also Gurr and King, 1987, ch.2; Clark and Dear, 1984, ch.7). This judgement was upheld in City of Trenton v. New Jersey (1923) 262 US 182. In practice, this status of mere creatures - commonly known as Dillon's Rule - has been modified: many local governments have been granted considerable powers by their states, including powers to devise and implement taxes. Local governments are general-purpose governments, which places certain requirements upon the services they provide and how they respond to citizen demands, which entails exercising some autonomous decision-making. Thus as well as exercising those powers expressly granted to them, local governments can exercise powers necessarily implied by the express powers.

Dillon's Rule has been modified also as a result of the 'home rule' movement, a movement which sought to give local governments the right to pursue some policy initiatives without direct legislative authority from their state legislature. Many municipal governments enjoy some measure of home rule though the variation between states and amongst local governments within single states remains considerable; as Jones observes 'there is a vast amount of state-to-state variation in the meaning of the term home rule. Some states supervise their local units of government so closely that self government is a sham. In other states, home rule grants important self governing power' (1983, p.206). For our purposes, the significant point is the existence of variation and the willingness to consider alternative methods of organizing revenues in the United States compared with British practice.

Local Finance in the United States

The Responsibilities of Cities

Cities in the United States are responsible for the provision of a wide range of services including fire protection, police, streets and sanitation, water systems, libraries, public works, health and welfare, inspection and regulatory services, government administration and general purpose services (see Table 5.1). Given this set of functions - vital to the working of the American polity - it is clear that local governments constitute an integral part of the political and administrative structure of the United States reflecting the strong decentralist principles of American federalism. Politically, the absence of strong national political parties and the development of urban party machines in the late nineteenth century, rendered cities and city politics central to the way in which politics was to be conducted in America. Recently, one scholar has argued that a fundamental cleavage of American politics derives from urban politics (Katznelson, 1981): according to Ira Katznelson the American polity is characterized by 'city trenches' constituted by a division between 'work' and 'community'. This has had profound consequences for the class structure, political action and the formation of group interests, according to Katznelson. Thus, urban activity is central to American political practice, at least as important, if not more so for some citizens, as national government. Since municipal finances are at the core of local government, they enjoy a prominence in urban political debate and discussion.

Internal and External Sources of Local Revenue

Local governments and municipalities raise the finances to cover these expenditure responsibilities from a number of sources, which can be grouped into two main areas: internal or local, that is, revenues collected from within the jurisdiction of the local government (including property taxes, borrowing and user fees); and external or intergovernmental, that is, revenues which come from outside the local

Table 5.1: Major state activities by tier of government in the United States

	Local governments	State governments	Federal government
National Defence	-	x	X
Transportation & communication	x	x	x
Education	X	x	x
Social security	-	x	X
Highways	x	X	X
Property protection	X	x	x
Metropolitan development	X	x	x
Health	X	x	x
Natural resource development	-	x	x

X = principal responsibility
x = secondary responsibility
- = no or marginal responsibility

Source: see Leach (1970), Table 3.1, p 60.

government's jurisdiction (including federal and regional state aid). It is necessary to discuss these different sources of revenue in some detail.

Internal Revenue 1: Taxes

For local governments, revenue generated through property taxes are especially important, with up to 80 per cent of local revenue deriving from this source for some local governments in 1978 - a fall from 87 per cent in 1960 (Walker, 1981; see also Jones, 1983). This is less true of many larger municipalities who rely less upon property revenue than other sources of income (see Table 5.2): 'reliance on the property tax dropped to 29.0 per cent for all municipalities by 1980; ten years earlier this tax had generated 39.1 per cent of all local revenues' (Judd, 1984, p.210). (School districts are an example of local government which continue to rely predominantly upon the property tax for its revenues, because they have no alternative revenue source.) For cities located in the Frostbelt (that is, Midwest and East) property taxes have been of declining importance to municipal revenues (for example, by 1975 they constituted 12 per cent and 14 per cent for St Louis and Philadelphia respectively (Walker,1980) as the deindustrialization of this region and attendant city fiscal stress have persisted.

Economic decline has been accompanied by demographic loss and a concentration of welfare dependants in central cities whose contribution to city revenues are minimal but whose consumption of public services is considerable. High inflation during the 1970s was particularly problematic for municipal property tax revenues, since their assessments did not keep apace with rapidly rising prices (Peterson, 1976; Shefter, 1977). In Sunbelt cities (that is, those in the South and West) the property tax has been of increasing importance to municipal revenue, because property values have increased with this region's economic transformation.

There is variation across local governments about what types of property constitute apposite objects of taxation. Tax rates also vary considerably: thus in 1984 the effective tax rate per $100 varied from 6.29 per cent in Newark (NJ) to 0.59 per cent in Casper (WY) (see Table 5.3). In general, property taxes are calculated on the basis of estimated capital (not rental) values rather than on the basis of realised value. Municipal officials produce assessed valuations for all property - a judgement about what

Table 5.2: Municipal revenues in the United States

(A) PROPERTY AND OTHER TAXES IN SELECTED CITIES

City	Property tax as % of city budget (1) (1983)	Property tax as % of all city taxes (2) (1981)	% Revenues from sales/gross receipts (2) (1981)
New York	24	44.9	25.9
Chicago	19	43.6	44.5
Los Angeles	19	36.7	43.8
Philadelphia	16	23.9	0.9
Houston	47	55.4	42.5
Detroit	10	50.0	12.0
Dallas	37	55.0	43.0
San Diego	15	32.8	59.7
Phoenix	18	33.4	61.6
Baltimore	37	64.3	9.6
San Antonio	15	54.0	42.8
Indianapolis	33	95.3	2.2
San Francisco	27	48.4	29.8
Memphis	24	71.1	17.1
Washington	19	24.8	34.5
Milwaukee	25	94.4	1.7
San Jose	15	26.9	49.7
Cleveland	14	29.2	0.5
Columbus	4	10.6	1.5
Boston	38	98.8	-
New Orleans	6	30.3	53.3
Jacksonville	24	67.1	26.8
Seattle	19	33.2	44.1
Denver	16	64.8	16.3
Nashville	53	58.5	33.1

Sources: (1) from Stanfield (1983);
(2) from County and City Date Book 1983 (US Department of Commerce, Bureau of the Census)

Table 5.2 (cont.):

(B) REVENUES FOR ALL CITY GOVERNMENTS (percentages)

	1970		1983	
General Revenue	81.4		77.8	
Federal and state grants	24.2		25.8	
Taxes	41.7		32.0	
Property		27.9		16.7
Sales and gross receipts		7.4		9.0
Income, licenses and other		6.4		6.4
Charges and miscellaneous	15.5		20.0	
Utility and liquor store revenue	15.8		18.0	
Water system		6.7		5.5
Electric power system		5.8		9.2
Gas supply system		0.9		1.9
Transit system		2.1		1.1
Liquor stores		0.4		0.2
Insurance trust revenue	2.8		4.2	
Total	100.0		100.0	

Source: see Statistical Abstract of the United States 1986 (US Department of Commerce), table no. 475.

the property would fetch if placed on the open market. Controversy surrounds this process, since many property owners will dispute their assessed valuation, and there are a number of possible inequities in the system. One important source of inequity concerns those properties whose market value is increasing rapidly, which tend to remain undertaxed since assessed valuation does not always increase apace. According to one scholar, 'tax assessors do not always update the estimated values for the properties in their jurisdictions. Properties do not increase (or decrease) in value uniformly. If such changes are not regularly taken into account, properties that were taxed at the same real rate (the tax rate relative to market worth) five years ago will not be taxed at the same real

Table 5.3: Residential property tax rates in large cities, 1984

City	Effective tax rate per $100	Assess-ment level	Nominal rate per $100
Newark, NJ	6.29	50.0	12.58
Detroit	4.04	49.1	8.22
Wilmington	3.47	70.0	4.95
Providence	3.36	48.3	6.96
Milwaukee	3.34	99.9	3.34
Baltimore	2.70	43.5	6.21
Des Moines	2.68	72.5	3.69
Philadelphia	2.62	35.0	7.48
Indianapolis	2.56	20.0	12.78
Portland, OR	2.37	96.0	2.47
Minneapolis	2.31	20.4	11.30
St Louis	2.15	33.2	6.45
Chicago	1.99	19.8	10.05
Cleveland	1.87	35.0	5.16
Jacksonville	1.85	94.0	1.97
Boston	1.71	100.0	1.71
Houston	1.68	100.0	1.68
Memphis	1.54	22.3	6.91
NYC	1.42	15.6	9.10
Louisville	1.27	90.0	1.40
Atlanta	1.23	24.4	5.03
Charlotte	1.20	94.5	1.27
Washington, DC	1.14	93.0	1.22
New Orleans	1.06	10.0	10.57
Phoenix	1.00	10.0	10.02
Seattle	0.95	94.5	1.00
Denver	0.70	7.8	8.99
Los Angeles	0.66	61.2	1.07
Casper	0.59	7.4	7.90

Source: Statistical Abstract of the United States 1986 (US Department of Commerce: Bureau of the Census), table no. 480.

rate today (except in the unlikely event that their market values have changed in exactly the same ways)' (Jones, 1983,pp.273-4). One way to counteract this disparity is to institute assessment-sales ratios: that is, to compare sales value (derived from recent property transactions) with assessed value in a given jurisdiction. Inequities in property values between jurisdictions also occurs as a result of the difficulty of valuing particular types of property such as commercial or industrial property.

Inequity arises further through individual municipalities' tax exemption policies: for example, enterprise zones frequently include a waiving of taxes as an incentive to attract new business; or various charitable, educational and religious institutions enjoy tax exemption on their property holdings. The total of tax exempt property in any one city can be substantial: for example, in 1969 '54 per cent of the real property in Boston was tax-exempt' (Judd, 1984, p.211), though this is exceptionally high. A related problem is the declining congruity between property tax paying and service usage: 'Since we now move about freely, the beneficiaries of today's education or welfare expenditures financed by the property owners of one community are tomorrow likely to be the residents of another community (Ecker-Racz, cited in Reagan and Sanzone, 1981, p.41).

Collection of property taxes can be stalled by delinquency, that is, failure by property owners to pay their tax, frequently because of bankruptcy. Cities acquire the property for which taxes have not been paid and then face the problem of selling off the property. This latter can become a substantial activity for the municipality and 'often results in properties remaining unproductive while the city follows legal procedures for acquiring private property' (Jones, 1983, p.277). During periods of recession tax delinquency becomes a major problem for cities, as it did for Detroit in the post-1975 period. Historically, property taxes in the United States have been regressive, allowing a heavy burden to fall upon low-income groups; this has changed somewhat, as some local governments give tax breaks to the elderly and poor, and middle-income groups spend proportionately more upon housing. This has by no means rendered the property tax progressive but has made it less glaringly regressive.

In addition to property taxes, an increasing number of American cities rely upon sales and income taxes (see Table 5.2). These originated in larger cities in the crisis of the 1930s: 'in 1934 New York City adopted a retail sales tax, and in 1938 New Orleans followed suit. Philadelphia in 1939 varied the pattern by adopting an earnings tax' (Maxwell and Aronson, 1977, p.167). There is variation regarding this tax amongst the large cities: for example, Boston does not use one, Houston, Baltimore and Columbus hardly at all; but for Phoenix, San Diego, Seattle and San Jose taxes on sales and gross receipts have become very substantial in the 1980s. Some cities use also a wage or income tax: for instance, a wage tax constitutes 48 per cent of Philadelphia's revenue (Stanfield, 1983). Thus the general trend amongst municipal local governments is diversification in the forms of tax revenues; this has required authorization from their regional states but reflects the capacity for local governments to articulate and pursue some independence in this area. Local governments do not have an automatic right to implement new taxes but nor are they restricted to a uniform pattern of taxes.

However, there are local limits to such expansion. Property taxes are vulnerable to shifting economic conditions, which explains in part the erosion of property tax dominance in northeastern cities; and to political factors: Proposition 13 (1978) in California, along with similar measures elsewhere, suggests that a threshold exists amongst the populace concerning the level of taxation that can be levied. This constitutes an additional constraint upon internal revenue sources and hence local autonomy. Proposition 13 was the initiative of a businessman in California, Howard Jarvis, who was determined to impose some limitations upon taxes levied for what he argued was a wasteful public bureaucracy. Despite the opposition of most politicians, Proposition 13 received a large majority from the voters. In California during the 1970s there was serious incongruity between real property taxes and the capacity of individuals to pay their taxes, because property assessments doubled (in some cases, tripled) in short periods; these regular reassessments reflected high rates of inflation. This initiative has been followed in other states and local jurisdictions, with considerable success. Prior to Proposition 13,

> four other states had adopted expenditure limits and subsequently eleven more caught some variant of Proposition 13 fever. Of the fifteen enactments, seven were constitutional, and all but two occurred in regions outside the Northeast and Great Lakes. In addition to these tax and expenditure lids, six states in the late seventies (Arizona, Colorado, and California in 1978 and Wisconsin, Iowa, and Minnesota in 1979) indexed their personal income taxes. By requiring that certain fixed dollar features of their income tax code be adjusted annually in the light of the rate of inflation, these states sought to curb the collections 'windfall' that occurs simply by inflation's capacity to push a family's income into a higher tax bracket. (Walker, 1981, p.162)

Such proposals are usually initiated by business people or landlords and resistance to them has been organized by public employees and state beneficiaries. One important caveat needs to append discussion of Proposition 13: this is that many contextually specific factors contributed to its success in California (see Danziger, 1980, p.604), which implies caution in the interpretation of this event - it should not necessarily be viewed as a general phenomenon. On the other hand, Proposition 13 has certainly acted as a stimulus to other states and localities to follow similar measures, and as Danziger notes, 'fully twenty three states passed some major fiscal limitations during the 1970s; (1980, p.609).

In sum, local governments levy a variety of taxes depending upon what the state to which individual municipal authorities belong allow them to do. But the general trend is toward increased diversification in the taxes which local governments can levy. By the early 1980s, all local governments had a property tax permitted by their states while '29 states permit a local general sales tax, and 13 states permit a local income tax' (Wolman, 1982, p.174). For some large cities nonproperty taxes provided over 40 per cent of their total tax collctions, which meant their dependence upon the local property tax was diminished; examples include, in 1973, Philadelphia, New Orleans, Los Angeles, Seattle, New York. For city governments as a whole property tax as a percentage of total taxes levied has dropped from 41.7 per cent in 1970 to 32.0 per cent in 1983 (US Department of Commerce, 1986). Thus those cities with diversified economies and diversified revenue systems are the strongest in the face of recession and shifting levels of economic activity. But the possibility of developing a diversified set of revenue sources depends largely upon the degree of local autonomy enjoyed by municipalities in the United States. Comparatively, it is important to note that experimentation with alternatives to the property taxes has been undertaken by municipal governments in those states where the state governments have agreed: 'development of new sources of revenue has, then, been mostly an urban phenomenon confined to a limited number of states. In these states - whether from a strong and positive home rule sentiment, or from a disinclination of legislatures to lift local problems to the state level - local governments have been allowed to experiment with taxes' (Maxwell and Aronson, 1977, p.169). This is a striking exercise of local autonomy denied British local authorities.

Internal Revenue 2: Borrowing

The second local source of revenue is borrowing. Borrowing is undertaken by municipalities for capital, rather than current or operating, expenditures: that is, for substantial infra-structural investments or improvements. Thus it is unlikely that a municipality would draw upon borrowing to meet current expenditures such as salaries or purchases. The exception to this is that municipalities can undertake short-term borrowing for pressing current or operating costs. Local governments borrow by issuing bonds, which guarantee to repay the purchaser the value of the bond as well as any interest accruing to it within a specified time period. The price of bonds is determined in a bond market where valuations of different cities' financial health are estimated and ranked. This is to avert the danger of cities defaulting on their bonds as New York City and Cleveland, Ohio, almost did in the 1970s because of their respective budgetary crises. In general, most cities in the United States have acquired fairly sizeable levels of debt (see Table 5.4).

Such debt can be either long term or short term: bonds issued for long term borrowing are used to finance capital expenditures. Long term borrowing is usually through general obligation bonds, which guarantees priority to the bond holder should the municipality go bankrupt. An alternative form - nonguaranteed bonds - are less securely based, to sidestep state limitations upon bond issuance by municipalities; they consist of revenue bonds issued in respect of specific projects, rather than general services which means that municipal underwriting is not necessary for repaying them in the event of bankruptcy. In the post-1945 period these nonguaranteed bonds have been extensively used by local governments. Thus as in nonproperty taxes, municipalities enjoy considerable local discretion/autonomy in this area: 'between 1977 and 1978, long-term debt outstanding for municipalities increased 9.8 per cent, while revenues from all sources increased only 8.6 per cent (and local tax revenues increased only 6.8 per cent). Municipalities are often unwilling to increase taxes, but they seem far less reluctant to increase debt' (Jones, 1983, pp.280-1). Municipal governments also engage in short-term borrowing which, as the name suggests, is for short-run fiscal needs - for example, meeting payrolls - giving the municipality increased budgetary flexibility. Local governments' notes are issues guaranteeing repayment plus interest for this purpose.

It is noteworthy that American cities have substantially increased the volume of municipal bonds issued during the last few decades, for both

Table 5.4: City Government Borrowing in the United States

	1970	1983
	%	%
Long-term debt	88.8	95.6
(as % of total debt)		
Full faith and credit	50.3	37.6
Nonguaranteed	38.5	58.0
Short-term	11.2	4.4

Source: Statistical Abstract of the United States 1986 (US Department of Commerce: Bureau of the Census), table no. 475.

long-term and short-term borrowing. As Judd (1984, p.220) records, 'between 1950 and 1970, the outstanding long-term debt of the nation's cities increased from $11.0 to $40.8 billion' Local government bonds are exempt from federal taxation: that is, 'the federal government does not tax the interest on state and local securities through income tax' (Maxwell and Aronson, 1977, p.200), which obviously increases their attraction to investors. This tax exemption status was established by Congress in 1913; federal Treasury efforts to abrogate this exemption status have failed so far.

Internal Revenue 3: User Charges

The third major internal source of revenue is from charges exacted for the use of local government services including water, city inspections, sewer services, licences and permits, etc. This is quite an important source of revenue for local government, increasing from 15.8 per cent of city revenues in 1970 to 18.0 per cent in 1983 (US Department of Commerce, 1986). Municipal authorities are able to price directly these governmental services: for example, water users pay for the amount they consume; consequently municipal water authorities forego the use of revenues from the municipal government. Municipalities are often urged to extend this system to other services by academics and government professionals for a number of reasons: they are argued to improve how public resources are allocated; user charges are frequently judged fairer than taxation, since they can be linked directly to service consumption; and user charges can modify private market practice (see Mushkin and Vehorn, 1980).

However, there is good reason to believe that greater application of user charges would generate significant inequities (for example, fire services would be more heavily used by those in poorer, less safe buildings) and that some services would not be provided (for example, public transport). At present, the level of charges for particular services is determined by

> some rough estimate of the value of a particular benefit or of the cost of rendering the service. But the charge will usually fall short of the benefit value or unit cost, and this shortfall may be justified either for reasons of equity - that is, for welfare or redistributional reasons - or as spillovers or benefits or costs (Maxwell and Aronson, 1977, p.183).

For the most part, local governments make little effort to incorporate a principle of equity into these user charges contending that such objectives can only be fulfilled by national public policy; that is, there is no effort to make these user charges progressive in their distribution of either costs or benefits. User charges constitute a relatively small but constant proportion of local governments revenues.

Detering efficiency in the public provision of services is a further problem as Peterson (1981, p.33) observes: 'public services cannot be provided efficiently because no pricing mechanism pinpoints misallocation of public resources'. A further issue is the difficulty of charging each consumer for the exact proportion of public services that they consume: there are conflicts between taxation principles, based for example on property value, and use of services, which may differ with individual household practices; Peterson (1981, p.34) also notes that 'cities are constitutionally or practically constrained from charging tolls to limit access to their services. Schools cannot charge tuition; access to streets and sidewalks is free and open to the general public; and police and fire protection is not conditioned upon payment for the service. Since these charges cannot be related to use, some residents subsidize the benefits received by others'. Thus it is unlikely that local governments will pursue the Pareto optimum equilibrium advocated by the Tiebout hypothesis; but, events like Proposition 13 do suggest that the revenue-raising practices of local governments must heed consumer preferences to some extent, and that these must influence decisions about service provision.

EXTERNAL REVENUES: FEDERAL AND STATE AID

Supplementing these internal sources of revenue are the substantial funds received from intergovernmental or external sources. The contemporary intergovernmental financial (at least, pre-Reagan) system was initiated during the 1930s when federal government began to provide funds for cities to use for the relief of Great Depression hardship (see Gelfand, 1972; Gurr and King, 1986; Mollenkopf, 1983), a process further stimulated by the failure of the regional states to assist adequately the local governments and municipalities within their jurisdictions. This system expanded steadily, if undramatically, in the 1940s and 50s, but increased exponentially from the early mid-1960s under the impetus of the the Great Society, peaking in 1978. However, during the 1960s and 70s the intergovernmental's (federal and state) proportion of municipal revenues expanded significantly, allowing cities to initiate new services and to maintain existing responsibilities: 'the ultimate engine of local public sector expansion during this period (1965-73) was the federal government, which channelled massive amounts of aid to the cities both directly and through the intermediation of the state' (Peterson, 1976, p.58). Howitt (1984, p.7) argues, correctly, that:

> the Great Society represented a significant turning point in the development of the intergovernmental system. By moving into many new policy areas and greatly extending its involvement in others, the federal government became a more significant - and highly active - presence in the daily lives of state and local officials and in the delivery of government services to citizens. The relationship with local government, in particular, was altered significantly. As the country politically recognised an 'urban crisis', many of the new grant programs were set up to provide aid directly to municipal governments or local agencies rather than through the states as intermediaries.

This latter development is very important in that it heralded vastly increased federal aid for cities provided directly from Washington. By the late 1970s close to 40 per cent of municipal revenues came from intergovernmental aid. The Reagan administration has sought to implement significant changes in the intergovernmental financial system, primarily through retrenching the key federal role: states are to have greater rights in the federal system but at the cost of reduced federal funding. For cities and local governments, reductions in federal aid can have potentially disastrous results, particularly for those which have used federal funds to finance the provision of basic municipal services like fire, police, sanitation, etc. (Fossett, 1983); this is the case for some cities in the Midwest and East whose property tax base has been most eroded under the process of structural deindustrialization evident since the late 1960s.

The Reagan Administration

Consequences for Internal and External Revenues

The Reagan administration's determination to reduce non-defence federal outlays has resulted in consistent efforts by this administration to withdraw federal funding from the US intergovernmental financial system. The Reagan administration has pursued a 'New Federalism', with two main elements: first, increased independence to states and local governments in the administration of their own affairs; second, as a corollary, reduced federal fiscal assistance to these subnational tiers of governments. Combined with the serious fiscal difficulties encountered by many cities during the 1970s and early 80s (illustrated, most spectacularly by NYC's fiscal crisis of 1975) this has had profound implications for sources of municipal revenue. The major federal retrenchment was embodied in the 1981-2 budget: federal grants-in-aid to local governments (as well as to states) fell by 12 per cent as a consequence (Bowles and King, 1986, Table 2). While the subsequent budgets have not yet instituted such drastic cuts, the general trend has continued. This has forced municipal governments either to find alternative means of raising revenues or to reduce their service provisions. Concerning the latter, many American cities have reduced the number of their employees (principally through non-replacement rather than actual firing) with some consequences for the provision of services. Stanfield (1983) reports that although most cities felt the effects of employee cutbacks on services, it was not yet as damaging as it might be. However, if cities are forced to continue this pattern then local service provision will suffer significantly.

Local Government Responses

Many cities have sought to offset the falloff in federal aid by raising their property taxes. Thus in

1983 'New York City imposed a temporary income tax surcharge; Los Angeles increased its hotel tax and utility users tax; Philadelphia, its income and real estate transfer taxes; and Washington, which had not increased direct consumer taxes since 1980, raised taxes on utilities' (Stanfield, 1983, p.2361). Thus most of the large cities have responded to the loss in intergovernmental revenue by increasing local tax revenues; in per capita terms in fiscal year 1982, 'local property tax revenues increased by 11.0 per cent, other local tax revenue by 14.3 per cent, and fees, user charges, and miscellaneous revenue by 12.4 per cent' (Wolman, 1986, p.321). Thus despite the political unattractiveness of raising property taxes, many municipalities followed this option. Those cities which did not follow this practice (for example, Californian cities in the post-Proposition 13 period - similar measures exist in Massachusetts and New Jersey), user charges have been a substitute and this is a second major city revenue response to the Reagan administration's policies: in 1983 'Los Angeles imposed a fee for having garbage collected, San Diego charged for the use of public tennis courts, San Jose increased charges to developers, San Francisco instituted admission fees to the art museum and the zoo and increased the fares on the municipal transit system from 25 cents to 60 cents' (Stanfield, 1983, p.2362). A major disadvantage of user charges, however, is that they rarely embody any redistributive or egalitarian principle in that they apply to the well off and disadvantaged similarly. And some cities - such as Cleveland - have resisted user charges for this very reason (see Table 5.2). In the United States, municipalities have the local autonomy or discretion to follow such imperatives in their revenue policies.

LOCAL GOVERNMENT FINANCE IN BRITAIN

Internal and External Sources of Revenue

Local government finance in Britain can be divided also between the two categories of internal (users fees and charges, local property tax/rates) and external (central government grants). Local authorities can borrow as in the United States in order to finance capital investment projects. Since the details of British revenue-raising practice are well known only key points require highlighting. As in the United States, external finance (that is, central government grants) were until the late 1970s of increasing importance to the revenues of local authorities in Britain, and still constitute 42 per cent of local government revenue in England in 1984/5 (Cmnd. 9714, p.78). The other most important source of local revenue is internal - rates, both domestic and non-domestic, which together provided 28 per cent of local government revenue in England in 1984/5 (ibid.). Other internal local sources of revenue (sales, fees and charges, rents, etc.) constitute a relatively small proportion of local government revenue. Consequently, it is central government grants and rates (domestic and non domestic) which have been two key components of local authorities' revenues in Britain. Local autonomy is so restricted that authorities do not have the option of adopting and experimenting with alternative revenue sources as do American local governments.

Since 1979 central-local financial relations have been fraught with conflict and controversy as the central government has sought to reduce substantially local government spending as part of its macro economic strategy; this is, it should be noted, despite the fact that British local government is not a particularly large spender in comparison with other countries. Accordingly, the 1980 Local Government Planning and Land Act included legislation to realise this objective through a new grant system and the stipulation of penalties for authorities which exceeded centrally determined expenditure levels. The 1980 Act incorporated a new Block Grant to each local authority within the RSG; and allocation was no longer to meet the shortfall between what each authority raised from its rates and its predicted spending, but rather the new system relied on central assessments (grant-related expenditure assessments) of what each authority should spend. The system of central-local relations has been fundamentally altered: the scope for local authorities to decide upon their own expenditures has been reduced as central control has increased. Thus the centuries-old principle that local authorities have the right to determine their own spending and revenue-raising needs has been abandoned. The sheer heterogeneity of municipal authorities and urban conditions suggests that divesting municipalities of such a key role in favour of centrally formulated levels of spending and taxing is misguided. Municipalities are given much less scope to determine what its officials think the key areas of need are for its locality, which is one of the principal rationales for the existence of local authorities with elected leadership.

REVENUE RAISING IN THE UNITED STATES AND BRITAIN COMPARED

In Britain the activities of local authorities are strictly constrained by legislation. Parliament specifies the functions which local government must undertake, and services cannot be provided which have not been authorised in this way. And Parliament has the power to alter these arrangements quite easily and to institute new arrangements as in, for example, the types of local revenue local authorities can collect. But before 1979 British local authorities were, in principle, able to levy whatever tax rate they deemed appropriate and to determine their own expenditure. In the United States municipalities and local governments are, for purposes of constitutional law, 'mere creatures' of their states.

In both countries the type and level of internal revenue-raising is ultimately determined by either the central government (in Britain) or the states (in the United States). In Britain local authorities are restricted to one tax, the rates, and have no recourse to additional taxes, while in the United States the regional states delineate the types of taxes which local governments can utilise, leaving discretion over choices and combinations (of taxes) to the local officials. Britain's formal position has been rendered flexible by the right of local authorities to settle on their own tax rate and to determine their own expenditure level. The importance of fiscal issues to central-local relations can hardly be emphasized enough. The scope and limitations of these respective practices reflect the different political systems (federal in the US and unitary in Britain) and their consequences for local autonomy. However, in both countries there are strong traditions of local democracy and belief in the importance of local accountability through decentralised mechanisms (see Magnusson,1986; Gurr and King, 1987). In the United States 'there is a widespread belief that strong local governments are vital to successful democracy, and that their strength can be maintained only by possession of appreciable financial independence' (Maxwell and Aronson, 1977, p.164). In Britain, lipservice is regularly paid to the role of local government in democracy, and the principle of accountability is central to the current government proposals for local government finance. The difficulty or inconsistency with this position concerns the degree of local autonomy (either internal or external) which is necessary for successful local democracy and local accountability. It is far from clear that the new proposals for local government finance will allow sufficient local autonomy over revenues to make local government as meaningful an organ of democracy as it might be. This issue is addressed in the conclusion.

CONCLUSION

Figure 5.1 summarizes the two dimensions of local autonomy in revenue raising, alluded to at the beginning of this chapter. Traditionally British local authorities have enjoyed high autonomy over local or internal revenues in that they could determine their own rates in the one existing revenue type; and they had autonomy over external revenues in that these served to balance shortfalls in local revenues without specifying usage. In the United States, local government autonomy over the types and level of local or internal revenues has been, and remains high, while autonomy over external funds varies since some federal aid is allocated for specific projects and some is available for allocation by the local government itself. However, in Britain, local autonomy over both sources of revenue has declined since the late 1970s, principally as a consequence of the increased centralization initiated by the post-1979 Conservative government. As Newton and Karran (1985, p. 129) remark in their recent book: 'Britain stands within sight of a form of government which is more highly centralised than anything this side of East Germany'. The combined effect of changes in central-local fiscal relations since 1980 and the restructuring of local authorities reflects powerful trends toward centralization in the British political system, which diminish significantly the autonomy of local authorities over revenue-raising.

Figure 5:1 Revenue-raising powers of local government after current reforms

Autonomy of local government over external revenue		Autonomy of local government over internal revenue: HIGH	LOW
	HIGH		
	LOW	United States	Britain

But the implications of the current proposals are more dramatic: essentially, they represent a merging of the distinct internal and external sources of local revenue in the one centralised authority. The proposal that non domestic rates should be set by the central government at a uniform rate, collected and pooled centrally and then redistributed across all authorities as a common amount for each adult represents a startling erosion of local authorities' control/autonomy over a key part of their own local/internal source of revenue. Likewise, the introduction of a Community Charge applicable to all adults at a standard rate reduces the capacity for local authorities to formulate local revenues relative to their perceived local needs, though the level of the Community Charge is to be determined locally. Collectively, the policies pursued by the central state in the area of central-local relations reduce the scope for local initiative, discretion and autonomy in most policy areas including revenue-raising.

Such policies contrast with American practice: there local governments enjoy considerable autonomy/control over local sources of revenue, have been able to introduce new local taxes, fix rates as deemed appropriate and, most importantly, develop a diversified revenue base. Such options have now been largely ruled out for British local authorities. What are the reasons for the differences between the two systems? And what does the future hold for local autonomy over revenue-raising in the United States?

Part of the reason for the differences lies in the contrasting principles informing the respective political cultures and hence institutional arrangements. The American system of government is intrinsically and necessarily decentralist, providing a constitutionally-guaranteed set of institutional safeguards for the values of local democracy which in turn are espoused by political leaders. This commitment to local democracy facilitates, in the area of local revenues, diversity of taxes and the capacity to experiment with alternative schemes as deemed necessary: instead of placing complete faith in one system American local governments can experiment with a number of systems deriving a mix most suitable to their circumstances. It is important to note that local governments in the United States have some autonomy over both the type of tax adopted and their rates, whereas in Britain autonomy has been restricted to rates only and even then has been limited.

In Britain, similar principles of local democracy are regularly praised by politicians which is hardly surprising given the similarities in liberal democratic values; they do not, however, resonate with citizens in a remotely comparable way. This provides political opportunities to a centralizing government with clear fiscal policies of the kind presently offered. But institutional safeguards on behalf of local democracy are lacking in Britain as the post-1979 centralization indicates. The Government has interpreted accountability in a narrow fashion: paying for services on a centralized standardized basis. An alternative, and arguably more valid, interpretation of local accountability would be to increase, not diminish, the autonomy of local political institutions in their relations with their electors.

The future of American local government revenue-raising practice is likely to reflect recent changes initiated under the impetus of the Reagan administration. The latter's determined inroads into federal assistance to municipal authorities has forced many of these to expand their revenues generated locally. This they have done through a variety of taxes. Such a strategy is likely to persist amongst most local governments who are committed to the services currently provided. However, two factors will constrain this in the future. First, some local governments - traditionally those located in Southern States - are less fully committed to aspects of welfare policies initiated by the federal government in the 1960s and may withdraw these provisions, thus creating regional differentials in welfare provision. This was the pattern prior to the 1960s federal commitment to welfare. Inevitably such cuts fall most heavily upon the least advantaged members of American society. The second factor concerns the capacity of local economies: some municipal economies - and hence revenue bases - are economically weaker than others, and this places limits upon the amount of taxation which can be levied. This applies especially to the older industrialized cities - located in the Northeast and Midwest - who were most fiscally strained by the 1970s crisis (see King and Gurr, 1987). Thus while most local governments retain a commitment to those services retrenched by federal government and will seek to maintain them with local revenues, there are limits to the local taxes which can be raised. But, that said, American local governments retain considerable control over the level and types of taxes which they can implement, certainly when contrasted with British local authorities. Local government revenue is much more 'local' business in the United States than in Britain, despite similar rhetorical commitments to local democracy in both countries.

REFERENCES

Bahl, Roy (ed.) (1978)
The Fiscal Outlook for Cities, Syracuse University Press, Syracuse, NY

Bowles, Nigel and King, Desmond S. (1986)
''States' Rights in Modern Guise: The Aggrandizement of the Presidency under Ronald Reagan', unpublished conference paper.

Byrne, Tony (1985)
Local Government in Britain, Penguin, Harmondsworth

Caraley, Demetrios (1986)
'Changing Conceptions of Federalism' Political Science Quarterly, vol.101, no.2, pp.289-306

Clark, Gordon L. and Dear, Michael (1984)
State Apparatus, Allen & Unwin, London and New York

Danziger, James N. (1980)
'California's Proposition 13 and the Fiscal Limitations Movement in the United States', Political Studies, vol. 28, no.4, pp.599-612

Elazar, Daniel J. (1972)
American Federalism: A View from the States, Thomas Y. Crowell, New York

Fossett, James W. (1983)
Federal Aid to Big Cities, Brookings, Washington DC

Gelfand, Mark (1972)
A Nation of Cities, Oxford University Press, Oxford

Gurr, Ted Robert and King, Desmond S. (1986)
The State and the City, Macmillan, London; University of Chicago Press, Chicago

Howitt, Arnold M. (1984)
Managing Federalism: Studies in Intergovernmental Relations, Congressional Quarterly, Washington DC

Jones, Bryan D. (1983)
Governing Urban America, Little, Brown, Boston

Judd, Dennis R. (1984)
The Politics of American Cities, Little, Brown, Boston

Katznelson, Ira (1981)
City Trenches, Bantheon Books, New York

King, Desmond S. (1987)
Capital, State and Urban Change in Britain', *The Capitalist City*, Joe Feagin and Michael P. Smith (eds.), Basil Blackwell, Oxford and New York

--and Gurr, Ted Robert (1985)
'The State and the City: Economic Transformation and the Autonomy of the Local State in Advanced Industrial Societies', *Rhythms in Politics and Economics*, Paul M. Johnson and Willaim R. Thompson (eds.), Praeger, New York

--and Gurr, Ted Robert (1987)
'Federal Responses to Urban Decline and Fiscal Strain in the United States', *British Journal of Political Science*, vol. 17, no.1

Layfield, Frank (1976)
Local Government Finance, HMSO, Cmnd. 6453

Leach, Richard H. (1970)
American Federalism, Norton, New York

Magnusson, Warren (1986)
'Bourgeois Theories of Local Government', Political Studies, vol. 34, no.1, pp. 1-18

Maxwell, James A. and Aronson, J. Richard (1977)
Financing State and Local Governments, Brookings, Washington, DC

Mollenkopf, John H. (1983)
The Contested City, Princeton University Press, Princeton, NJ

Mushkin, Selma J. and Vehorn, Charles L. (1980)
'User Fees and Charges', in Managing Fiscal Stress, Charles H. Levine (ed.), Chatham Publishers, Chatham, NJ

Newton, Ken and Karran, Terence (1985)
The Politics of Local Expenditure, Macmillan, London

Peterson, George E. (1976)
'Finance', in The Urban Predicament, William Gorham and Nathan Glazer (eds), Urban Institute, Washington, DC

Peterson, Paul E. (1981)
City Limits, University of Chicago Press, Chicago

Reagan, Michael D. and Sanzone, John G. (1981)
The New Federalism, 2nd ed, Oxford University Press, New York

Shefter, Martin (1977)
'New York City's Fiscal Crisis: The Politics of Inflation and Retrenchment', Public Interest, no. 48, pp. 98-127

Stanfield, Rochelle L. (1983)
'America's Oldest, Largest Cities Seem to Have a Formula for Survival', 'National Journal', pp. 2357-62

Thomas, Robert D. (1986)
'Cities as Partners in the Federal System',

Political Science Quarterly, vol. 101, no. 1, pp. 49-64

Tiebout, C.M. (1956)
'A pure theory of local expenditures', Journal of Political Economy, vol. 64, pp. 416-24.

US Department of Commerce (1986)
Statistical Abstract of the United States 1986, US Department of Commerce, Bureau of the Census

Walker, David B. (1980)
'The New System of Intergovernmental Relations: More Fiscal Relief and More Governmental Intrusions', in Managing Fiscal Stress, Charles H. Levine (ed.), Chatham Publishers, Chatham, NJ

-- (1981) Toward a Functioning Federalism, Winthrop Publishers, Cambridge, MA

Wolman, Harold (1982)
'Local Autonomy and Intergovernmental Finance in Britain and the United States', in Fiscal Stress in Cities, Richard Rose and Edward Page (eds), Cambridge University Press, New York

-- (1986) 'The Reagan Urban Policy and Its Impacts', Urban Affairs Quarterly, vol. 21, no. 3, 311-35

6 MUNICIPAL FINANCES IN CANADA: ISSUES OF LOCAL FINANCE AND THE CASE FOR USER CHARGES

Douglas J. McReady

While urban government in Canada is no longer the focus of a federal government department, a great deal of attention has been directed to urban problems in the past two decades. Most of that attention has been at the provincial level where the financial relationships between municipalities and the provincial governments have been of prime importance. Since there are ten provinces and two territories in Canada, each with their own municipal organization, it is difficult to generalize about the relative importance of differing aspects of local government finance in Canada. This chapter looks at one aspect of Canadian local finance, the revenue base of the municipalities and the arguments for introducing user charges as a means of augmenting the local fisc.

THE CURRENT STRUCTURE OF CANADIAN MUNICIPALITIES

The consequence of local government being a creature of the provincial governments, not recognized in any constitutional documents, means that the responsibilities (read expenditures) and revenue sources differ greatly as does the structure of the municipalities (one-tier and two-tier). New Brunswick, for instance, took over many functions that had traditionally been a municipal responsibility during the 1960s. Ontario has established 13 two-tiered regional governments, each with its own Act. Generally water, sewage, arterial roads, health, welfare, and police protection are

Table 6.1: Current Expenditures, 1983

Province	Sales of goods and services	Total Revenues	Per capita Sales of goods and services	Percent of total revenues
Newfoundland	20,028	185,906	34.77	10.8
Prince Edward Island	5,718	95,511	46.11	6.0
Nova Scotia	78,984	1,113,598	92.06	7.1
New Brunswick	43,053	281,574	61.07	15.3
Province of Quebec	949,294	8,780,207	145.71	10.8
Ontario	1,444,168	14,272,895	164.11	10.1
Manitoba	133,258	1,543,188	127.52	8.6
Saskatchewan	145,003	1,521,954	146.32	9.5
Alberta	810,371	5,302,530	345.57	15.3
British Columbia	493,807	3,714,842	175.23	13.3
N W Territories	16,805	85,013	240.07	19.8
TOTAL	3,816,802	36,897,218	153.61	10.3

Source: Statistics, Canada, Local Government Finance, 1983 and Consolidated Government Finance: Revenue, Expenditure, Assets and Liabilities: Fiscal Year Ended Nearest December 31, 1982.

assigned to the upper tier while street lighting, fire protection, garbage collection, parks and recreation, and libraries remain the responsibility of the lower-tier municipalities (Canadian Tax Foundation, 1983). British Columbia also has two-tiered governments at the local level. The lower tier has generally been left with greater responsibilities than in Ontario.

Table 6.1 indicates the variation between the provincial/local sources of revenues for 1983. Note the heavy reliance on local government's own revenues in Manitoba, British Columbia, Saskatchewan and Ontario in contrast to the low reliance on local government taxes in Newfoundland, Prince Edward

Island and New Brunswick. Historically, Manitoba's provincial government had increased its share of the contribution since the late 1970s but the local portion grew by 4 per cent or more in Newfoundland, Nova Scotia, Ontario and Saskatchewan.

As for reliance on different revenue sources, there is also a great deal of variation. Property taxes on real estate (land and improvements) have been the chief source of municipal revenue, accounting for 46 per cent of municipal revenues in 1967 and 38 per cent in 1980 while transfers from provincial governments accounted for 40 per cent of municipal revenues in 1967 and 46 per cent in 1980 (Bird and Slack, 1983). Heavy reliance on property taxes and the vilification of that tax has resulted in many studies of assessment methods and the relationship of property tax to provincial responsibility and grants.

Generally, most of the task forces or Royal Commissions tackling the problems of urban finance have been pushed at public hearings and by municipal and provincial politicians to consider the role of provincial grants to the municipalities since those are seen as being more equitable than real property taxes. 'The personal income tax based on progressive rates is generally regarded as the most fair form of taxation, particularly if care is taken to ensure that the system does not have excessive deductions and "loopholes" ' (Saskatchewan, 1986, p.254).

Furthermore, municipal politicians wanted to be able to increase services at a faster rate than inflation but felt constrained to keep property tax increases to 'not much more than the rate of inflation' and the personal income tax revenue elasticity in Canada being greater than one permitted this so long as the provinces were cooperative in sharing the revenues through increased grants.

Provincial funds can bring about equalization too. Reliance on the property tax means that the poorer areas have a smaller tax base and consequently are less able to afford to provide basic services.

> There is considerable variation among local governments in terms of the size of their local tax base relative to expenditures they are

> required to make. Some local governments have relatively large tax bases and are able to provide extensive services with low or moderate mill rates even without provincial funding. (Saskatchewan, 1986, p.22)

Not one of the reports, mentioned above, leaves the impression that other sources of revenue are to be extensively tapped. In most instances, that would appear to be a result of the terms of reference rather than a deliberate decision on the part of commissioners or task forces to recommend against other types of revenue. Indeed, most often, the issue to be investigated was the assessment function in real property tax and thus only one aspect of municipal finances were reviewed, property tax and provincial grants to municipalities dominated. Even a study carried out by Bird and Slack (1983) for the Ontario Economic Council entitled Residential Property Tax Relief in Ontario (which one would think from the title might refer to prices for government-provided goods and services) contains nothing on 'other' revenues.

Typically, since the major local revenue from their own sources is the property tax, constituting 55.5 per cent of those revenues and since school boards get approximately half of those revenues (usually a little more), there is an assumption on the part of many that the property tax is itself like a user charge. Many references are made to the fact that police services, for instance, are worth more to the higher-valued property and consequently there is a presumption that property taxes are not income redistributive. The property tax being seen as a user charge is accentuated by recent moves on the part of provincial governments to give seniors property tax credits when they pay personal income tax to compensate for the amount of the property tax going into schools from which it is said they receive no direct benefit.

One excellent source of material on user charges in Canadian municipalities, although now dated is Richard M.Bird's (1976) Charging for Public Services: A New Look at an Old Idea. While that document examines in some detail the theoretical issues related to user charges, it also undertakes a rather thorough empirical compilation of user-charge situations (in the municipal field there is more on Ontario than the other provinces). Unfortunately, his more recent Urban Public Finance (1983) avoids the issue of user charges which is in line with the emphasis by municipal and provincial politicians on general taxes rather than product pricing.

HISTORICAL PERSPECTIVE

The British North America Act of 1867 established a federation of British Colonies in the northern sphere of North America. The Act was passed by British Parliament and given Royal Assent by Queen Victoria, thus creating a new Confederation. Discussions leading up to the formation of Canada had been proceeding in earnest since 1864 but Newfoundland and Prince Edward Island after initial discussions preferred to remain colonies outside the federal agreement.

The distribution of powers in the British North America Act, particularly fiscal powers, can be best understood only by reference to the situation of the British North American colonies at the time of Confederation. The bulk of the colonial revenues were derived from customs and excise duties and that was most true in Nova Scotia and New Brunswick where virtually all revenues were derived from these sources. In fact, except for two or three cities, municipal government functions were carried out by the provinces. In the province of Canada (which became the provinces of Quebec and Ontario at the time of Confederation) municipalities were more fully developed and had undertaken road maintenance, education support and public welfare by 1867. Revenues for these functions were basically derived from real property taxes (taxes on land and the improvements attached thereto).

When the Quebec Resolutions were agreed to by the colonies, the general (central) government was to assume responsibility for defence, transportation and most colonial debts and consequently it was only natural that it should also be given the most lucrative sources of revenue including both direct and indirect taxation.

The provinces (the former colonies) were left with the responsibility for the maintenance of a civil government, the administration of justice, education, local works and undertakings, welfare, etc. It was anticipated that these responsibilities would entail little in the way of future expenditures in addition to their current modest levels. Thus direct taxes were assigned to the provinces jointly with the federal government and those taxes were not ever expected to be significant and thus transfers of 80% per capita from the federal government, were to make up nearly half the provincial revenues. Direct taxation was viewed as being sufficient to ensure 'that no extravagance is committed by those placed in power over them' and ' that responsibility will be exacted by the people in the most pre-emptory manner'. It was clear that taxes on realty were considered to be direct taxes. While the politicians considered direct taxes to be broadly defined, the real constraint they perceived was the political difficulty they envisaged in imposing such taxes.

In December 1981, the House of Commons and Senate in Canada passed the Constitution Act which included a request to the Houses of Parliament at Westminster to enact an Act transferring the Canadian constitution including amendment powers back to Canada. The subsequent Canada Act, 1982, passed by the Parliament of Great Britain transferred to Canada the constitutional provisions of the British North America Act of 1867 as amended and a Canadian Charter of Rights and Freedoms along with full amendment powers. On 17 April, 1982 Queen Elizabeth II proclaimed the new Canadian Constitution and any powers they might have derived from the provinces delegating authority to conduct business, collect taxes and pass laws.

Between the formation of Canada on 1 July, 1867 and the passing of the Canada Act 1982, there were a number of adjustments to the British North America Act. As new provinces entered Confederation, they had to be enticed with more liberal provisions than the original document had provided, whether a railroad (British Columbia) or subsidies based on a falsified larger-than-true population base (Manitoba). Nova Scotia and New Brunswick both had to be encouraged to remain part of the federation by an increase in subsidies.

On the prairies the federal government owned the lands and consequently, as those lands were divided into provinces, there was some impact on the raising of revenues. In the more settled provinces there was considerable property in the hands of private persons from which revenue could be raised by municipal rates. In the prairie provinces, section 125 of the British North America Act precluded an imposition of a tax on lands owned by the Crown and there were also special provisions for lands held by the Hudson's Bay Company and the Canadian Pacific Railway. Settlers on the prairies initially held only partial interest in Crown lands since the federal government wanted to retain the ability to influence and speed the settlement of those lands but the courts ruled that provincial and consequently municipal governments could impose a tax on owners of a partial interest in federal lands.

It was not long after 1867 when it was realized that the powers that had been given to the provinces under the British North America Act were going to expand in cost. The general result was that the provinces found the need to tap new revenue sources. Licence and fee income had been rising quickly, but was too small in absolute terms to pay for developmental expenditures. Consequently, municipalities were formed and with them taxes on real property became important. The progression towards municipal development quickened after the start of the twentieth century and as is the case today a tax on realty provided the financial wherewithal. One is almost tempted to hypothesize that the real reason for the formation of municipalities was to tap the realty tax and to eliminate some direct provincial expenditures - a means of reducing provincial debt incursion.

PROPERTY TAXES

The Atlantic Provinces

There are four provinces in the Atlantic region. Nova Scotia and New Brunswick have been part of Confederation since Canada became a separate entity in 1867. Prince Edward Island rejected initial membership in Confederation but became a part of Canada in 1871, four years after Confederation. Newfoundland waited until 1948-9 to join Confederation and even then did so only after extensive and sometimes bitter debate.

Table 6.2: Property and related taxes, 1982 (in thousands of dollars)

	Local		Consolidated Provincial and Local	
	Per capita including grants (current)	Per capita excluding grants (current)	Per capita excluding federal grants	Local as % of consolidated
Newfoundland	327.48	175.77	1,781.74	9.9
Prince Edward Island	779.64	141.98	1,747.38	8.1
Nova Scotia	1,314.07	453.20	2,011.12	22.5
New Brunswick	404.33	181.26	1,725.83	10.5
Quebec	1,363.72	612.58	3,349.65	18.3
Ontario	1,654.81	911.88	3,089.32	29.5
Manitoba	1,503.73	704.17	2,688.39	26.2
Saskatchewan	1,571.76	806.26	3,482.22	23.2
Alberta	2,369.61	1,202.25	6,383.96	18.8
British Columbia	1,353.58	745.68	3,196.61	23.3

Source: Statistics Canada, Consolidated Government Finance, 1982 (Ottawa: Supply and Services, 1986), table 5.

Newfoundland does not have mandatory property taxes for all local governments, only those where more than half of the properties are serviced by water and sewer systems. Real property includes land, buildings and machinery or fixtures attached thereto. Assessment is on an 'actual' basis with exemptions for farmland, woodlots and buildings associated with either. Some relief is given to those with incomes of less than $6,000 (increased according to number of dependents).

Prince Edward Island imposes a general property tax at both the provincial and municipal and includes provincial and municipal property in the tax base. While assessment is at 'market' value, the rates are fixed for provincial property taxes. There is the possibility of deferral of the tax for senior citizens receiving guaranteed income supplemental payments.

Nova Scotia includes in the tax base underground improvements as well as trees and other growing things. Local councils have the option of exempting those over age 65, widowed, or single parents with dependents if income is below an amount to be determined by the local government.

New Brunswick uses a province-wide property tax as well as a municipal tax. Machinery and equipment is included in the tax base only if it services the land and/or buildings. Many institutions such as schools and universities are classified as residences so as to qualify for the lower tax rates associated with residential property. Agricultural land taxes may be deferred until the use of the land is converted to another use and those with low incomes who are unmarried may be exempted from paying property taxes.

In all provinces in this region, but particularly in New Brunswick, we see a desire on the part of provincial authorities to maintain relatively weak municipal governments and stronger provincial governments. Whether that stems from the historical strength of the colonial government and the relative lateness of municipal development, this region has relied less on local tax sources in general and property taxes in particular.

Central Provinces

Ontario and Quebec were part of the province of Canada prior to Confederation. Thus they started with a common government and so Confederation introduced differences. Some differences had always been evident because of the legal systems and language barriers.

Quebec introduced substantial land tax reforms in 1980 and included all immoveables in its assessment but not including underground improvements or railway, natural gas, electricity, or telecommunications systems. Relief from property tax burden is borne solely by the province since there is a refundable tax credit in the personal income tax. Also, the province has an equalization scheme to help those municipalities with smaller fiscal potential.

Ontario relies very heavily on municipalities to raise revenues and spend monies. While the assessment function is provincial, municipalities have been given the option of introducing the provincial market value assessment and consequently there are significant discrepancies in the bases of many municipalities and between municipalities. Ontario, like Quebec, has an equalization of assessment scheme and a property tax credit through the personal income tax system.

The Western Provinces

As the western provinces each entered Confederation after 1867 and on the prairies at least there was the possibility of organizing local governments after 1867, there are certain similarities in the way the land tax is handled in this region. Generally, local assessors handle only the larger municipalities while provincial authorities handle the rest. Also, unorganized areas have their property taxes imposed provincially while local governments do that elsewhere. In Alberta school taxes include a province wide mill rate on nonresidential property.

In each of the provinces relief is available in the form of grants, tax credits or exemptions for low-income individuals. An examination of Table 6.2

Table 6.3: Transfers to local governments, 1983

	Real property	Special assess-ments	Busi-ness	Other	Total Per capita
Newfound-land	39,451	158	15,412	5,920	107.35
Prince Edward Island	22,916	60			187.50
Nova Scotia	209,340	4,175	28,354	3,172	289.20
New Brunswick	143,009	122			205.50
Quebec	1,837,119	406,701	318,817	184,088	426.60
Ontario	4,407,591	37,400	686,438	108,692	607.50
Manitoba	396,817	20,663	31,301	18,876	455.70
Saskatch-ewan	469,636	11,393	26,031	4,659	528.50
Alberta	1,140,724	50,823	111,622	129,571	640.30
British Columbia	1,227,939	61,847	42,489	1,707	486.10

Source: Statistics Canada, Local Government Finance, 1983, table 1.

shows the difference on a per capita basis of the reliance on the property tax. When compared to the first column in Table 6.1 it is evident that in some provinces a larger portion of the local revenues are coming from property taxes, varying from over 36 per cent in Ontario to closer to 25 per cent in Prince Edward Island and Alberta.

PROVINCIAL TRANSFERS

Provincial transfers include conditional and unconditional grants to municipalities, grants in lieu of property taxes, and specific funding that varies from province to province. There are also federal government transfers in lieu of property taxes.

As can be seen in Table 6.3, there are extreme differences. Not only are transfers different as a percentage of local government revenues, varying from 40.8 per cent in Newfoundland to 78.5 per cent in

Prince Edward Island. The differences in philosophy become more evident in the larger provinces where in Ontario, the provincial government has been inclined to give more autonomy to municipalities as compared to New Brunswick where local governments remain very much a creature of the provincial government. Thus, at $714 per capita, Ontario's grant to local governments remains more than three times that of New Brunswick's and yet constitutes a smaller percentage of local revenues. It has already been shown that New Brunswick has most of the functions normally provided by local government supplied by the provincial government.

CURRENT STATUS OF PRICING PUBLIC SERVICES

Despite the heavy emphasis in official documents and in public discussion on property tax and provincial grants to municipalities, there have been and will continue to be sales revenues for goods and services sold by municipality. These include remittances from enterprises like Edmonton City Telephones (the corporation's shareholder being the City of Edmonton) and various public utilities owned by municipalities. The amount, however, remains small relative to other sources of revenue, varying from 15.3 per cent of local government revenues in Alberta and New Brunswick to 6.0 per cent in Prince Edward Island.

The most current information is found in Table 6.4. Note there that Alberta on a per capita basis pays almost six times as much as New Brunswick in user fees, the same percentage of local revenues comes from pricing in both provinces. In general, as one moves west, per capita payments for goods and services rises, the lowest being in Newfoundland and the highest being Alberta. While the figures in Table 6.4 include water, it is unclear whether they include hydroelectrity or natural gas (which in some cities is distributed by the local public utility).

Note that in Tables 6.1 to 6.4, despite some pretty basic differences regarding their reliance on locally-raised funds (per capita) and despite differences in the degree to which user charges are

Table 6.4: Sales of goods and services, 1983 (thousands of dollars)

	Gross general revenue	Provincial grants	Provincial as a percentage	Per capita grants
	(in thousands of dollars)			
Newfoundland	185,906	75,801	40.8	133.53
Prince Edward Island	95,511	74,954	78.5	611.84
Nova Scotia	1,113,598	700,536	62.9	826.65
New Brunswick	281,574	145,033	51.5	208.26
Quebec	8,780,207	4,769,873	54.3	740.85
Ontario	14,272,895	6,158,696	43.1	714.04
Manitoba	1,543,188	784,349	50.8	764.29
Saskatchewan	1,521,954	704,130	46.3	727.17
Alberta	5,302,530	2,550,617	48.1	1,139.83
British Columbia	3,714,842	1,620,024	43.8	592.47

Source: Statistics Canada (1986), Local Government Finance, 1983, Ottawa

relied upon, there are striking similarities across provinces. Almost 50 per cent of all local revenues derives from provincial transfers (Prince Edward Island and Nova Scotia being the only provinces that deviate greatly) and of own revenues, real property taxes constitute the major source of revenues. This homogeneity is surprising when one considers the heterogeneity as between provinces (culture, historical development, ethnic background) and the fact that it is a provincial responsibility to determine the role of local government.

It is difficult to uncover much information on the variety of pricing policies for a wide range of activities. There is even less in the way of rational statements of the objectives of municipal user charges. The homogeneity mentioned above is true here as well. No province differs in making the principles clear. In many instances, the activities which earn municipalities sales revenues are legally those conducted by special-purpose legislative bodies. Water is a prime example with Public Utilities Commissions, which are elected at the same time as municipal councils, being responsible for setting the prices. Public library boards and transit commissions are usually appointed but their decisions are only dealt with in a cursory manner by municipal politicians as the charges they impose are only a minor part of their total revenues.

In the cases of library boards that this author is familiar with, the prices charged for borrowing privileges are viewed as making up the difference between the grant given by the municipality and the costs of salaries, new books, utilities, etc. Pricing borrowing privileges has nothing to do with average or marginal cost and very little to do with the desire to redistribute wealth, except on occasion there may be an extra fee for non-taxpayers in the municipality.

DISCUSSION AND CONCLUSION

While local government finance in Canada appears to differ from province to province, there are strong similarities. Clearly, in all provinces the property tax and provincial grants to local governments constitute the two largest sources of local finance. The reliance on the property tax reflects a view that local government must have a tax base of its own. Yet differences abound when it comes to the issue of assessment for in some provinces the assessment function has been centralized under the provincial government whereas in other provinces the function is purely local while in still others provincial assessors work beside local assessors. Also the tax base or what is to be assessed differs from rental value to actual value to market value with inclusions and exclusions changing from one province to another.

Provincial funding of local government also varies both on a per capita basis reflecting the wealth of the area and the responsibilities assigned to local governments. Further, as a percentage of local revenues, provincial funding varies reflecting the degree of reliance the provincial government wants to put on the property tax. Ontario, for instance, historically always had a heavy reliance on the property tax and that fact remains. New Brunswick at Confederation had no property tax and virtually no municipalities and still the provincial government undertakes many normally local functions and consequently reliance on the property tax is small. As for the western provinces, provincial resource revenues have permitted larger per capita provincial grants than in the east and consequently a decreased emphasis on property taxes (if not a decreased per capita dollar amount).

Reliance on user fees and other sources of income remains small. Again, however, there are philosophical differences which appear as between the provinces. The two most western provinces rely more heavily on user fees on a per capita basis and this is consistent with the market orientation of their Social Credit governments (Alberta has had a Social Credit government for 25 of the last 40 years but now has a Progressive Conservative government which is also noted for a strong market orientation). Thus, again while there are similarities in the degree of reliance on user fees there are strong philosophical differences about their importance.

From this author's perspective as a public finance economist, the greatest potential for future work lies in the need to expand market financing through user fees. The property tax has been studied and restudied and there is not a great deal more in revenues that can be derived from playing any more with the base or the rates. In an era when federal tax reform will be limiting provincial revenues from the personal income tax, there is not a great deal of possible increase in provincial grants to local government. Consequently, user fees will have to be looked at not as making up the shortfall (although that may be the motivation) but as a means of efficiently and equitably allocating resources.

REFERENCES

Bird, R.M. (1976)
Charging for Public Services: A New Look at an Old Idea, Canadian Tax Foundation, Toronto

--and Slack, N.E. (1978) Residential Property Tax Relief in Ontario, Ontario Economic Council, Ontario

--and Slack, N.E. (1983)
Urban Public Finance in Canada, Butterworths, Toronto

Canadian Tax Foundation (1983)
Provincial and Municipal Finances, 1983, Canadian Tax Foundation, Toronto

Kitchen, H.M. (1984)
Local Government Finance in Canada, Canadian Tax Foundation, Toronto

7 FEDERALISM AND THE BOLSTERING OF AUSTRALIAN LOCAL GOVERNMENT FINANCE

Ronan Paddison

In Australia local government is of growing importance. Recent developments, and particularly those involving Commonwealth-local links, have enhanced the status of local government and bolstered its fiscal base while as a result of federal and state initiatives the list of service functions for which local councils are responsible has grown. Though, as Jones (1981) argues, some states have shown a preference for devolving functions to ad hoc agencies rather than local government, the growing visibility of local councils, from an intergovernmental perspective (Chapman and Wood, 1984) and from the viewpoint of service delivery, defy popularly held views that by comparison with other economically advanced nations, and, more appropriately, by comparison with the 'classic federations' of North America, Australia is distinctive by virtue of the relatively minor role played by local government. Successive observers of Australian local government have described it as having 'stagnated' (Neutze, 1974, p.76), as being 'unnoticed, unesteemed and under-financed' (Bowman, 1976,p.3), and being 'not a robust and vigorous institution' (Purdie, 1976, p.2).

It remains true that local government expenditure accounts for a small proportion of total expenditures - in 1983/4 its outlays accounted for only 6 per cent of all public sector outlays, and had fallen slightly over the decade - but within the last 15 years the role and financing of local government has occupied a more important position on the political agenda.

In so far as federal involvement in local government has increased, its effect has been to draw the 'third tier' more fully into the administration of the state, countering the argument (probably overstated) of local government being the creature of the states. The trends could be easily overemphasized, however. Critically, local government lacks constitutional status, while its functional and fiscal basis, and its disabilities on both counts, remain a matter of reform for the state governments. The failure to implement local fiscal reform other than at the margins remains a source of weakness. As the Australian ACIR was to argue the paradox was that the 1970s witnessed a growing awareness of the importance of local government, but also a recognition that in its present form it was unlikely to be able to meet its potential (ACIR, 1984).

The key to federal involvement has been expanding fiscal assistance to local government, leading, after 1976, to the introduction of general revenue-sharing. The extension of untied grants to local government - the states have received such payments since the federation was established (AGPS, 1983) - has been premised on the need to bolster the revenue base of local authorities. The councils themselves had long been drawing attention to the weakness of their revenue base, and, indeed, had been petitioning Canberra for direct funding since 1947. Their claims were not without justification, yet until the 1970s they were to fall largely on deaf ears as far as the Commonwealth government was concerned. Beyond the payment of some specific grants, such as for roads, the federal government eschewed the possibility of direct funding. Local government, it was argued, was a state concern, and that, in particular, compensating councils for any shortfall in fiscal need should be a question of state transfers.

This chapter reviews the background against which Commonwealth direct funding has emerged and the implications for some of the major canons of local taxation - particularly autonomy, accountability and equity - raised by it. Briefly, the functional responsibilities and revenue bases of local government are discussed, the major problem of Australian local government revenue being commonly perceived as its dependence on property rating. State governments have not been unaware of the fiscal disabilities of local government, each of them having established inquiries to make recommendations on improvements to the property rating system and/or the encouragement of alternative revenue sources. A critique of the proposals, including the recommendations in some states for a poll tax, forms the basis of the following section. The failure to achieve radical local fiscal reform is a common denominator among the states, the reasons for which partly lie in the pronounced vertical fiscal imbalance which characterizes the Australian federation. Yet, paradoxically, the failure was also to provide a rationale for the national government to venture into direct funding. The growth and implications of this are discussed in the final section.

AUSTRALIAN LOCAL GOVERNMENT: SERVICE RESPONSIBILITIES AND REVENUE BASE

One of the truisms of Australian local government is its diversity. Nor is the diversity simply a reflection of country's federal status and because local government is essentially a state concern. As Bowman (1975) has remarked, 'local government authorities vary widely in area, population, revenue, organisation and activities, most markedly between, but also within, States' (p.66). Nationally, the differences vary from an outback council, serving a large area but a small, widely scattered population in which the largest settlement may be scarcely more than several hundred, to the large central city authorities. Even within the same type of settlement there are considerable variations: while most of the populous capital cities are divided into a patchwork of municipalities, this is less true of Queensland where Brisbane has been under a unitary authority since 1925, although the metropolitan area now extends beyond the city boundary (Greenwood and Laverty, 1959).

While ecological diversity in the range of population and areal sizes and settlement types has resulted in variations in the mix of services provided by local authorities, there is a core of activities found in all local authorities (Sitlington, 1985). These focus on property-related services and include roads, bridges, footpaths, drainage, street cleaning and lighting, garbage collection and disposal, parks and gardens and regulatory services, notably covering public health and town planning. Including water supply and sewerage but excluding parks and recreational activities, these services accounted for 63.5 per cent of total expenditure by local government in Queensland in 1981, 56.5 per cent in Tasmania, 49.9 per cent in New South Wales, 45.7 per cent in Victoria, 36.3 per cent in South Australia and 33.9 per cent in Western Australia. The local provision of physical infrastructure has been the traditional function of local councils, a fact given organizational expression in the importance of property voting in the local franchise. All states with the exception of Western Australia have now extended the franchise to all residents over the age of 18, though in all except Queensland the corporate vote remains, while in general residents who own more than one property are allowed to vote in respect of each of their properties.

More recently, local government has become increasingly involved in the provision of people-related services. These include health and welfare services, libraries and recreation provision. By 1981 they accounted for over 20 per cent of all local expenditures in three states, South Australia, Western Australia and Victoria, the commitment to people-related services being greatest in the latter.

The movement into the social development field marks a significant departure. Preoccupied with 'roads and drains', local government in Australia has not been concerned historically with improving social equity. The criticism that this involvement has been less a product of local initiative than it has been of tapping into a financially assisted programme initiated by higher tier of government has some justification. Further, to some critics, the health and welfare services were more appropriately provided for by the well-developed voluntary sector. Yet, the demands for these services to be provided by local government have generally risen and increasingly so since the economic recession has taken effect.

While the diversity of Australian local government defies classification, Power, Wettenhall and Halligan (1981) have sought to identify two polar types of local government systems, viz.:

(1) Constitutionalist - systems in which there is a 'relatively high degree of local autonomy, cautious fiscal policies, a weak mayoralty and a property-based franchise' (p.21). The prime examples are Victoria and South Australia.

(2) State-interventionist - systems which differ historically from the constitutionalist because rather than being established by local demand, local government was often imposed by the state. This has influenced its 'malleability', so that in state-interventionist systems - Queensland and New South Wales are the best examples - there has been less reluctance to restructure the territorial pattern of local government areas.

State-local relations do vary in Australia, as the classification of Power _et al._ suggests, but the base line is that the powers, duties and responsibilities of local government are the prerogative of the state parliaments. The status of local government in the Australian constitution was defined in a 1904 High Court judgement stating that:

> The State, being the repository of the whole executive and legislative powers of the community, may create subordinate bodies, such as municipalities, hand over to them the care of local interests and give them such powers of raising money by rates or taxes as may be necessary for the proper care of those interests. But in all such cases these powers are exercised by the subordinate body as agent of the power that created it. (1904) 1. C.L.R. 208, 240

However much legal definitions gloss over the nuances in the political relationships between the states and local government, local autonomy operates within more or less strictly prescribed limits.

The main characteristic of the tax base of Australian local government is its narrowness. Locally raised revenue is limited to property rating and to a variety of user charges, fees for town planning permits, parking fines and the running of local businesses. Property rating is overwhelmingly dominant, accounting for over 95 per cent of the local tax collection, while comprising nearly half of all local government incomes (Table 7.1).

Table 7.1: Components of Australian local government income, 1978/9

	$A (millions)	%
Rates	1216	47.5
Fees and fines	49	1.9
Grants (including PIT share)	530	20.7
Loans	506	19.7
Public enterprise and property income	262	10.2
Total	2563	100.0

Source: Advisory Council for Inter-government Relations (1981), Additional Revenue Sources for Local Government, Discussion Paper No. 4, ACIR, Hobart, p.7.

Much as there are differences between the states in terms of the service responsibilities of local government, so does the operation of property rating differ within Australia. Valuation systems differ and in each of the six states, except Queensland and

New South Wales, local governments have a choice of systems. In Victoria (for example) local councils can use net annual value (similar to the British method) or site value, or a combination of these, as the basis for rating. Besides the general rating powers, local councils are usually empowered to levy special rates. In Victoria these include rates to cover the provision of particular services - sanitary, water and drainage - together with a betterment rate for planning purposes and a Country Road Boards levy. In South Australia extra rates can only be charged following the approval of a majority of electors in a local referendum - this applies either to a special rate to be set for a particular year and normally levied when the general rate is insufficient to meet the financial requirements of the council, or for the purposes of a loan rate when the council wants to renegotiate or repay a loan.

The growth of special and separate rate charging, while variable between and within states, is symptomatic of the failure of the basic rating system to provide adequately for the financial requirements of local government. But their growth also represents an attempt to make local taxation more equitable. Rates are usually seen as a type of benefit taxation, in which the benefits of the services provided by rate revenue accrue mainly to the property-owners in the local area. In practice, the benefits are more widely dispersed, the equity implications of which can be countered through specific rating.

Partly to meet the apparent inequities in the rating system all states, but particularly New South Wales and South Australia, have passed enabling legislation to allow local councils to levy differential rates within their area. Differential rating is the levying of general rates at varying amounts in the dollar on different types of property or locations, the argument being that local councils are in the best position to a judge the equitable incidence of rates. The bases for differential rating vary (Table 7.2) and some systems are at best only partial. Where, however, a more comprehensive and flexible approach has been adopted, as in South Australia, the advantages claimed for differential

Table 7.2: Types of differential rating bases in the Australian states

	1966/7 Base year	%	1970/1 Constant prices	%	1974/5 Constant prices	%	1978/80 Constant prices	%
Rates	292.5	69.0	349.7	64.0	412.2	58.4	470.3	58.2
Fees, fines, etc.	14.0	3.3	12.1	2.2	15.0	2.1	19.4	2.4
Public enterprise/ property income	55.8	13.2	80.8	14.7	84.8	12.0	198.0	13.4
General Revenue sharing grants					32.9	4.7	77.6	9.6
	61.4	14.5	104.4	19.1				
Specific purpose grants					161.0	22.8	132.9	16.4

Note: The System in Tasmania has an undefined base.

Source: Advisory council for Inter-government Relations (1982), Sources of Local Government Funds, ACIR, Hobart, p.33.

rating are that it bolsters local autonomy, increases the local revenue take, and does so more equitably in relation to the benefits distributed by local government. Futhermore, though there may be difficulties in identifying different categories of ratepayers, land uses or other criteria which are used, it is a workable adaptation of the rating system. To its advocates, full differential rating (together with the adoption of other schemes such as rate rebates) would avoid many of the inequities of property rating.

Differential rating provides the one means for augmenting local revenue raising, though in general, the opportunities for increasing local revenue collection are limited. User charges and fees, particularly in relation to the regulatory services of local government, could be more fully exploited, though even here local discretion is catered for by state legislation. Were local councils to seek to broaden the range of service charges and fees, this would necessitate amendments to state legislation or state approval of alteration of council ordinances or

Table 7.3: Changes in the components of Australian local government revenue, 1966-80($Am)

Base used	NSW	VIC	QLD	SA	WA	TAS
1. Between or within electoral districts		x		x	x	
2. Between areas, parts of areas, designated financial divisions	x		x	x		
or centres of population	x		x			
3. Between rural and urban areas						
4. According to land use category	x			x		

Source: Adapted from Advisory Council for Inter-government Relations (1982), Sources of Local Government Funds, ACIR, Hobart, p.4.

by-laws. Equally, the opportunities for local governments to make substantial profits from trading operations are limited by state legislation. More generally, the potential for local government to increase rate revenue collection is limited by the action of other levels of government, and in particular, by the Commonwealth government. Assuming that the size of the national tax take is constrained by policies concerning economic stabilization and the desired level of public sector borrowing, Howard (1985) argues that because of the dominance of the Commonwealth government in the direct taxation field, especially income tax, it has been able to 'crowd out' the possibility of local bodies increasing their share of household taxation.

While rates remain the major source of locally-raised revenue their importance within the overall revenue base has tended to decline within the recent past (Table 7.3). Between 1966/7 and 1979/80 the proportion of local government revenue accounted for by rates fell from 69 per cent to 58.2 per cent, while it was the grant element which accounted for much of the 'gap' caused by the relative decline in property rating. Until the mid-1970s, specific grants dominated, with only a few states, such as New South Wales, initiating untied grants. The development of Commonwealth untied funding has altered the balance and not just in the type of grant, for there is evidence to show that as federal grants have increased, the level of state grants has decreased, eroding the possible gains for the local revenue base.

STATE INQUIRIES INTO LOCAL FISCAL REFORM

As far as local government is concerned the over-dependence on property rating is a major obstacle to its ability to meet its full potential as service provider. Summarizing the responses to its survey on local finances, the ACIR concluded that:

> From discussions ... it has become apparent that local government believes it essential for its revenue base to be broadened to include sources of revenue additional to rates and financial transfers from other governments. The reasons for this belief are twofold. As the responsibilities of local government become wider, it is no longer appropriate for property rates to be the only significant source of local taxation revenue. Further, local government finds itself unable to provide adequately those services now often expected by the community (ACIR, 1981, p.1).

Property rating was seen as restrictive, not only because increasing the levy would impact negatively on those with limited capacity to pay, but also because of its lack of buoyancy.

The weakness of the revenue base of local government and its reliance on property rating has not fallen on totally deaf ears within the state capitals, at least in so far as there has been a willingness to set up inquiries examining the problem.

During the last 20 years each of the state governments has established an inquiry examining local government finance (while a joint study of local fiscal problems in Australia and New Zealand was published in 1976). State inquiries have varied in their comprehensiveness, ranging from the Royal Commission in New South Wales, which examined the rating and valuation systems together with alternative sources of local revenue, to the much more restricted inquiry in Queensland limited to valuation problems.

If the number of inquiries held is a general indication of the lack of satisfaction with the present system of funding of local government, most of these inquiries have been content to make recommendations only as to how the rating system, including the method of valuation, might be improved. That is, while other revenue sources for local government have been considered by at least some of the inquiries - notably tourist and sales taxes, business licence fees, betterment levies, a local income tax, and a poll tax - little concerted attention has been given to the adoption of any of these by state governments, even as additions to the continued retention of rates. Perhaps as a reflection of the 'partial' approach to local fiscal reform which has been assumed - actual reforms have been limited mainly to modifications of the rating system, including reducing the period between revaluations - few state inquiries have treated the issue in practical terms. There has been little discussion as to the criteria to be met by a local taxation system.

One modification of the rating system to which considerable attention has been directed is the question of compensating local authorities for exempt property. Commonwealth and state property dominate the exempt category and are excluded from payment by the constitution. The loss to the local government revenue base can be considerable, especially in the capital cities where administrative functions are clustered. In their submission to the National Inquiry into Local Government Finance the Council of

Capital City Lord Mayors showed that the loss to the rates attributable to exempt property as a proportion of the rates paid averaged 17.8 per cent, and was as high as 35 per cent in Perth. Full compensation would substantially improve the local revenue base, but assuming this meant that all Commonwealth and state agencies would pay rates direct to the local authorities, the likelihood of this within the present economic climate is negligible.

Among the discussion of alternative sources of local revenue the introduction of a poll tax has been raised by a number of state inquiries, and in some cases advocated. A number of submissions to the New South Wales Royal Commission suggested the imposition of a poll tax and in its final report the Commission argued for its adoption. To the Commission the rationale for its adoption arose from the changes in local service provision; that as the expenditures of local councils were being devoted increasingly to 'people services' so residents who were not ratepayers should be obliged to contribute towards the revenue of local government. In spite of the real administrative complexities a poll tax would raise, particularly the upkeep of a residents' list, the Commission argued its advantages were of greater weight, not only on equity grounds but also, as in the British case, because of the enhancement of the accountability criterion. Rather than recommending that a mandatory poll tax be implemented the Commission favoured the possibility of Councils being able to experiment with it. Councils that chose to introduce a poll tax, however, would do so within a maximum set by the state, the presumption being that it was to be a supplementary, rather than replacement, source of local income, in distinction to the British proposals.

In South Australia the Local Government Act Revision Committee (1970) similarly found in favour of the poll tax, giving more discussion to the practical problems raised by its introduction than had been devoted by the New South Wales Commission. One such question concerned the base on which the tax would be levied, either the place of residence or the workplace, though both harboured problems. Other state inquiries in Victoria, Tasmania and West

Australia, to the extent that they considered the introduction of a poll tax, rejected it as impractical.

The poll tax is one of a number of possible options which have been considered by state inquiries, usually as a supplementary source of income. Of the various options the poll tax, together with tourist taxes, business licence fees and betterment levies, have been the more favoured in the state reports. Nevertheless, no state has seen fit to introduce legislation allowing local government to implement such supplementary sources. In several state inquiries the idea of potential taxing options was rejected virtually out of hand, without any detailed research or analysis to support the rejection. Even where attention on reforming the local government revenue base has focused mainly on modifying the rating and valuation systems, comparing the recommendations of the state inquiries and legislative reform, the one striking feature has been subsequent state inaction.

While state governments have been silent on the failure to implement fiscal reform there are at least two plausible reasons for it. Following from the argument of taxable capacity introduced earlier, and given that the Commonwealth government has assumed responsibility for approximately 80 per cent of all taxes collected, state governments have become the major victim of the vertical fiscal imbalance which characterizes the Australian federation. In consequence, state governments are reluctant to allow local government access to other tax options. As a corollary, because some state inquiries have advocated local experimentation with different tax options, the reluctance of state governments to sanction even this 'half-way house' is because of the greater fiscal autonomy this would lend to local government. The interpretation depends on the relationships between the two levels of government and to the meaning to be given, as far as the higher tier is concerned, to local autonomy. Restricting local fiscal autonomy may simply signify the trend which has persistently characterised state-local relations, that it is an arm of local administration rather than a local government.

In defence of the states, it could be argued, their conservatism is borne out of having little to devolve. That is, until there is a major tax devolution from the Commonwealth to the states, there is little chance of the latter devolving tax options to local government. Thus the states have resisted demands for the transfer of the land tax to local government because of its importance to their own economies. Yet this does not explain why local governments have not been allowed to introduce business licence fees, an innovation which would have some, but not major, disadvantages for the states, and which has gained support within local government. Jones (1981) asserts that state governments have been giving declining support to local government, in general, preferring to establish parastate bodies for the provision of particular services: the reluctance to allow local government to experiment with different tax options, as a number of inquiries have advocated, is symptomatic of a more general attitude of state governments towards local councils, and the small importance attached to local autonomy.

DIRECT COMMONWEALTH FUNDING AND ITS GROWTH AND RATIONALE

Since 1973 local government income has been bolstered by direct payments from the Commonwealth government. Initially, the policy to give direct assistance to local government was effected through an extension of the Commonwealth Grants Act of 1933. This Act was amended to allow for the direct payment of grants to regional groupings of local government, the major purpose of which was to reduce fiscal inequalities between local councils. Thus under Section 6 of the 1973 Act grants for local assistance were to enable

> all the local governing bodies in a region to function, by reasonable effort, at a standard not appreciably below the standards of the local governing bodies in other regions.

In fact, while fiscal equalization is a means rather

than an end, the objectives of which were only partly articulated, the Grants Commission was soon to find that both the methodology and the necessary data base to achieve equalization were lacking, problems which were compounded by the very diversity of local government in Australia. Accompanying the Grants Commission assistance were direct Commonwealth payments aimed particularly at the improvement of the urban and regional infrastructure, plugging a gap which had been a manifest failure of the state governments, according to the Whitlam government.

At root the development of the Commonwealth direct funding, and in particular the extension of Grants Commission to local government, might be traced to the historical antipathy of the Australian Labour Party, or at least of its federal wing, to the fact of federation (Paddison, 1983). The philosophy of a Commonwealth Labour government's approach had been stated by Whitlam in a speech made a few years prior to assuming office when he declared that

> were a new system of government to be devised for Australia there would be neither a federation nor so few intermediate local governments as the States, but a system of delegated but supervised local government based on assemblies for the cities and regional assistance for the rural areas (Whitlam, 1969).

The centralist aspirations of the Commonwealth government, which were to bring accusations of 'bypassing the states', and the rationale for direct funding were to be argued differently, however, emphasizing the overriding concern of the national government to aim for equity in service provision within Australia as a whole, and the functional interdependencies between the different levels of government. Thus the argument was that, on the one hand, there are clear national demands in terms of health, education, public transport, utilities and other services, which for reasons of equity, the Australian government has the responsibility to pursue national standards, while, on the other hand, the interdependency of policy decisions between different levels of government and the national government's overall responsibility for economic management logically pointed to its involvement in the planning and allocating of resources for expenditures of both state and local governments.

Aside from the specific grants directed to improvement of the urban and regional infrastructure, payments to local governments by the Grants Commission between 1973 and 1975 had both symbolic as well as practical importance. The intention was that the payments should be considered as 'topping up' grants, but that, because of their untied nature, the supplementation of the revenue base would enhance local autonomy. For the less-well-endowed councils, in particular, 'topping up' could mean the provision of services which would otherwise not have been possible. Symbolically, the expansion of direct payments from the Commonwealth were to raise the political stature of local government, making the abandonment of the precedent by a different Commonwealth government less likely.

The arrangements for bolstering the local government fisc under the New Federation policy of the Liberal-National Country Party government were to extend and modify the previous methods. Revenue-sharing was to be achieved through the earmarking of a fixed percentage of personal income tax to local government. This share was set initially at 1.52 per cent of the income tax collections, increased to 1.75 per cent in 1979/80 and to 2 per cent after 1980/81. The grants were to be distributed through the states, the payments to each local council being decided by the State Grants Commission established in some cases especially for the task. Only two conditions were stipulated under the enabling Local Government (Personal Income Tax Sharing) Act 1976 as to how the states should allocate payments, viz.:

(a) not less than 30 per cent of the total amount for a state for a year should be allocated on a population basis (Element A).
(b) the remainder should be allocated on a general equalisation basis (Element B).

These guidelines are sufficiently flexible to allow

for considerable state autonomy as to how PITS money has been allocated between local governments. Three states distribute more than 30 per cent of the grant under Element A and for a number of years the figure was as high as 80 per cent in Western Australia, leaving only a modest proportion to meet the objective of fiscal capacity equalization. These differentials have narrowed, so that (for example) Western Australia has given increased emphasis to Element B, yet substantially different methodologies on which the equalization element is assessed have been developed by the states. The outcomes of these different approaches, however, is less variable than might be expected. In all states rural shires receive substantially more in PITS grants per capita than do metropolitan and other urban authorities, a trend which, from the viewpoint of equalization, is to be expected, given the expenditure disabilities of the more sparsely populated councils, particularly in the provision and maintenance of roads.

Both by its nature, as an untied grant, and by the methods used to distribute the Element B payment, notably the widespread adoption of the 'effort neutral' principle, local autonomy has been bolstered by revenue sharing. Neither factor, however, has been uncontentious. Rather than being available for all services, and, indeed, in some authorities for holding down the level of rates increases, it has been argued that PITS money should be restricted to non-property-based services. The argument stems from the benefit principle. As, traditionally, local government services have been property-based, rates are an appropriate charge; this is not so for people-services, for which there is a case for grants to cover the cost of services. The argument for keeping the grants untied have been more persuasive, particularly in increasing local autonomy.

Equally important to maintaining local autonomy has been the use of the effort neutral principle. In determining the distribution of Element B payments the application of the principle means that the size of the grant is not affected by the effort made by local governments to raise revenue - both the level at which rates are struck and the standard of services to be provided are considered as matters of local concern. The alternative, involving some degree of fiscal discipline, would incorporate a measure of taxing effort. As Groenewegen (1976) showed of New South Wales local governments, there are considerable disparities in taxing effort between councils and that (arguably) low rating authorities are under-exploiting their tax base. From the submissions to the national inquiry into revenue-sharing some high-rating councils were even willing to abandon the effort neutral principle, arguing that its application was unfair to those local governments who, by increasing the local tax burden, were already providing a good standard of service. Quite apart from the fact that the revenue-raising disabilities would probably preclude all councils from being able to raise collections to the level of the high-rating authorities, the obvious drawback to abandoning the effort neutral principle would be the erosion of local autonomy.

CONCLUSIONS

With the weakness of the local tax base, and given the unlikelihood of tax devolution, the development of untied federal grants have assumed an important position in Australian local finance. In the major inquiry initiated by the Commonwealth government into local finance, it was concluded that the general purpose support given to local government under PITS should be continued. Indeed, the inquiry argued that the percentage allocation of the income tax collection might be increased, and that the programme of assistance be reviewed regularly in the light of the changing responsibilities of local government and the depth of grant support provided by the states. Some of the changes recommended by the inquiry were subsequently included in the 1986 Local Government Finance Assistance Act.

The arguments for retaining PITS funding are persuasive. Vertical fiscal imbalance between the different levels of government, more pronounced in Australia than in most other federations, is the starting point from which the necessity for a system of grants is generated (McClure, 1983). Further, as local government takes on increasing functional responsibilities, particularly in people-services, the ability to meet demands from the property tax is limited. Arguably, in terms of the benefit principle, there is less justification for meeting the cost of these services from the property tax, given that the benefits accrue to more than the set of local property owners. Indeed, there is some logical support for the introduction of a poll tax to meet such services (where user charges are not possible) but because of the commonly perceived difficulties in implementing the tax, Element A in the PITS funding provides a 'second-best' substitute. Applying the benefit principle in this way leads into difficulties, however, not least because of the hazy division between property and people-services and because the accumulation of benefits is not a clear-cut division. Finally, PITS funding has found widespread favour because of its contribution to horizontal equalization between councils on a state-wide basis. Admittedly, the equalizing effect has been only partial, and to be achieved more completely would require a substantial increase in the overall level of funding. On the grounds of its fairness in providing for a maximum standard of service, and of its efficiency, in offsetting the undesirable effects of fiscal migration the commitment to horizontal equalization is widespread, though never so intense that any submissions to the National Inquiry proposed that PITS funding be only provided for the poorer authorities.

As important as revenue-sharing under the PITS scheme might be, its drawbacks, as a grant, are that accountability is fudged, local autonomy is potentially impaired and the level of support is more directly vulnerable to macroeconomic controls. Whatever its disadvantages, property rating will continue to dominate the field of local taxation so that its augmentation, through such proposals as compensating local councils for property exempted from rates, provide the more feasible solution for bolstering the fiscal status of Australian local government. The outlook for the continued level of funding has become more uncertain, however, with the programme of expenditure cutbacks installed by the Commonwealth government in 1985 and 1986. With the states unwilling or unable to implement local fiscal reform - and where the New South Wales' precedent for fiscal control through rate-pegging may be adopted by other states - local fiscs are likely to be increasingly squeezed.

REFERENCES

Advisory Council for Inter-government Relations (1981)
Additional Revenue Sources for Local Government, Discussion Paper No. 4, ACIR, Hobart

--(1982)
Sources of Local Government Funds, Discussion Paper No. 8, ACIR, Hobart

--(1984)
Responsibilities and Resources of Australian Local Government, AGPS, Canberra

AGPS (1983)
Equality in Diversity, Australian Government Publishing Service, Commonwealth Grants Commission, Canberra

--(1985)
National Inquiry into Local Government Finance (3 volumes), Main Report and Research and Consultancy Reports, Australian Government Publishing Service, Canberra

Bowman, M. (1976)
Local Government in the Australian States, AGPS,Canberra

Chapman, R.J.K. and Wood, M (1984)
Australian Local Government: The Federal Dimension, George Allen & Unwin, Sydney

Greenwood, G. and Laverty, J. (1959)
Brisbane 1859-1959: A History of Local

Government, Ziegler, Brisbane

Groenewegen, P. (1976)
The Taxable Capacity of Local Government in NSW, Research Monograph No.13, Centre for Research on Federal Financial Relations, ANU, Canberra

Howard, J. (1985)
Local Government Revenue Raising, Report to the National Inquiry into Local Government Finance, AGPS, Research and Consultancy Reports (2), Canberra, 157-332

Jones, M.A. (1981)
Local Government and the People: Challenges for the Eighties, Hargreen, Melbourne

McClure, C.E. (ed.) (1983)
Tax Assignment in Federal Countries, Centre for Research on Federal Financial Relations, ANU, Canberra

Neutze, M. (1974)
'Local, Regional and Metropolitan Government', in R.L Mathews (ed.) Intergovernmental Relations in Australia, Angus & Robertson, Sydney

New South Wales (1967)
Royal Commission into Rating, Valuation and Local Government Finance, Government Printer, Sydney

Paddison, R. (1983)
'Intergovernmental Relationships and the Territorial Structure of Federal States', in N.Kliot and S. Waterman (eds.) Pluralism and Political Geography, Croom Helm, London, pp.245-58

Power, J., Wettenhall, R. and Halligan, J. (eds.) (1981)
Local Government Systems of Australia, AGPS, Canberra

Purdie, D.M. (1976)
Local Government in Australia: Reformation or

Regression, Law Book Co, Sydney

Sitlington, J.A. (1985)
Local Government Functions, Report to the National Inquiry into Local Government Finance, AGPS, Research and Consultancy Reports,1, Canberra, pp.1-156

Whitlam, E.G. (1969)
An Urban Nation, First Annual Leslie Wilkinson, University of Sydney, Sydney

8 LOCAL GOVERNMENT REFORM AND FINANCE IN FRANCE

Michael Keating

POWER AND INFLUENCE IN FRENCH LOCAL GOVERNMENT

The debate on the reform of local government finance has revolved around three principal themes, the need to ensure independence for local government, the need to ensure accountability for local spending, and the requirements of fairness. In all three respects, the debate in France parallels that in Britain but the local government system and traditions are so different as to make direct comparisons between reforms and proposals for reform extremely difficult. Crucially important here is the way in which power is distributed. In France, power is less dependent on the structure and functions of local government than on relationships among the actors involved and this has long been understood as the key to the system.

In structural terms, French local councils have always appeared weak. The basic unit is the commune, an ancient entity whose counterparts (such as the small burghs of Scotland) have been largely swept away in other Western European countries. There are some 36,000 communes and while some, like the city of Marseille, have large populations, a substantial resource base and their own bureaucratic and technical services, most are very small and rely for advice as well as the implementation of their decisions on the field services of central government. The reform of March 1982 formally abolished the _tutelle_ of the prefect but the effects of this were limited as, in the large cities, this had become a formality, while in the small rural communes the mayor continues to rely on the prefect (renamed _commissaire de la rêpublique_) and his sub-prefects (_commissaires de la rêpublique adjoints_) for advice and support.

Above the commune is the département, a technocratic creation of Napoleon but which, though no longer able to claim the same functional logic as in 1800, has proved resistant to reform. The 1982 Act, indeed, strengthened the département by transferring the executive power from the prefect to the council president.

The third tier is the region, established in 1972 but directly elected only since March 1986. Demands for regional government have a long history in France but for many years central governments resisted it, fearing for the unity of the state and of encouraging ethnic and separatist demands. Under the Fourth Republic, however, the state increasingly used regions as a unit for physical and economic planning and under the Fifth Republic nominated councils, the CODER, were introduced, very much along the lines of the contemporary Regional Economic Planning Councils in Britain. Finally, after a false start in 1969 (which provoked the resignation of de Gaulle), indirectly-elected regional councils were established in 1972. The inclusion of all members of Parliament and Senators in the region, along with representatives of départements and cities, ensured that the regions could not emerge as challengers to the existing power structure. The region was also structurally weak, boundaries being drawn to correspond neither to traditional provincial loyalties nor to the facts of contemporary social and economic geography, though some have nonetheless established themselves as significant policy actors. Much was hoped for from regional government in the early days of the decentralisation programme but, with the delay in direct elections (first provided for in the 1982 Act), it has lost the political initiative to the département.

Functionally, too, French local councils were weak despite the general competence power which in principle they possessed. Few functions belonged unambiguously to one tier or another and many services were run directly by the field services of central departments. Indeed, almost any initiative for the provision of capital facility or the establishment of a new service has required a collaborative decision by several agencies of central and local government. It had been intended, in the second phase of the reforms of the 1981-6 Socialist government, to clarify responsibilities, devolve more power to local councils and replace the general competence power with power of attribution. In practice, however, the complexities of modern government, together with the unwillingness to grasp the nettle of structural reform, has made this impossible. So, while the reform legislation does give one tier the lead responsibility in each sphere - the commune in local planning and urban development, the _département_ in social services and the region in economic planning and intervention - it is recognized that all three levels, together with the field services of the state and the _ad hoc_ agencies will be involved jointly in most areas of activity.

The interlinking of responsibilities in the French system also makes international comparisons of functions and spending patterns extremely difficult. In Britain, for example, one can attribute the administrative responsibility for primary and secondary education quite unambiguously to the county or regional council (policy, admittedly, is more complicated). In France, however, the commune may provide the building, the _département_ the school meals and transport, the regional council the land or subsidies to teach minority languages, and the state employ the teachers. So, within each policy field, responsibility is divided.

A mere examination of the structure and functions of French local government, however, largely misses the point for its weakness in these respects disguises the real power of the local politicians. This is based on the _cumul des mandats_, the tradition whereby ambitious and successful politicians are able to accumulate offices at all levels throughout the system. Most Members of Parliament hold local government office, usually as mayor of their commune, with many holding office in both commune and _département_, while the Senate is elected from local government; and the regional councillors, until March 1986, comprised all Members of Parliament and senators in the region plus representatives from the communes and départements and thus were by definition cumulards. The process works both ways. Not only does the mayor of a big city seek election to Parliament as a matter of course, but politicians who start from the top, as members of Parliament or brought in directly as ministers, feel obliged to dig local roots by getting themselves elected to local office. Nor does the ambitious politician give up his local office on election to a higher one. In recent years, Pierre Mauroy and Jacques Chirac have remained as mayors of Lille and Paris respectively while Prime Minister and Gaston Defferre was setting no precedent in the early years of the Mitterrand government by serving as mayor of Marseille at the same time as Minister of the Interior, making him the hierarchical superior of his local prefect.

An accumulator of offices becomes in due course a notable, a figure of great influence, able to act on the system at various levels, to circumvent opposition from the prefect or field services and to put together the complex policy and financial packages necessary to make the system work. The prefect, in turn, has usually seen his interest in lying in collaboration with his local notables rather than in conflict and has tended to defend his locality in Paris. Indeed, to prevent them going totally native, prefects have usually been moved around every two or three years. The result is that a system which, from the centre appears a model of uniformity, dissolves at the periphery into a myriad of individual decisions, negotiated on the basis of local compromises.

The contrast with Britain is striking. For many years, a school of thought in France has admired the 'Anglo-Saxon' system of local self-government, with its independent councils controlling their own resources and administrative machinery - the comparison emerged again during the debates on the recent reforms. Foreign admirers of the French system (Ashford, 1977; Wright, 1978), however, have a very different view, contrasting the isolation of British local government from the centre with the access of the French mayor and claiming that these features provide for the exercise of local power to a degree unavailable in Britain, although it is a 'democracy of access' rather than a democracy of deliberation and decision. Ashford (1982) goes further to claim that the French tradition of negotiation and bargaining across the territorial divide makes for better policy outcomes than the British system with its rigid functional divisions and 'dogmatic' attitudes. Even conceding this point, it is hard to draw any prescriptions for British local government from this. If French governments are forced to negotiate with territorial power-holders and cannot unilaterally change the terms of the relationship, this stems from a feature of French political culture and the strong territorial roots of politicians, not from purely institutional mechanisms which could be transplanted. Certainly, proposals have frequently been made for a second chamber representing local or regional government - the French Senate does this - but second chamber representation is no substitute for having the Prime Minister and half the Cabinet serving simultaneously as mayors.

French critics of the system (Thoenig, 1979) are less generous than some foreign observers and, while conceding that the 'jacobin' myth of all decisions being taken in Paris is a far cry from reality, claim that the system has neither the merits of a centralized, hierarchical bureaucracy nor a 'horizontal' local democracy. Rather, it is a 'honeycomb', with lines of communication and control rendered extremely complex and accountability obscured. If one's local *notable* has succeeded in bringing home a new concert hall or an improved bus service, it is often impossible to tell whether it was in his capacity as mayor, as councillor in the *département*, as Member of Parliament or Minister or as a director of some intergovernmental quango. So power belongs neither to the Ministers in Paris nor to the electors in the localities but to a complex political bureaucratic network which, by its control over the distribution of resources, is able to sustain its own power indefinitely. It is because the *notables* gain in power and influence from the system that, while rhetorically declaiming against centralization, they are in practice its firmest supporters (Grémion, 1976). So attempts to reform the structure of French local government in the past have sunk in the consultation process or been destroyed in the *notable*-dominated Parliament, and new procedures and policies become items for the *notables* to circumvent and turn to their own advantage. It is because of this and the connected failure to reach agreement within their own party that the Socialists' proposals, implemented after 1981, left the existing three-tier system alone (Keating and Hainsworth, 1986).

The 1981-6 reform of French local government was intended to increase local accountability by giving councils more responsibilities for taking decisions on their own account and removing the central controls (such as the vestigial *tutelle*) which were less a means of enforcing the centre's dictates than of allowing local politicians to escape the responsibility for their actions. The 'democracy of access' was to give way to the deliberative model. The main provisions were:

- the abolition of the *tutelle* over the communes;
- the transfer of the executive responsibility in the *départements* and regions from the prefect to the president of the council;
- the direct election of the regional councils;
- firmer control by the *commissaire de la république* (prefect) over the field services of the various ministries, making him, in principle, the sole interlocutor for local government;
- a transfer of functions to local councils, with some transfer of personnel or, failing this, provision for central civil servants to be placed at the disposal of councils;
- a reform of local government finance;
- a reform of the local civil service;
- a gradual limitation of the *cumul des mandats*, to be introduced over a period of years and which would eventually restrict politicians to two offices. Great scepticism has been expressed over this provision which, by limiting offices to three in the first stage, would actually allow some people to extend their accumulation in 1987 and whose full implementation has been put back safely to the far side of the presidential (and, presumably, legislative) elections.

The programme has produced some real changes, though not always those anticipated in 1981. Politicians have seen their power strengthened at the expense of bureaucrats but the failure to tackle the issue of structural reform has left this power in the hands of the traditional political class. The entity which has gained most is in fact the _département_, the unit most widely considered redundant before 1981 by reformers, who conceded that the commune was close to the people and had a democratic vitality while insisting that the region was better tailored to the needs of large-scale planning and intervention. It is no accident that it is the _département_ in which the practices of notabilism are most strongly rooted. There is evidence, indeed, that they are being strengthened, with presidents of councils building up personal power systems and even conceding individual councillors powers of patronage within their electoral districts. In the large cities, on the other hand, most of the powers were already effectively in the hands of the mayor, who had usually built up his own administrative apparatus, while city politics are conducted on a party political basis rather than through patronage and personal links. Here the reforms have had limited impact, though they have increased the accountability of the mayor, who can no longer hide behind the prefectoral veto.

The failure to tackle the question of structural reform, together with the failure clearly to demarcate functions, has meant that the essentials of the old system have remained. Local power holders have demonstrated their influence by moulding the reform to their own interests and access to other levels of decision-making continues to be the main source of power. Finance was to have been a key element of the reform but, as elsewhere, has proved a political and technical minefield.

LOCAL GOVERNMENT FINANCE

If the network of local power and decision-making in France is everywhere complex, nowhere is this more true than in relation to finance. As with so many other matters, the administration is in the hands of a central government official, the Trésorier-Payeur Général. It is he who writes the cheques and settles accounts and, in the past, was able to ensure that council expenditure was within the law. Of course, the boundaries between what is illegal, what is bad financial practice and what is merely politically undesirable from the point of view of the centre are, in France as in Britain, difficult to define. The role of the Trésorier-Payeur Général certainly often went beyond mere questions of legality or accounting and by creating difficulties with contentious items of spending or referring matters to Paris, effectively constituted another type of tutelle. Clear parallels exist here with some of the fears expressed about the English Audit and Scottish Accounts Commissions, whose actions have been seen by some as trespassing into areas of political judgement.

The 1981 Act sought to clarify matters by providing that the mayor or president of the département could requisition funds from the Trésorier-Payeur Général who would no longer have the power to refuse. To ensure respect for legality, it was initially proposed that the mayors and presidents could be arraigned before the new Regional Courts of Accounts if suspected of exceeding their legal powers but, under heavy pressure from the mayors, this provision was withdrawn. There remains the obligation to prepare a balanced budget and respect national laws on what constitutes legitimate spending but local politicians do not face the awesome penalties threatening their British colleagues for non-compliance. Instead, on a declaration from the Administrative Tribunal or Court of Accounts, the commissaire de la république has the power to substitute legal acts for illegal ones. Here is another possible lesson for Britain, where councillors face the prospect of surcharges and disbarment, while their sponsoring Minister at the Department of the Environment can simply get his Parliamentary majority retrospectively to legalise his illegal acts and does not even face any pressure to resign.

Beyond this, the Socialists had promised a

comprehensive reform of local finance. This proving as intractable a subject in France as in other Western countries, an assurance was given that, in the meantime, transfers of functions would be accompanied by transfers of finance, through a combination of assigned revenues and global subsidies. In fact, reform efforts had already started under the previous government of Giscard d'Estaing but the complexities of the subject and the weight of entrenched interests had stalled progress. In 1980, local government was responsible for some 30 per cent of public expenditure, amounting to 9.7 per cent of Gross National Product. Of this, 65 per cent was accounted for by communes and groupings of communes. Councils were raising some 35 per cent of their own revenue expenditure through taxes and charges, mainly through four taxes. The most important - accounting for half of tax receipts - was the taxe professionelle. Introduced in 1976 by Jacques Chirac, this is based on local payrolls and industrial property values. It is highly unpopular and widely criticized as a tax on jobs and industrial investment and for the inequitable distribution of revenues - according to the level of industrial activity - though over the years equalization mechanisms have been introduced (Belorgey, 1984). The other taxes, the taxe d'habitation and those on foncier bâti and foncier non-bâti are property taxes. In addition, councils raised small amounts from various archaic taxes and charges.

Following an Act of 1980, under the Giscard government, councils now have the power to alter the rates of individual local taxes and to change the balance among them. Previously, they could only inform the revenue services of the tax product they desired and leave it to the latter to adjust the rates proportionally. In practice, the new system has made little difference except in the large cities with their own administrative services, as it is immensely complicated to change the balance of the taxes, putting it beyond the competence of most communes. Regions had limited taxation powers subject to a ceiling on the amount which could be raised per inhabitant; the amount raised by the regions was in fact very small. Charges are used mainly by _régies_, semi-autonomous trading services for transport, low cost housing and the like and by groupings of communes. For communes and _départements_, they accounted for less than 1 per cent of revenue. While French local government might appear to have a wider tax base than its British counterpart, therefore, this consists of largely non-buoyant and unpopular taxes, so that the scope for independent decision-making is similarly limited.

Capital expenditure is defined to include loan charges, so making comparisons with Britain difficult, and in 1979 comprised some 26 per cent of local expenditure. Of capital finances, 21 per cent came from subsidies, slightly over half of this from the state and the rest passed down from regions and _départements_, 36 per cent came from loans, 15 per cent from capital receipts and 27 per cent from revenue.

Transfers within the local government system were, as we can see, an important element. About a third of the communes' income came from subsidies from the _départements_, which had a responsibility for redistributing resources and helping small communes. In the case of the regions, all their spending was directed to other agencies since they had no power to under-take work at their own hand. Some regions merely engaged in _saupoudrage_, an even scattering of subsidies around the region, with limited impact on the ground. Others sought to gain more policy leverage by selective targeting of larger subsidies on a few key projects. This feature, of large transfers within the local government system, is a product of the French system of interlocking responsibilities and finds no parallel in Britain, though suggestions have been made that, were regional government to be established in England, the distribution of part of Rate Support Grant and capital allocations could be handled by the regions (Keating, 1986). This was also provided for in the Scotland and Wales Acts and is an element in all the current proposals for Scottish devolution.

Transfers from central government traditionally took the form of specific subsidies for individual investments and services. The conditions attached to these, and the need to get approval from the various central government technical services before subsidies could be granted, were the basis for many of the financial and technical tutelles under which local councils suffered. Indeed, a whole subsidy culture developed so that councils would put their efforts into subsidised investments and avoid others, even where the value of the subsidy was negligible. Since the early 1970s, a debate has continued on how to replace these subsidies with global grants for investment and services.

In 1979, as one of the few practical products of the decentralization efforts of the Giscard government, the Dotation Globale de Fonctionnement (DGF) was introduced for revenue expenditure. This transfers revenue to all local councils and attempts to equalize for resources, though not for needs. Its main components are (Belorgey, 1984):

- a guaranteed sum for all councils, diminishing year by year;
- an equalization element, based on the fiscal potential of individual councils and growing year by year;
- specific elements for categories of council such as small communes or inner city areas;
- a dampening mechanism to attenuate the sudden effects of the changes on individual councils from one year to the next.

The amount of the grant, which councils are free to spend in their own way, is linked to the national product of Value Added Tax on the assumption of an unvaried rate and coverage.

Capital expenditure has since 1976 benefited from a global subsidy in the form of the Fonds de Compensation de la TVA. This originated in a demand by councils for a rebate on the Value Added Tax paid on their public works. Given the complexities of this, central government opted for what is in effect a direct subsidy to completed capital expenditures, extending it eventually to a range of public bodies such as housing agencies and mixed public-private development companies. The system was widely criticized as open-ended and indiscriminate, subsidizing everyone at the same rate and biassing budgets towards capital expenditure rather than service development. The fund has been retained, however, despite the latest reforms.

The major reform of the system of subsidies for capital expenditure has been the Dotation Globale d'Equipement (DGE), outlined in principle in the 1982 Act and enacted in a series of laws in 1983. It equalizes for both resources and needs, albeit in a rather unsophisticated manner and is being implemented over a period of three years, gradually bringing specific subsidies into a single block. For the communes, the principles for distributing the total are (Belorgey, 1984):

- at least 70 per cent according to the actual investment of communes;
- at least 15 per cent among small communes according to the length of communal roads, mountainous conditions and fiscal potential;
- the remainder according to the fiscal potential of communes relative to others of the same size bracket, and to districts and urban communities (groupings of communes).

The original proposals had placed more weight on actual capital expenditure but this was changed after objections in Parliament that, by favouring communes which invested most, it insiduously encouraged communal mergers and regroupments. We see here again how attempts at reform of any part of the system come up against the entrenched interests and jealousies of the notables.

For départements, the grant is in two parts. The first part is distributed as follows:

- at most 75 per cent according to actual capital expenditure;
- at most 20 per cent according to the length of departmental roads;
- the rest according to fiscal potential.

There is a dampening mechanism to prevent too rapid changes for individual councils.

The second part is distributed as follows:

- 80 per cent according to actual capital expenditure in rural areas, including the subsidization of the capital expenditures of communes and other agencies;
- the remainder according to fiscal potential.

There is no doubt that the introduction of the DGE is a move of great significance, giving councils much greater freedom in determining their investment programmes. Not all the ministries, however, had been playing the game equally enthusiastically. New specific funds were introduced in education, culture and professional training, covering capital as well as revenue expenditure. Like so many of the decentralization measures, too, it benefits mostly the big councils who are in a position to take advantage of the new freedom. Small communes will need to co-operate with each other and with départements to realise investments. They will also continue to be subject to control by the département which will allocate much of their capital finance. The evidence so far shows that départements have been unwilling to carry through the logic of the programme and globalize their own subsidies to the communes. Some presidents justify this by pointing out that the aid is an instrument of departmental policy, not an automatic entitlement or a means of reducing communal taxation. In some areas, however, it appears to be becoming the instrument of a new patronage, with departmental councillors able to distribute the money among the communes of their own cantons (electoral divisions).

So far we have been discussing the financing of the traditional functions of local government. For the newly transferred functions, the Government promised new resources, maintaining a balance between assigned or transferred taxes and direct subsidies. The major new subsidy is the Dotation Globale de Décentralisation, a block grant calculated initially on the basis of the cost of transferred services. In future, its growth will, like the DGF, be linked to the product of Value Added Tax. The main taxes to be transferred have been those on the carte grise to the regions and vehicle exise duty to départements, together with some taxes on changes in property use.

For the regions, the ceiling on taxation has been lifted with their direct election in 1986. In the meantime, it was raised, with regions taking considerable advantage of this in the first year (1983), to increase their budgets between 30 per cent and 50 per cent . While the large percentage rise in regional taxes which this entailed caused some cries of anguish, the absolute levels of regional expenditure and taxation remain tiny in relation to those of the communes and départements.

Loans account for some 13 per cent of councils' income and 36 per cent of their investment expenditure (in 1982). Most of these come from public funds at special rates of interest, notably the Caisse des Dépôts et Consignations and the Caisse d'Aide à l'Equipement des Collectivités Locales. In the past, Keynesian considerations of demand management played less of a part in central regulation of local borrowing than in Britain (Ashford, 1982), though in practice global control was achieved through state control of the credit system in France. The availability of loans and the rates of interest were tightly controlled by the Ministry of Finance. In any case, few capital projects proceeded without a central subsidy - even when these were tiny, they tended to guide investment decisions in the collaborative tradition of French local government. The globalization of subsidies lifts this constraint but councils' borrowing is still subject to state control of the credit system. A liberalization of credit as promised under a government of the Right could presumably affect this, allowing councils more freedom to borrow on the market, but, given the restrictive attitude of the Right to local government and to public spending in general, new controls would presumably emerge. In comparison with Britain, then, the mechanisms of control are quite different, reflecting the differing structures of capital markets, but the effects are similar, central control over the level of local borrowing and debt.

Finance has proved to be one of the most controversial aspects of the whole decentralization programme, with councils almost unanimously complaining that they have not been given the means to discharge their new responsibilities. The Government, on the other hand, insisted that it had scrupulously transferred resources and taxes corresponding to the present cost of services. The problem seems to be that many of the transferred services are ones in which expenditure is growing for demographic or economic reasons - for example in the social services - while transfers are linked to taxes, including Value Added Tax, whose yield is likely to be restricted in the conditions of austerity anticipated in the Socialists' post-1983 policy of rigeur and the Right's preference for Thatcherite deflation. It is also alleged that much of the property whose maintenance central government is transferring suffers from a large backlog of neglect. Hence the suspicion that the centre is transferring the burden of the most difficult and expensive services to the localities. Meanwhile, the promised radical reform of local finance never found time in the 1981-6 Parliament and is unlikely now to resurface for many years to come.

CONCLUSIONS

At the beginning of this chapter, we set out the criteria to judge proposals to reform local government finance as local independence, accountability and fairness. The French reforms have attempted to move in these directions, albeit with limited success. The greater freedom to alter the levels and mix of local taxes will benefit the large councils, which have the administrative capacity to do this and the globalization of revenue and capital grants will help to increase local autonomy. On the other hand, the extreme interdependence of levels of government and the lack of a clear functional differentiation will continue to obscure local accountability. The criterion of fairness has been taken into account in the equalization systems introduced at all levels, though the local taxes themselves continue to come in for criticism.

As in the United Kingdom, the central Ministry of Finance remains obdurately opposed to further devolution of fiscal powers and sought to transfer fiscal capacity in the form of assigned rather than devolved taxes. The local notables have gained considerably from the reform, especially in the départements, but are deeply worried that the state plans to transfer to them the political burden of coping with the fiscal crisis, without real powers of decision-making. This is too cynical an explanation of what the Socialists planned and there was a genuine urge to reform the system in the direction of greater transparency and accountability, but it does remain an option for French governments. The Ministry of Finance is concerned always to control expenditure but, while it deplores high local spending levels, there is no suggestion that these or the local tax levels associated with them are a central issue of policy. I would not, therefore, anticipate French governments going down the British road to intervene in the expenditure decisions of individual councils or take away powers from local government. The notables would not stand for that and, if it did come about, they are skilful enough to circumvent any conceivable system, bending the rules to the cases in time-honoured fashion. So the centre has, under successive governments, sought to simplify central-local relations and devolve the powers over individual cases, along with the political responsibility. At the same time, fiscal pressure is being maintained by the continued absence of a reform of local taxation, together with tight control on central grants.

REFERENCES

Ashford, D. (1977)
Review article in Comparative Politics, 9

-- (1982) British Dogmatism and French Pragmatism. Central-Local Policymaking in the Welfare State, Allen & Unwin, London

Belorgey, G. (1984)
La France Décentralisée, Berger-Levrault, Paris

Grémion, P. (1976)

Le Fouvoir Périphique. Bureaucrates et Notables dans le Système Politique Francais, Seuil, Paris

Keating, M. (1986)
'Regional Government', in M. Goldsmith (ed.), The Future of Local Government, West Yorkshire County Council

-- and Hainsworth, P. (1986)
Decentralisation and Change in Contemporary France, Gower, Aldershot

Thoenig, J-C (1979)
'Local government institutions and the contemporary evolution of French Society', in V. Wright and J. Lagroye (eds.), Local Government in Britain and France, Allen & Unwin, London

Wright, V. (1978)
The Government and Politics of France, Hutchinson, London

9 FINANCIAL DEVELOPMENT IN NORWEGIAN LOCAL GOVERNMENT

Tore Hansen

INTRODUCTION

Debates on local government autonomy, democracy, activity and efficiency often turn into debates over the financial basis and strength of local government, with a particular emphasis on the revenue system. The sources of local revenues and the way in which the revenue system is organized - as well as the proportion of total public revenues at the disposal of local authorities - are considered as affecting not just the role of local government as producer and provider of welfare services, but also the more ideological fundaments upon which the very idea of local self-government rests. However, the objectives and ideas of the welfare state - as expressed in terms of universality, justice and equality - do not necessarily coalesce with increased local autonomy and local accountability (Sharpe, 1970; Kjellberg, 1980).

In fact, the history of local government reforms in Norway since World War II may be viewed as a continuous process aiming at striking a 'correct' balance between localist and more centralist welfare state values. A common complaint, voiced particularly by and among local political leaders, has been that centralist values have had the upper hand on the development and the reforms introduced over this period. To a considerable extent this is obviously correct; local government has been turned into a major agent in the development of the Norwegian welfare state, a welfare state which has given higher priority to national equality than to local autonomy. On the other hand, this very development has also provided local authorities with far more tasks and resources than they ever have had before. If we consider the development of local expenditures, measured in constant prices, they were five times higher in 1986 than in 1950. Measured as a proportion of GNP, local government expenditure almost doubled between 1950 and 1986, from 14 per cent to approximately 27 per cent.

To be sure, a major force behind this expansion has been national legislation and policies initiated by central government - e.g. in the fields of education and social welfare policies. In this sense one may speak of a national standardization of local government responsibilities and tasks. On the other hand, it would be an overstatement to suggest that this growth and standardization has undermined local autonomy completely - as is frequently suggested in Norwegian public debates about these matters.

In the first place, the general principle upon which local government activities is based - namely that local authorities are free to do what they want to, unless other authorities by legislation have been provided with such powers and tasks - has remained unaltered since the introduction of the current system of local government in 1837. Secondly, transfer of tasks from central to local government has often been justified by the need to let local preferences determine how such policies should be implemented and accommodated at the local level. From this perspective it may be argued that local authorities have been given more influence in setting and implementing national priorities, while at the same time preserving their own autonomy vis-a-vis the state within their traditional areas of activity. Thirdly, the national legislation aiming at regulating local government activities, almost never gives any detailed instructions as to how much of a certain activity local government should perform, or how it should be performed. This legislation is rather characterized by providing general guidelines, within which local authorities may enjoy a fair degree of discretion in forming their activities (Hansen and Kjellberg, 1976). There are exceptions to this, as in the case of primary education where the curriculum is centrally determined, but such exceptions are of limited importance seen in relation to the total level of local government activity. In fact, one may even suggest that national legislation and regulations are of less importance in determining the actual content of municipal tasks than are informal professional values and standards as well as general technological possibilities (Hansen and Sorensen, 1986).

Generally, the argument that the imposition of tasks on local authorities by central government has undermined local autonomy completely is hardly tenable, at least not without important qualifications. One such qualification relates to the organization of the local revenue system, a question which will be addressed in the following sections. After that I will give an outline of the recent development of Norwegian local government finances, with a particular emphasis on the distributive effects (between various types of municipalities). In a final section I will return to the general theme addressed in the introduction, presenting some empirical evidence on the perceptions of and attitudes to local autonomy among local officials.

DEVELOPMENT OF LOCAL REVENUES

As suggested in the introduction, the organisation of the local revenue system has been at the core of the debate over the financial development of Norwegian municipalities. Apart from the recurrent demand for providing the municipalities with more financial resources, considerable attention has been paid to the way in which central government grants have been distributed to local authorities. Two issues have been pertinent in this context. The first relates to the question of accomplishing a 'just' distribution across the country's 450 municipalities, in the sense that total per capita revenues should be kept above a certain - although not specified - level in all municipalities. This was the prime concern when the first major state grant to the municipalities - the tax equalization grant - was introduced in 1936 (Myhren, 1977). The second issue relates to the way in which central grants have been distributed between various areas of local government activities, an issue which became increasingly important as a consequence of a fast and steady growth in specific - or earmarked - grants over the whole postwar period. While the first issue relates to the problem of achieving distributional justice and equality across various jurisdictions and geographical areas, the second issue concerns the question of local fiscal autonomy and accountability - the extent to which local authorities are free to use their total revenues according to their own priorities, and to what extent they should be made accountable for the actual outcomes of the budgetary decisions.

Before we consider these issues further, it will be useful to examine the actual composition of local government revenues. Here I will restrict my discussion to current revenues, leaving out revenues for investment purposes - such as loans. It should, however, be noted that loans and other revenues for capital investments added up to 19 per cent of total local government revenues in 1982, but the relative importance of such revenues vary considerably across the municipalities. As regards current revenues, we may distinguish between four major categories. The first category comprises local taxes, of which local tax on income and wealth is the most important, and has been the major local revenue source since such taxes were made mandatory by legislation in 1882. Since 1979 the local tax rate has been 21 per cent of taxable income, and is of far more importance to the individual taxpayer than income taxes to the state. Municipalities do, however, charge other taxes as well, of which property tax is the major one - although of far less practical importance than income taxes. In addition, the municipalities may also charge a business tax, but this is of even less importance than property taxes. Thus in 1985 only 0.4 per cent of total local revenues came from business taxes, while the corresponding figure for property taxes was 4 per cent. It should also be noted that, in contrast to taxes on income and wealth, it is up to the individual local authority to decide whether to charge property and business taxes. In 1985 altogether 66 per cent of all municipalities charged business taxes, while 44 per cent charged property taxes (Hansen, 1987). In the further discussion, I do not distinguish between these types of taxes.

The second major revenue category comprises specific state grants. These are earmarked, in the sense that they may be used only for specific purposes as defined by central ministries. Until 1986 there were nearly 200 such grants altogether, each of them granted separately without any central co-ordination. From 1986, as I will return to, the whole grant system was reformed by amalgamating all specific grants into four sector-based and one general block grants.

Apart from specific grants, the municipalities also received a general grant, aimed at equalizing differences in local taxing abilities. This grant has been financed by earmarking a certain proportion of local income taxes for a tax equalization fund. Since 1979 2 per cent of local taxable income has been earmarked for such purposes. Although this grant has been locally funded, the actual distribution of the grants has been the responsibility of central authorities. Since 1986 such grants have been included in the new state grant system, but still aiming at equalizing variations in local tax revenues

The fourth revenue category comprises fees and charges, particularly for various individual services, like day nurseries for children, water supply, garbage collection and so on. The incidence of such revenues may, however, vary substantially between the municipalities. Apart from those service areas where legislation explicitly rules out the charging of fees, it is up to the individual local authority to decide whether to make use of such revenue sources or not. Since such revenues are highly visible (in contrast to income taxes which are deducted at the source), decisions to introduce such payment systems - or to increase the prices - are likely to cause considerable political conflict, not least because of the distributive effects of such revenues. Local authorities have therefore been rather hesitant in making use of these potential revenue sources, although they have increased in importance over recent years as a consequence of a more squeezed financial situation in most municipalities.

Let us now consider the actual distribution of total current revenues according to these four categories. In Table 9.1 the actual amount - measured in constant prices - is reported for 1977, 1979 and 1982. In addition to these figures, the table also displays the relative distribution of revenues across the four categories.

Table 9.1: Per capita revenues from and relative distribution of taxes, state grants and fees and charges, 1977-1982 (constant 1980 prices: Kroner)

Year	Taxes	Specific grants	General grants	Fees/ charges
1977:				
Amount	3692	1446	997	1204
% of total	50.3	19.7	13.6	16.4
1979:				
Amount	3369	1767	1083	1383
% of total	44.3	23.2	14.3	18.2
1982:				
Amount	3861	1918	1358	1531
% of total	44.5	22.1	15.7	17.7

As is evident from the figures in Table 9.1, there have been some rather significant changes in the relative composition of local revenues over this 5-year period. The most important changes relate to the marked drop in taxes as a percentage of total revenues - from 50.3 per cent in 1977 to 44.5 per cent in 1982. Actually, if we just consider the changes between 1977 and 1979, tax revenues decreased in real terms by almost 9 per cent. The major reason for this decrease was a central government decision to lower the maximum tax rate by 0.5 per cent, while at the same time to increase the rate for the tax equalization fund by 0.5 per cent. This decision was primarily aimed at controlling and reducing further expansion of public expenditures - and to accomplish a more egalitarian distribution of financial resources across the municipalities. On this background it is therefore rather surprising to observe the fast growth that has taken place in state grants - specific as well as general - during this period. The decrease in tax revenues from 1977 to 1979 was more than compensated for by increases in central grants. If we consider the total revenue growth between 1977 and 1982, which amounted to 18 per cent, almost two-thirds of this growth was accounted for by increases in state grants. In other words, the attempt to curb the growth in tax revenues was more or less neutralized by increases in state grants.

The figures also show that the effect of the reduction in the maximum tax rate only was a temporary one. The marked decrease in taxes between 1977 and 1979 was followed by a growth in such revenues which was relatively stronger than the total revenue growth. However, this growth did not contribute to alter the relative distribution of all revenues, apart from certain minor changes seen in relation to the 1979 figures. This indicates that, apart from a temporary slow down in revenue growth, the long-term effect of the reduction in tax rate lies in the alteration in the relative importance of the various revenue sources. In the first place, taxes have become less important as a local revenue source, although they still remain the most important one. Secondly, the municipalities have become increasingly dependent on financial support from central government. Apart from the consequences this may have for local autonomy, this dependency has also made local government far more vulnerable to central government measures aimed at macroeconomic regulations. The 'protection' which local authorities enjoyed from a fairly autonomous revenue system - in the form of tax on income and wealth - is now in the process of deteriorating.

Thirdly, the growth of earmarked grants along with an increasing dependency on fees and charges makes the budgetary system far less flexible in terms of rearranging priorities according to changing needs and demands. In this sense local government activity may become less efficient and more wasteful.

REFORMING CENTRAL GRANTS

The above problems, as well as the problems of reduced autonomy and local accountability, have been a recurrent topic in the work on local government reforms that has taken place throughout the post-war period. The issues were thoroughly addressed in two major report during the 1950s and the 60s (Skatteutjamningskomiteen, 1956; Funksjonsfordelingskomiteen, 1967). Both reports were primarily concerned with the need to accomplish a more clear division of functions and responsibilities between state and local government. The last report, in particular, was concerned with the need to simplify the system of central government transfers by abolishing the increasing number of specific grants in favour of a general grant, not earmarked for any specific purpose. Two major arguments were put forward in favour of such a reform. In the first place, a transition of the transfer system into a general block grant would make the local authorities more accountable for their budgetary decisions. In the second place, the increasing number of specific grants was considered as having adverse effects on the total distribution of central government grants - and local fiscal abilities - across the municipalities. The redistributive effects of the tax equalization grants were to a considerable extent neutralized by the various specific grants. In this sense, the growth of specific grants was considered as threatening the egalitarian principles of the welfare state, stressing equal fiscal abilities across all local authorities.

Neither of these reports led to any specific policy measures, and the issue of financial reform was not given any further consideration until another government committee issued a report on 'objectives and principles for local government reforms' in 1974 (NOU, 1974, p.33). On the basis of more or less the same considerations as those presented in the 1966 report - relating to accountability and distributive justice - this committee suggested abolishing all specific grants in favour of one general grant. Furthermore, the allocation of such grants should be made on the basis of fixed objective criteria, rather than on discretion which so far had been the dominant way of determining the allocation. The principles laid down in this report were further developed by the committee into two specific proposals for reforms of the financial relationships between central and local government - one relating to regional government (NOU, 1979:44) and the second relating to the (primary) municipalities (NOU, 1982:15). In both cases, the committee proposed merging the various specific grants with the tax equalization grant into one comprehensive block grant, distributed on the basis of 'objective' criteria.

Although largely welcomed by the local authorities themselves, the proposals were opposed from particularly two different quarters. First, central ministries having the major responsibilities for tasks performed by local authorities objected mainly on the basis of the argument that the new grant system might violate the principle that all inhabitants, irrespective of their place of living, should have equal rights and access to the major services provided by local government. Even stronger was the opposition voiced by various organizations of municipal employees and representatives of individual functional sectors at the local level, who found that 'their' areas would suffer cutbacks as a consequence of this reform. The teachers' unions reacted strongly to the proposal, and issued a counterproposal aimed at preserving the system of earmarked grants.

Common to those opposing the proposed reform was that they considered the legislation as too weak an instrument to guarantee that the activity within their areas of responsibility would be maintained at the current level. In this context it is also interesting to observe that even locally elected members of e.g. municipal school boards - as well as local administrators - considered more local fiscal autonomy as endangering their own autonomy as representatives of individual sectors.

On the background of this opposition, the Ministry of Municipal Affairs modified the original proposal by proposing the introduction of five grants, of which four were aimed at broader policy sectors according to 'objective needs', while the fifth grant aimed at equalizing differences in local taxing abilities across the municipalities. The reasons given by the Ministry for preferring a sector-based grant system rather than one general block grant were fourfold. In the first place, a sector-based grant system would allow Parliament - as well as the Cabinet - to signal their priorities as regards local government activities more efficiently than would be possible by the use of legislation. In the second place, this system would make central ministries responsible for the individual sectors more accountable, in the sense that they were made responsible for securing sufficient financial resources on their own budgets when imposing new tasks on local authorities. Thus the proposal recognized that any increase in local accountability would imply a reduction in the accountability of central authorities. In this sense the proposal represented a compromise between these two conflicting considerations.

A third reason for choosing a sector-based grant system rather than a comprehensive one related to the practical difficulties of defining a set of objective criteria for calculating the distribution of grants across the municipalities. The argument was that it was easier to construct such formulae on the basis of needs criteria within the individual sectors rather than attempting to establish one comprehensive formula for the whole area of municipal activities. In addition, sector-based allocation criteria were considered as being more flexible and easier to change. Furthermore, although not suggested in the White Paper, a system of sector-based grants would probably be regarded as more legitimate among representatives of the municipalities, not least in the sense that distributive effects across various municipalities would become less visible to those concerned. In fact, one of the issues creating most conflict and discussions in connection with the original proposal to introduce a comprehensive block grant related to the distributive effects across variously sized municipalities. In particular, a minority in the committee put forward a proposal to introduce a 'big city factor' into the distribution formula, a proposal which was rejected by the

Ministry.

Fourth, and lastly, it was argued that a sector-based system would create a better financial stability in the individual municipality than would a system based on one general block grant. This would ease local financial planning and allow the municipalities to adjust their policies and activities over a longer period than would otherwise be the case.

The Ministry's proposal was unanimously accepted by Parliament and came into force from 1986. Despite this decision, several issues - of both a principle and practical nature - were still unsolved. In the first place, a basic assumption when introducing the new grant system was that no municipality should be made worse off as compared to the situation in advance of this reform. This necessitated certain adjustments in the grant formulae, as well as the exertion of some discretion in deciding the final amount to be granted to the individual municipality. Secondly, and probably of far more importance, the question whether the sector grants should be regarded as earmarked was still unsettled. According to the Ministry of Municipal Affairs, the sector division of the grant was merely a device for calculation - an intermediate step in arriving at the total amount to be granted to the individual municipality. Thus the actual payment of the grants was made in the form of one cheque, with no indication as to the amount to be distributed across the sectors upon which the calculation was based. In this respect - and seen from the perspective of the individual municipality - the new grant system functions as if it consists of one comprehensive block grant.

DISTRIBUTIVE EFFECTS

An overriding consideration behind the central government's policies, including the various reforms that have been implemented since World War II, has been to accomplish equality in the distribution of financial resources across the municipalities - irrespective of their geographical location and differences in the tax base. This was also one of the objectives of the most recent reform of the state grant system, but the debate on the proposals centred more around the question of local autonomy than on distributive issues. It was particularly one group of municipalities who claimed some sort of preferential treatment in connection with the construction of the formulae upon which the allocation of grants should be made, namely the larger cities. In this respect the debate over the reform indicated a kind of turning point, in the sense that up to the late 1970s, demands for preferential treatment as regards the distribution of state grants always came from smaller and peripheral municipalities. Apart from signifying increasing financial problems in the larger cities (Hansen, 1986), these claims also evidenced the actual development that had taken place in recent years as far as redistribution of resources across the municipalities is concerned.

The factor most frequently used in Norway to indicate 'expenditure needs' and financial problems in a municipality, has been population size. The assumption has been that 'fiscal abilities' or the level of local service provision has been negatively related to population size. This assumption has also guided the central government's policies towards the municipalities both in relation to broader structural reforms (e.g. the amalgamation reform) and in relation to the choice of criteria for the distribution of state grants. Generally speaking, central government has given priority to smaller municipalities - and sometimes at the expense of larger ones. Let us therefore consider to what extent this policy has succeeded in terms of accomplishing an egalitarian distribution of financial resources. In Table 9.2 the total average percentage change in some major financial indicators in the period from 1972 to 1981 are presented for variously sized municipalities. All figures have been calculated on the basis of per capita expenditures/revenues measured in constant prices.

For all five indicators we find a fairly clear negative relationship between aggregate growth and population size. The clearest exception to this pattern relates to investments, where the middle-sized municipalities suffered real cutbacks, while larger municipalities experienced a growth - although a rather modest one. We also observe that the largest municipalities experienced a slightly faster growth in government transfers and fees/charges than those in the second largest category. The most prominent pattern of this table is the considerable average growth on all indicators among the smallest municipalities. It is particularly worth noting that this group was the only group to experience a significant growth in tax revenues during this period - despite the reduction in tax rate in 1979.

Table 9.2: Total average percentage change in current expenditures, investment, taxes, government transfers and fees and charges by size of municipality, 1972-1981

Population size	Current expen- diture	Invest- ments	Taxes	Trans- fers	Fees/ charges
<3,000	59	44	25	59	71
3- 7,000	36	31	6	39	63
7-10,000	29	-14	3	21	55
10-20,000	17	8	-7	17	33
>20,000	16	7	-8	20	40

Previously we noted the duality in the Government's policy as regards local taxes and transfers, in the sense that increases in transfers compensated for the cutbacks in tax revenues. As is evident from the figures in Table 9.2, this compensation applies only if we consider the aggregate development for the total local government sector. In fact, as illustrated in the table, it is those municipalities who suffered most from the reduction in tax rate who benefited least from the growth in central government grants - namely the largest ones. These are also the municipalities who were most dependent on taxes measured as a proportion of total revenues. In this sense, the reduction of the maximum tax rate in 1979 may be viewed as yet another measure aiming at accomplishing a redistribution of resources between the municipalities. It is also worth noting the strong positive correlation which is indicated between growth in current expenditures and government grants; the figures in the two columns are almost equal. This is still further evidence of how dependent local authorities are on financial support from central government, a dependency which hardly will be less under the new grant system - although of a different character.

So far we have just considered the relative growth of various financial indicators. To what extent have the observed differences been caused by differences in the actual level of each indicator in the various municipalities? Is the fast growth in the smallest municipalities simply a function of a lower spending and revenue level in 1972 than what was the case in the larger municipalities? And to what extent have these different growth rates led to a more egalitarian distribution in the level of spending across the municipalities? In order to assess these questions, we will look at the resulting level of expenditures and revenues - measured per capita - in the five groups of municipalities. For the sake of simplicity, I have calculated an index, based on data from 1982, where the smallest municipalities constitute the base for all indicators, in the sense that they have been given the index value of 100. The index values are presented in Table 9.3.

The almost linear relationship between the growth rates and size of municipality which we observed in Table 9.2 is not repeated when we look at the per capita level of the individual indicators - with the exception of transfers which are negatively related to population size, and fees and charges where the figures indicate a positive relationship. For the two measures of expenditures we are actually faced with two separate groups of municipalities: one group with a population less than 3,000 and another group with more than 3,000 inhabitants. This applies to a lesser extent to taxes, where the figures indicate a U-shaped relationship.

Table 9.3: Per capita level of current expenditures, investments, taxes, transfers and fees and charges Index-figures 1982

Indicator	Population Size				
	<3,000	3-7,000	7-10,000	10-20,000	>20,000
Current	100	76	75	74	77
Investment	100	68	60	60	66
Taxes	100	84	92	97	111
Transfers	100	57	42	36	28
Fees/ charges	100	109	140	144	182

Altogether, the table clearly demonstrates that the central government has 'more' than succeeded in bringing about a redistribution in resources across the municipalities, and where the smallest municipalities are able to keep an average per capita expenditure level which is in the area of 30 per cent higher than that in other municipalities. In this context it should also be noted that this group includes altogether 160 municipalities, which means that this distribution is not the result of a few extreme values within that group. On the other hand, the table also tells us that the Government has succeeded in accomplishing a rather egalitarian distribution of expenditures between those 290 municipalities who have got more than 3,000 inhabitants. The 'cost' of this rather massive redistribution - and equalization process - has been an increasing dependency among the smallest municipalities on central government grants. On the other hand, their level of tax revenues is only exceeded by that of the largest municipalities who on their side have become heavily dependent on rather controversial fees and charges. In this respect it is therefore no surprise that the claim for preferential treatment in connection with the new grant system came from the largest municipalities.

MORE AUTONOMOUS MUNICIPALITIES?

In the preceding section I argued that the cost of the financial equalization that has taken place was an increased dependency on state grants - and by implication less local autonomy. To what extent is this increased dependency felt as a problem among the local decision-makers themselves? Has the price been worth paying, and do they feel that the new grant system will contribute to a strengthening of local autonomy? Space does not allow me to give any thorough assessment of these issues, but some empirical evidence from a recent survey among local councillors and administrators may serve to elucidate these questions.(1)

Apart from the central government's need to exert some control over local finances as a measure of macroeconomic policy - a need which has become increasingly important as a consequence of fast local financial growth - the most important aim of central government's policy vis-à-vis the municipalities has been to secure geographical and social equity in the local service provision. To what extent is this objective being accepted as legitimate among local decision-makers? According to the survey, altogether 73 per cent of the local councillors and 70 per cent of the administrators were of the opinion that local autonomy had to be subordinated to the aim of securing equity in the provision of local services. Furthermore, more than 60 per cent of all respondents considered that local fiscal autonomy depended more on the way in which local councillors and administrators support the policy that has been conducted by the state, and they consider local authorities to be fairly autonomous in financial matters, depending on the willingness - and ability - of local councillors to act independently and in accordance with their own priorities. Seen in relation to the views normally expressed in Norwegian public debate about such issues, these answers are rather surprising. On the other hand, the answers to these questions lend support to the conclusions drawn on the basis of various local expenditure studies, where local political factors turn out to have a significant effect on budgetary decisions (Hansen, 1981; Hansen and Kjellberg, 1976). In this respect, the answers seem to represent fairly realistic assessments of the actual situation in most Norwegian municipalities. This is, of course, not the same as suggesting that local authorities have been satisfied about the state of the art concerning central-local fiscal relationships. In particular, more than 80 per cent of the respondents found that the system of earmarked grants had hampered progress in rearranging priorities in relation to changing needs and demands. In the background of these answers it is therefore quite surprising to observe that 60 per cent of the respondents did not expect the new grant system to affect the pattern of priorities established under the system of earmarked grants. In fact, when asked to indicate what service areas they expected to be given higher or lower priority under the new grant system, a majority of the respondents did not expect any great changes. This may be interpreted as if legal constraints or other central regulations are of as much importance as specific grants in imposing constraints on local decision-makers. On the other hand, the answers may be taken as an expression of a fairly broad consensus among local decision-makers on the pattern of priorities that was established under the 'old' grant system. Whether this suggestion is tenable is, however, only possible to assess in future studies.

NOTE

1. The survey was conducted as a part of a larger research programme on the consequences of the new grant system. The survey is based on a random sample of 60 municipalities, where all members of the executive boards of the municipalities as

well as the heads of the administrative departments received a questionnaire. I am indebted to Rune J. Sorensen and Ole Wiig - as well as the director of the research programme, Professor Francesco Kjellberg - for giving me access to the data. For more details about the survey and some major results, see Sorensen (1986 and 1987).

REFERENCES

Funksjonsfordelingskomiteen (1987)
Om funksjons - og utgiftsfordelingen mellom staten, fylkeskommunene og primaerkommunene. Innstilling II., Oslo, Ministry of Municipal Affairs.

Hansen, T. (1981)
'Transforming Needs into Expenditure Decisions', in K. Newton (ed.), Urban Political Economy, Frances Pinter, London, pp. 27-47

-- (1986) Territorielle fordelinger og bykommunale finanser, Oslo, Universitetsforlaget

-- (1987) 'Norwegian Local Tax Policy', Government and Policy, forthcoming

-- and Kjellberg, F. (1976) 'Municipal Expenditures in Norway: Autonomy and Constraints in Local Government Activity', Policy and Politics, vol.4, pp. 25-50

-- and Sorensen, R. (1986) Professionalism and Public Resource Allocation, Paper for the ECPR Joint Sessions, Gothenburg

Kjellberg, F. (1980)
'Et perspektiv pa utviklingen av Kommune institusjonen', in F. Kjellberg (ed.), Den kommunale virksomhet, Universitetsforlaget, Oslo, pp. 9-19

Myhren, K. (1977)
Gjeldstrykk og skattetrykk, Universitetsforlaget, Oslo

NOU (1974:33)
Mal og retningslinjer for reformer i lokalforvaltningen, Kommunal - og arbeidsdepartementet, Oslo

--(1979:44) Nytt inntektssystem for fylkeskommunene, og arbeidsdepartementet, Oslo

--(1982:15) Nytt inntektssystem for kommunene, Kommunal - og arbeidsdepartementet, Oslo

Sharpe, L.J. (1970)
'Theories and Values of Local Goverment', Political Studies, vol. 18, pp. 153-74

Skatteutjamningskomiteen (1956)
Om inntekts - , utgifts - og funksjonsfordelingen mellom staten og kommunene, skatteutjamning m.v. Innstilling V., Kommunal - og arbeidsdepartementet, Oslo

Sorensen, R.J. (1986)
Nytt inntektssystem for kommuner og fylkeskommuner: holdninger, erfaringer og forventninger, Institute of Political Science, Oslo

Sorensen, R.J. (1987)
Ønsker Kommunene større Kommunalt selvstyre?, Institute of Political Science, Oslo

10 LOCAL GOVERNMENT FINANCE IN SWEDEN - PRESENT STATUS AND RECENT TRENDS

Ernst Jonsson

Local self-government has a long tradition in Sweden. There are two kinds of local government units: the municipalities (Kommuner), which are the smallest, and the county councils (landsting), i.e. the regional units. There are 284 municipalities and 23 county councils with, on average, 30,000 and 340,000 inhabitants, respectively.

The tasks of local government fall into two discrete categories: those performed within the general powers of municipalities and county councils, as defined by the Local Government Act, and those based on special legislation. General powers granted to the municipalities cover such sectors as cultural services, leisure activities, streets and roads, parks, communications, public lighting, water and sewerage, refuse collection and electricity generation. Special statutory powers - normally compulsory - principally cover the following sectors: primary and secondary education, social services, public health, site development planning, social planning and fire protection. An estimated 70 per cent of municipal expenditure falls within the sphere of state-regulated activities. The county councils' overwhelmingly predominant task is medical care, which is a state-regulated activity.

Currently, municipalities and county councils together account for almost three-quarters of overall consumption and investment in the Swedish public sector. This means that local government accounts for 23 per cent of GDP. Of aggregate local expenditure, the municipalities account for 68 per cent and the county councils 32 per cent.

AUTONOMY

The municipalities and county councils are free to establish the rates of local government income taxation without intervention by the central government, subject only to the constraints of local economic and political circumstances. Local income tax has been regarded as the cornerstone of local autonomy. If, at the local level, people prefer public provision to private enterprise and are prepared to pay for it out of local taxes, they should be permitted to do so. Local authorities are also entitled to levy charges and fees for specific services (e.g. water and refuse collection). The central government determines only one-quarter of the local authorities' current income, i.e. the portion derived from state grants.

Most mandatory obligations imposed on local authorities are general, empowering them to perform certain functions while granting discretion regarding the level and scope of services provided. Moreover, the general powers entitle local authorities to deal with and decide on matters of local concern. Summing up, local governments in Sweden enjoy a high degree of autonomy, defined as the scope for local action.

Decentralization and deregulation

During the past decade, the central government has endeavoured to raise the degree of local autonomy even further. Political, administrative and financial decentralization and deregulation have been the common denominators of the efforts to revitalize public administration and tackle the new problems of economic contraction (Larsson, 1985). The aim is to promote local and regional autonomy and reduce central control and bureaucracy. Matters requiring considerable knowledge of local conditions and specific details should be decentralized, i.e. transferred to local authorities. An attempt has been made to delegate functions to the lowest level at which it is thought that they can be competently handled. Decision-making in the sphere of school administration, for example, has been transferred to regional and local levels.

The central government also aims to curtail central control of local authorities by removing detailed regulations. Paving Acts relating, for example, to social welfare, medical and child-care services have been passed. These constitute merely the broad organizational framework of a service sector. Similarly, the detailed regulation on which specific grants are based has been reduced.

In addition, the central government encourages and supports the trend towards local service programmes and away from central direction by legislation and regulation. The objective is to make bureaucratic organizations more responsive to citizens' demands and to enhance their speed and efficiency of action. To this end, the central government has initiated an experiment involving 11 local authorities, whereby they have been asked to state which regulations and control procedures they regard as unnecessary.

The central government has also issued an Ordinance prohibiting new regulations liable, directly or indirectly, to raise local and regional units' expenses without direct government approval.

Proposed switch from special to general grants

Of the total funds disbursed in state grants, 80 per cent is composed of specific grants. Some of these are designed to help finance a service (e.g. compulsory schooling) which the local authorities are obliged by law to provide for all citizens concerned. However, the purpose of most specific grants has, instead, been to encourage local authorities to provide a voluntary service (e.g. care of the elderly) benefiting local residents exclusively. Evaluations conducted to date also suggest that these open-ended grants have achieved the desired stimulus effect (Jonsson, 1986).

Once the voluntary service has become firmly established, the municipality's decision whether to continue providing it is probably unaffected by the existence of a state grant. From being a stimulus to action, the state grant has thus changed to serve primarily as financial support. In times of shrinking resources, on the other hand, the state grant may affect the municipality's choice of which service is to suffer marginal cutbacks. Every pound pared away from an activity funded by a state grant also entails a reduction in state-grant revenues. This fact may give the municipality an incentive for initial cutbacks in activities lacking state grants. Specific grants may thus prevent municipalities or county councils from impartially distributing necessary cutbacks according to what their own requirements or local conditions demand.

To enhance the municipalities' financial scope of action, it is desirable to cut the strings imposed by the specific grants, which serve mainly as financial support. To this end, a large proportion of specific grants (70 per cent of the sum total) may be replaced by a general or 'block' grant whose size is determined by needs (e.g. numbers of school-children or pensioners) in the sectors of expenditure no longer receiving any special state grants (Jonsson, 1986). This proposed change, which would give the municipalities greater freedom to use state-grant funds as they themselves wish, is currently being considered by the central government.

LOCAL ACCOUNTABILITY

According to the principle of local accountability, the full cost of local spending decisions should be borne by those who benefit from the services provided. In other words, local authorities should be obliged to balance the full marginal social costs of the services they provide against the marginal benefits. This marginal principle gives local authorities the incentive to reach decisions consistent with an efficient allocation of resources in the economy as a whole (Jackman, 1986).

To what extent is the requirement of local accountability satisfied in Sweden? In order to assess this, one must know what proportion of marginal benefits accrues locally and what proportion of marginal costs is borne locally. Of the municipalities' total current costs, 1.2 per cent comprises services (trunk roads, higher education) satisfying national interests; for the county councils, the corresponding proportion is 2 per cent. Moreover, 0.3 per cent of the municipalities' aggregate current expenditure comprises services (regional theatres or libraries) benefiting the inhabitants of the region rather than of the locality alone.

To the extent that young people, after completing their primary or secondary education, move from declining municipalities, corresponding positive external effects arise for the municipalities they move into (cf. Barnett and Topham, 1977). Future benefits of the costs of education already borne (on average, one-quarter of total current costs) then accrue to people other than the declining municipalities' own residents. How large can the costs which entail such external benefits be in relation to current costs as a whole?

In the period 1980-85, the overall net yearly exodus from declining municipalities in Sweden was, on average, 0.4 per cent of their population. The average migrant was 27 years old. At an estimated real interest rate of 8 per cent, this means that about half of the future benefits discounted at the date on which higher education is completed accrue to the host municipalities. For the sake of simplicity, this calculation is based on the assumption that these benefits are constant from one year to the next.

Thus, in all, an estimated 98 per cent of both the municipalities' and the county councils' current costs generate exclusively local benefits. How large a proportion of current costs, then, is locally borne? In 1985, 28 per cent of the municipalities' and 9 per cent of the county councils' total current costs were financed by state grants. Does this mean that the principle of local accountability is not fully satisfied in Sweden? To answer that question, one must investigate the objectives of the various state grants and their links with the marginal costs of local government services.

In order to even out the differences in taxation revenues and costs over which the municipalities have no control, the state provides a tax equalization grant. This state grant, which is designed to redistribute revenues from rich to needy municipalities, may be used freely by the municipality or county council as it wishes. This general state grant is thus intended to fulfil objectives relating to horizontal equity. The size of the equalization grant - which on average corresponds to 4 per cent of the municipalities' and 6 per cent of the county councils' total current costs - is independent of the scale of current costs. Consequently, there is no connection between cost increases and the size of the tax equalization grant. This state grant, therefore, does not conflict with the marginal principle; neither do specific grants (1 per cent of current costs) designed to compensate municipalities or county councils for the national or regional benefits they generate.

Certain specific grants are provided to promote objectives relating to vertical equity (i.e. between individuals with different incomes). The aim is to stimulate municipalities to give low-income groups a particular type of allowance, under conditions stipulated by the central government. State grants for this 'redistributive service' correspond to a certain percentage of the entire state-regulated allowance. Similarly, the state grant for child care is intended to give the municipalities an incentive to provide a beneficial service on a larger scale than they would otherwise do.

State grants of this kind for 'merit goods' are also compatible with the marginal principle, since their purpose is to stimulate the local authority to provide more service than that justified by a comparison of gross marginal cost (i.e. without deduction for the state grant) and marginal benefit. Owing to the state grant for these merit goods, the local authorities face marginal incentives which are consistent with the central government's objectives.

The remaining specific grants (10 per cent of current costs) are, on the other hand, seen to function primarily as financial support for services benefiting the inhabitants of the locality exclusively. These state grants (e.g. for home-help services for the elderly and disabled) are, as a rule, fixed in proportion to the municipality's expenses, i.e. open-ended. Thus if the local authority decides not to reduce the scale of a grant-subsidized beneficial service, it does not lose any state-grant revenues. It is for this kind of service, above all, that the local accountability principle is not fully complied with. To remedy this omission, it is desirable - as mentioned previously - to replace these specific grants with a general 'lump sum' or block grant.

To reinforce local accountability where the merit good of child care is concerned, it is also desirable that the present open-ended specific grant be replaced by a closed-ended one. Since such a grant is provided regardless of the service level adopted by the local authority, it is neutral where the local authority's spending decisions are concerned. With a grant of this kind, local authorities choosing to provide a higher level of services than that intended by the grant must finance it themselves by means of a a higher local tax rate.

EQUITY

The purpose of the tax equalization grant is to smooth out income and cost disparities arising from differences in tax capacity (= tax base per inhabitant) or spending needs. Disparities caused by variations in the level of service between local authorities should, on the other hand, be reflected in varying tax rates. Local area residents who opt for a high level of service should themselves pay for it by means of a higher tax rate.

The lower the tax base per inhabitant, the higher the tax equalization grant received by the local authority (R=-0.93 in a random selection of 70 municipalities). With the inclusion of this resource grant, the differences in tax base per inhabitant between local authorities in 1985 are only one-third as large as they would otherwise be. As Newton (1980) points out, this relatively small grant thus contains a major redistributive element.

In addition, compensation is paid in the form of a tax-base contribution to local authorities with large spending needs owing to unfavourable age composition in the population, or with high costs owing to geographical position or building stock. The local authorities of north inland Sweden are those for which the tax equalization grant is primarily affected by this needs or cost element. Including both the resource grant and the requirements/costs grant, variations in tax base per inhabitant were, in 1985, 25 per cent lower than they would otherwise have been (Table 10.1).

Table 10.1: Coefficient of variation for different variables in the municipalities selected, 1975 and 1985

	1975	1985
Tax base per inhabitant	0.117	0.090
-incl. tax equalization grant	0.108	0.068
Net costs per inhabitant	0.154	0.139
Local income tax rate	0.062	0.057

Without the tax equalization grant, local tax rates would have been a good deal higher - or service levels lower - in many municipalities or county councils, particularly in sparsely-populated areas. However, the tax equalization grant is not designed to give full compensation for low tax capacity, major expenditure needs or high costs. Residual differences in local income tax rates are therefore relatively large. In 1985, overall local income tax rates varied between 25 and 33.3 per cent of taxable income; in the municipalities they varied between 9.7 and 19.1 per cent, and in the county councils between 12 and 14.5 per cent.

Between 1975 and 1985, the tax equalization grant appears to have had no appreciable tax-equalizing effect over and above that attained in the introductory phase. In this period, it is true, differences in local income tax rates - as in net costs per inhabitant - diminished by one-tenth. This is connected with the fact that variations in the tax base (including the tax equalization grant) decreased by 37 per cent. Two-thirds of the decrease in these variations, however, arose from the diminution of tax-base differences (excluding the equalization grant) between local authorities. Only the remaining one-third is attributable to trends in the tax equalization grants over time (Table 10.1).

In order to reduce the remaining disparities in local income tax, the central government introduced a 'Robin Hood' tax on rich municipalities, with effect from 1986. A progressive tax equalization charge is levied on the local authorities with a tax base per inhabitant greater than 135 per cent of the nationwide average. This charge was paid primarily by three suburban municipalities in Greater Stockholm. The resulting revenue is transferred, in the form of a grant, to a number of small municipalities with a high tax rate, chiefly in north Sweden, thereby enabling them to lower their tax rate. This tax has to a large extent had the desired effect. In 1986, for example, the municipality with the lowest tax rate was obliged to effect a 16 per cent increase in order to pay the 'Robin Hood' tax. Simultaneously, for example, the municipality with the highest tax rate was able to lower it by 8 per cent. The gap between the highest and lowest tax rates was thus reduced by one-quarter.

Assessments conducted to date show that the municipalities with low tax rates do not fulfil their spending requirements less satisfactorily than those with high tax rates. With the exception of old people's homes, the tendency is rather the reverse in important areas of expenditure. Where secondary education, child care and free taxi transport for the elderly, in particular, are concerned, the higher the municipality's per capita income, the higher the level of service. The higher service level appears to be a consequence of wealthy municipalities with low tax rates deriving more stimulation from the open-ended specific grants provided for these three areas of expenditure than needy municipalities with high tax rates have done. These state grants have thus run counter to the purpose of the tax equalization grant. One remedy would be the replacement of the majority of specific grants by a general, needs-related grant. A reform of this kind would favour poor municipalities with least developed services. These could thereafter meet neglected expenditure needs or reduce taxation. Municipalities with a high tax base per inhabitant and low tax would, on the other hand, be penalized. To compensate for the loss of state-grant revenues, they would be obliged to raise tax (to finance their high service level) or lower the service level. The reform envisaged may thus be expected to have an equalizing effect on tax, services or living standards (Jonsson, 1986).

MACROECONOMIC CONTROL

High inflation, balance-of-payments deficits and growing foreign debts have been recurrent features of the Swedish economy since the mid-1970s. Between 1975 and 1985, real growth in the economy (= 1.5 per cent p.a.) was only half the OECD average. To restore the competitive strength of the industrial sector, the Swedish krona was devalued five times during this decade.

To reduce inflation and successively steer Sweden clear of its economic crisis, the central government has, in addition, been conducting a restrictive fiscal policy for several years. With the aim of reducing the state budget deficit, a stringent examination of expenditure has been carried out. As a result, between 1975 and 1985 real central government expenditure fell by an average of 1 per cent annually (Figure 10.1).

The post-war period has been one of rapid expansion of aggregate gross local government spending. However, from the late 1970s onwards, successive central governments have endeavoured to curb this expansion. At the same time, no government has ever questioned the local authorities' right to determine their own level of expenditure according to local needs and priorities. As a result, successive central governments have, in their economic policy, implemented a consistently decentralized approach, based on financial incentives rather than detailed control (cf. Dawson, 1983).

Figure 10.1: Trends in real expenditure (=investments and consumption) in Sweden, 1975-85. Index: 1975=100. Semilogarithmic scale

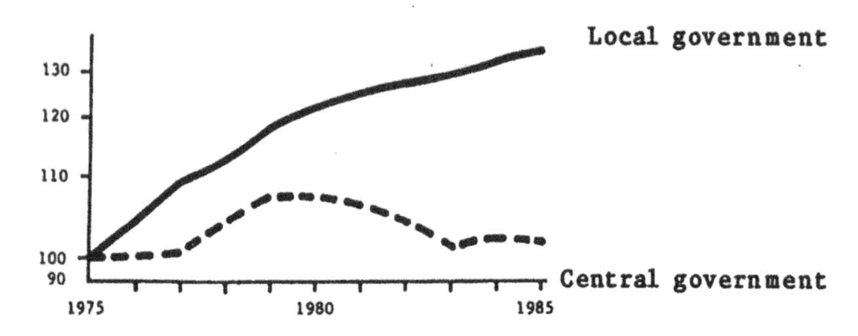

To enable local authorities to curtail their expansion, the central government has in recent years effected marginal cuts in the financial framework within which they may act. The total disbursed in specific grants was reduced in volume by 9 per cent between 1980 and 1985. Since the county councils' increases in both real expenditure and local income tax rates were particularly large, their grants have incurred especially large cuts.

In addition, some minor specific grants have been abolished or reduced in order to discourage local spending. The central government has, moreover, exerted a traditional control over aggregate borrowing to finance capital expenditure. It has thus been concerned with local government spending as a whole, rather than with expenditure in detail or with specific local authorities.

Owing to recurrent cuts in specific grants, the financial climate for local authorities nowadays is less stable and secure in the long run, i.e. over a number of budget years, than it used to be. On the other hand, since the central government has, as a rule, announced the cuts in good time before the local authorities' budget preparations, uncertainty has only slightly increased in the short term, i.e. within a one-year perspective. Nor have any cuts been imposed on local authorities in the course of a budget year. Thus, for each budget year, the financial framework has remained stable - this being, according to Jones et al. (1981), one condition of efficient local government.

To give the municipalities more time to prepare for future changes, the central government now seems to be striving to inform them of planned cuts in grants at least a year or two in advance. To a higher degree than previously, another condition of efficiency, i.e. predictability, is thereby being fulfilled (cf. Jones et al., 1981)

FISCAL PRESSURE

Fiscal pressure occurs where existing levels of expenditure can be maintained only by raising the level of taxation (Greenwood, 1981). Normally, Swedish local authorities are not exposed to such pressure, since the local income tax base tends to rise at least as fast as existing expenditure, i.e. as a result of ongoing price and pay increases. Income tax buoyancy tends to be sufficient to close the gap between existing expenditure and local resources. Between 1975 and 1985, for example, the tax base per inhabitant increased by an annual average of 11 per cent, and the implicit price index for overall local government spending by 10 per cent.

Cuts in state grants may also give rise to fiscal pressure at the local level. Although the central government has implemented such cuts since the beginning of the 1980s, they have been too marginal to bring about fiscal pressure in the traditional sense of the term.

During the post-war period, Swedish local authorities have, on the other hand, usually been exposed to fiscal pressure of another kind, and at a higher level. This fiscal pressure occurs where a marked expansion in real spending can be maintained only by an increase in the level of taxation. If the buoyant yield from income tax rises more slowly than the money spent if expansion plans are realized, such pressure results.

Until the end of the 1970s, the gap between sharply rising expenditure and less rapidly increasing local resources was usually bridged by means of recurrent increases in local tax rates

(Figure 10.2). In times of continuously rising real incomes, the majority of voters have clearly been prepared to pay an ever higher rate of local income tax to finance a continued expansion of local government services. As a result, between 1975 and 1980 local authorities' consumption and investments rose from 20 to 22.5 per cent of GNP.

Slack economic growth since the beginning of the 1980s has ushered in a new situation. In times of falling or stagnant real incomes, the taxpayers' willingness to incur continued tax increases appears to have diminished considerably. At the same time, one of the central government's objectives is to keep the overall tax burden more or less constant. Since most income-earners pay substantially more in local than in national income tax, the trend in local income tax is crucially important to whether this goal is attained. Pressure from both payers of local tax and the central government has thus lessened the political scope for further increases in local income tax. Simultaneously, the considerably slower real growth rate of the tax base has not sufficed to finance a continued sharp expansion in expenditure.

In this new situation, fiscal pressure has been

Figure 10.2: Average local government tax rate in Sweden, 1955-85

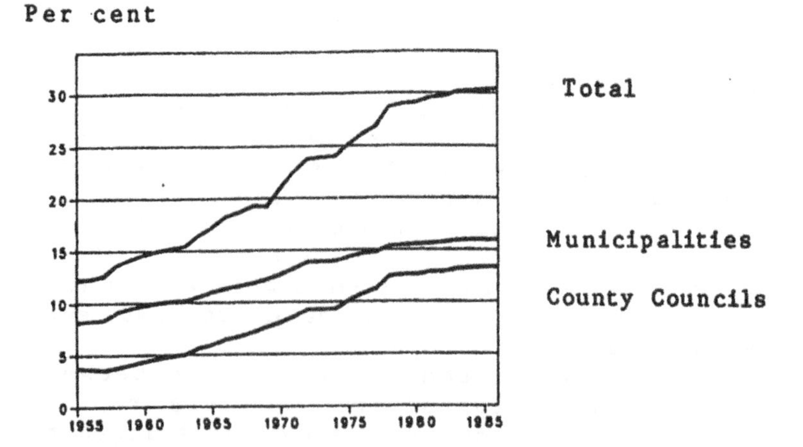

relieved primarily by a substantial curtailment of the growth rate of real expenditure. The rate of growth has fallen from 3.5 per cent annually in the period 1975-80 to 2 per cent in 1980-85 (Figure 10.1, Table 10.2). The local authorities have cut investment expenditure in particular: in terms of volume, it has declined by an annual average of 2.5 per cent since 1980. By the same token, borrowing has also become less significant as a source of finance (Table 10.3). Capital expenditure as a percentage of aggregate spending thus declined between 1980 and 1985, while the local authorities' real consumption continued to rise, although at a slower pace than previously.

Table 10.2: Percentage change in real expenditure of local authorities in Sweden, 1975-80 and 1980-85

	1975-80	1980-85
Municipalities		
Current costs	20	15
Capital expenditure	3	-15
Total expenditure	16	9
County councils		
Current costs	24	16
Capital expenditure	22	3
Total expenditure	24	14

Secondly, the gap between still expanding real expenditure and slowly rising revenues has been bridged by means of increases in fees and charges (Table 10.4). Thirdly, financial problems have been tackled by means of tax increases, although on a considerably smaller scale than before. Between 1980 and 1985, local income tax was raised by an annual average of 1 per cent, compared with 3 per cent annually between 1975 and 1980 (Figure 10.2).

Although the fiscal pressure exerted by the

government has not been particularly heavy, the municipalities seem as a rule to have reacted in the intended manner. Time-series analyses relating, for example, to specific grants which have been withdrawn or cut show that the desired effect on spending trends has been achieved. The local authorities have responded in a reasonably predictable and rational way to these financial incentives. For example, the

Table 10.3: Financing of capital expenditure of local authorities in Sweden in 1975, 1980 and 1985 (percentages)

A. Municipalities	1975	1980	1985
Income tax	40	50	51
State grants	9	7	6
Loan	34	27	24
Withdrawals from funds	0	0	4
Other sources	17	17	15
	100	100	100

B. County Councils	1975	1980	1985
Income tax	52	75	72
State grants	14	7	2
Loan	30	10	8
Withdrawals from funds	0	0	12
Other sources	4	8	6
	100	100	100

ceiling on the specific grant for free taxi transport, introduced in 1981, has had the intended effect of curbing the expansion of this service (Jonsson, 1986).

As Figure 10.3 shows, the local authorities' liquidity has tended to decline in recent years. This is only marginally a result of cuts in grants. This falling trend may indicate that macroeconomic control has not made local authorities markedly more

Table 10.4: Financing of current costs of local authorities in Sweden in 1975, 1980 and 1985 (percentages)

A. Municipalities

	1975	1980	1985
Income tax	40	41	40
Tax equalization grant	4	4	4
Specific grants	25	26	24
Fees and charges	18	21	22
Other sources	13	8	10
	100	100	100

B. County Councils

	1975	1980	1985
Income tax	58	61	59
Tax equalization grant	5	6	6
Specific grants	13	10	3
Fees and charges	15	16	25
Withdrawals from funds	2	0	2
Other sources	7	7	5
	100	100	100

uncertain regarding the future. In the event of a system-induced augmentation of uncertainty, it would presumably be in their interest to increase, or at least maintain, their capacity to pay, i.e. their liquidity.

Although macroeconomic control has had the desired effect, the expansion of real local government spending has not slowed down to the extent considered necessary by the central government. For the rest of the 1980s, the central government is therefore striving to curb this increase in spending from 2 to 1 per cent annually. To this end, the central government has intensified the fiscal pressure on local authorities with effect from 1986. The sum total of the tax equalization grant will be frozen at the 1985 level. Future real increases in this grant must be financed by the municipalities themselves by means of a tax equalization charge,

Figure 10.3: Local authorities' liquidity in Sweden, 1960-85

Liquid assets/expenditure

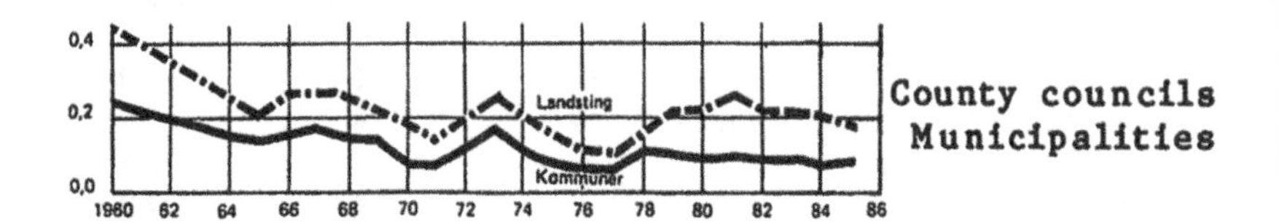

Source: SCB, 1986

which is to be levied on each municipality in proportion to the tax base per inhabitant. In addition, the full compensation hitherto paid to the municipalities in connection with the transfer of the tax base for juridical reasons to the state will be successively phased out. Moreover, in 1986 the central government made a temporary liquidity withdrawal of SEK 4.5 billion, equivalent to 2 per cent of the municipalities' current costs.

Despite heavier financial pressure, the local authorities have succeeded in keeping their income tax rates for both 1986 and 1987 largely unchanged.

INCOME TAX VERSUS POLL TAX

A poll tax is a flat-rate levy per head on adults residing in a locality. In Britain, a community levy of this kind has been discussed as an alternative to the current property tax (the 'rates'). No corresponding discussion has taken place in Sweden but, even so, it may be of interest to compare the distributive effects of a local income tax with those of a poll tax. In this comparison, the less wealthy are assumed to receive the type of rebate on the latter (up to a maximum of 80 per cent) which is mentioned in the 1986 Green paper, '<u>Paying for Local Government</u>' (diagram F7) HMSO (1986).

In 1985 Sweden had 6.5 million inhabitants aged

over 18, i.e. 78 per cent of the population. This number broadly agrees with the number of people with taxable incomes (6.4 million). How will the distribution of the tax burden be altered if local income tax is replaced by a poll tax, with rebates for those whose incomes fall below the median (SEK 60,000-80,000 p.a.)?

A reform of this kind would shift 14 per cent of the total local tax burden from those on the higher echelons of the income scale (with annual incomes exceeding SEK 100,000) to those on the lower (less than 80,000). The higher the income of a high-income earner, the greater both the absolute and the relative tax reduction becomes. For those with low incomes, the relative tax rise will instead be larger the lower their incomes (Table 10.5, columns 2 and 3).

If a poll tax with the proposed rebates (alternative A) were introduced in Britain, low-income earners would not, on the other hand, according to the diagram F5 in the Green Paper (1986), be hit by any rise in taxes. Instead, the

Table 10.5: Local income tax compared with poll tax per capita for persons in different income ranges in Sweden, 1985 (figures in SEK thousand)

Taxable income	No. persons (000s)	Local income tax per capita	Estimated poll tax per capita Alt A	Alt B
0 -20	1014	2.8	7.9	2.5
20-40	808	7.5	10.7	7.5
40-60	858	13.0	18.6	13.7
60-80	1049	18.1	21.7	26.1
80-100	1183	23.3	23.3	26.1
100-120	800	28.3	23.3	26.1
120-140	358	33.6	23.3	26.1
140-160	160	38.8	23.3	26.1
160-200	120	45.8	23.3	26.1
200-300	58	60.6	23.3	26.1
300-	13	115.1	23.3	26.1

community levy would be a slightly lower percentage of income after rebate than is the present property tax after rebate for the lowest-income group, i.e. with weekly net incomes of less than £50. The tax burden would be unchanged for those earning £50-75 weekly, and very slightly higher for those earning £75-100.

Since the average local income tax per capita in Sweden is considerably higher than the average property tax per head in Britain, rebate levels must be set substantially higher in Sweden in order that low-income earners are not hit by tax increases. The distributive effects of a poll tax with such rebate levels is shown in column 4, as compared with column 2 in Table 10.5. In this alternative, B, just over 10 per cent of the total local income tax burden is redistributed from people with higher incomes (exceeding SEK 100,000 p.a.) principally to those in the intermediate income range (SEK 60,000-80,000). Of the total redistributed tax burden, only 2.5 per cent would be transferred to the very lowest income earners in the form of reduced tax. As in alternative A, both absolute and relative tax reductions are greater the more a high-income individual earns.

If the local income tax is replaced by a poll tax, the tax burden would thus be redistributed from high-income earners to low-income earners (alternative A), or from high-income earners to middle-income earners (alternative B). Would this secure a more equitable distribution of the tax burden of local government services?

A poll tax takes no account of ability to pay. As the Green Paper also emphasizes, a poll tax would consequently be highly regressive, taking a larger proportion of income from the poorer than from the richer members of society (Figure 10.4). According to the ability-to-pay principle, which is essentially redistributive, a local income tax is therefore superior to a poll tax (cf. Bailey, 1986).

According to the benefit principle, people should be taxed according to the benefits they receive from the expenditure into which taxes are channelled. There is abundant evidence across a wide range of local services (education, leisure, libraries,

Figure 10.4: Hypothetical poll tax (alternative B) as a percentage of taxable income in various income ranges in Sweden, 1985

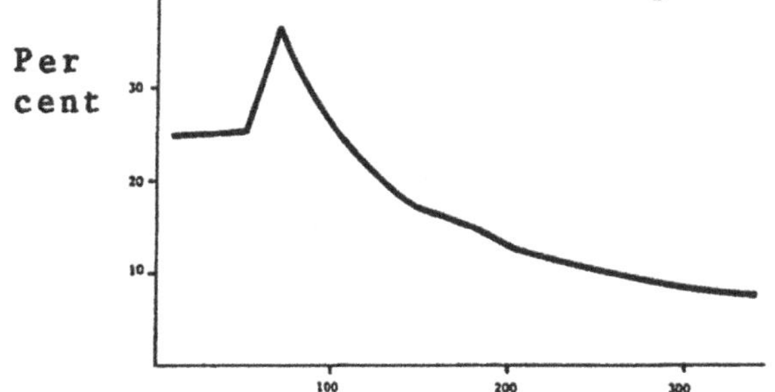

Taxable income p.a. (SEK thousand)

planning) that better-off groups systematically use services more (Le Grand, 1982; Bramley et al., 1983). Car ownership is also income-related and, with it, the use of roads maintained by local authorities (Jackman, 1986). The same applies to house ownership and the services (e.g. street maintenance, water and sewerage, fire protection, law enforcement, etc.) which complement it. Swedish surveys, too, show that high-income earners consume more child care, dental care, adult education, leisure and cultural services than low-income earners (Ostlin, 1984). Thus the use of most local services benefiting the community tends to rise with income (Jackman, 1986; Bramley, 1986). It is also conceivable that people with the ability to pay derive greater benefits (as measured by willingness to pay) for the same quantity of tax-financed services (Bramley, 1986; Foster et al., 1980).

Redistributive services comprise 10 per cent of current overall local government costs. It is also arguable that those who pay taxes for such services derive satisfaction from the relief of poverty (King, 1984). Thus the benefit principle, applied to local government services, suggests a local income tax rather than a poll tax (Jackman, 1986; Bramley 1986; Bailey, 1986).

INEFFICIENT INCENTIVES TO MIGRATION

Foster, Jackman and Perlman (1980) argue that a local

income tax is economically inefficient (in a Pareto sense) as a means of financing beneficial local services, since costs will vary for different taxpayers in different locations. The arguments they put forward may be questioned on both theoretical and empirical grounds (cf. Bennett, 1981).

First, they argue that, with a local income tax, marginal costs will equal marginal benefits only for people with the same incomes. Since the tax payment varies with income, high-income earners will pay more, and low-income earners less, than the marginal costs of services. Beneficial services are thus assumed to be fairly constant per head. However, this 'vertical inefficiency' does not arise if benefits increase with income and at roughly the same pace. Since the benefits of local services do, indeed, appear to be income-related, it is rather a poll tax that entails vertical inefficiency. Consequently, with a tax of this kind, high-income earners will pay less and low-income earners more than the marginal costs of services.

The second argument presented by Foster et al. is that, when average per capita incomes vary between local authorities, the rates of local income tax levied to finance the same level of local expenditure must also vary. This 'horizontal inefficiency' will create inefficient incentives for migration, since everyone will wish to move into the high-income localities so as to reduce their tax bills. However, if the costs of providing the same level or standard of beneficial or redistributive services vary from one local authority to another, a poll tax will encourage inefficient migration as well. A resident of an area with high spending needs or high expenses to satisfy these needs (owing, for example, to geographical circumstances) will have an incentive to migrate in order to escape the high tax burden.

Furthermore, the features of Pareto-efficient resource allocation may be assessed only with respect to a particular given income distribution. What is inefficient when income is distributed in one way may be efficient when it is distributed otherwise. As Foster et al. point out, the argument about horizontal inefficiency falls if, for example, the central government equalizes the tax base by a resource equalization grant. The risk that a poll tax may create inefficient incentives to migrants may, similarly, be eliminated by means of a needs or cost equalization grant which equalizes the costs of providing services at a uniform level.

Thus a local income tax (like a poll tax) cannot be altogether rejected on theoretical grounds as being Pareto-inefficient. That argument is valid only in the case when tax base and cost differences per capita have not been evened out sufficiently to prevent inefficient migration.

In Sweden, differences in the tax base per inhabitant have been reduced by about two-thirds by means of the resource equalization grant. Variations in costs per capita have, similarly, been reduced by means of the needs or cost equalization grant. Have these steps sufficed to prevent inefficient migration? The degree of equalization necessary for these purposes depends, for example, on how high the costs of migration are and how important the tax burden is as a factor in migration decisions. More detailed investigations of migration and its underlying causes are required before an assessment of these matters can be made. An alternative, simpler approach is to study whether the anticipated effects of a fiscal migration have arisen.

What are these effects? According to Foster et al. (1980), the fiscal incentive for migration is greater for higher-income groups, and social segregation is intensified as a result: high-income groups move to higher-income areas, and lower-income groups are left behind (Foster et al., 1980; Jackman, 1986; cf. Bennett, 1981). Fiscal migration is, in other words, expected to entail an increase in the differences in per capita income between localities over time. Instead, as Table 10.1 shows, these differences diminished somewhat in Sweden between 1975 and 1985. This fact suggests that, in general, the local income tax (combined with the resource equalization grant) in Sweden has not entailed any inefficient fiscal migration, at least not in this period. Variations in the tax burden between localities have evidently not been sufficiently large to create inefficient incentives to migrate.

THE PRINCIPLE OF BUOYANCY

Unlike a poll tax, income tax is elastic. Price and pay rises are reflected in the tax base, yielding automatic increases in tax revenues without the raising of tax rates. Foster et al. criticize this 'buoyancy' feature of income tax. In their view, a tax of this kind undermines the accountability of local government and encourages the expansion of spending.

However, the principle of local accountability must logically apply in real, rather than nominal, terms. If the automatic effects of price and pay rises cancel each other out on the expenditure and income sides of the budget, this principle is not jeopardized. If the real tax burden (i.e. as a proportion of income) automatically increases, on the other hand, local accountability may be undermined. This may occur if, for example, standard deductions are raised only at intervals of several years and more slowly than incomes. A similar effect arises if other deductions (e.g. for travel expenses) rise more slowly than ongoing increases in incomes: an ever increasing share of incomes then becomes taxable. With a proportional income tax, the real tax burden thereby becomes heavier. Between 1952 and 1965, for example, fiscal drag of this kind arose in Sweden. In this period, taxable income rose 10 per cent faster, on average, than earned incomes.

If, on the other hand, deductions from earned incomes follow income trends, a proportional income tax cannot raise the real tax burden. Another consideration is that ongoing price and pay rises can vary in impact on local authorities' expenditure and revenues. The net effect depends on how large a proportion of both follow pay trends rather than inflation, and how pay trends are related to inflation. In a random selection of Swedish municipalities in the period 1952-65, the automatic increase in tax revenues (i.e. with unchanged tax rates) was to a large extent cancelled out by the automatic rise on the expenditure side. However, the residual real rise in incomes sufficed, on average, to finance 60 per cent of the relatively pronounced real expansion in spending (on average, 6 per cent annually) which occurred in this period. This proportion is only half as large in the period 1975-85, owing to a considerably lower automatic real net increase in revenues (on average, 0.8 per cent annually). In other words, of the real annual increase in spending of 2.8 per cent on average, 70 per cent was financed by means of recurrent tax rises in this period (Table 10.6).

Thus between 1975 and 1985 the local authorities selected were, to a large extent, forced to balance the benefits of raised expenditure against the costs of increased taxation. In previous years of rapid economic growth, most of the expansion in spending was instead made possible by automatic rises in real revenues.

Table 10.6: Percentage change in different variables for local authorities in Sweden, 1975-85

	1975-80	1980-85	1975-85
Tax base per capita in current prices	90	50	185
Price index for total expenditure	78	47	163
Total expenditure in fixed prices	18.6	10.5	31.1
Tax base per capita in fixed prices	6.3	2.0	8.4
Income tax rate	15.3	4.4	20.4
Tax equalization grant in fixed prices	42	15	64
Specific grants in fixed prices	20	-9	10
Total grants in fixed prices	24	-4	19

SUMMARY

Local income tax has been regarded as the foundation of the high level of autonomy enjoyed by Swedish local authorities. In the last decade, the central government has extended this autonomy even further by decentralization and deregulation measures. To enlarge the local authorities' scope of action and, at the same time, the degree of local accountability, it is desirable to replace the majority of specific grants by a general, needs-related grant. A reform of this kind may also be expected to have an equalizing effect on tax rates and service levels, over and above what has already been attained via the tax equalization grant and the 'Robin Hood' tax on wealthy local authorities.

Using financial incentives rather than detailed controls, successive central governments have endeavoured to curb the expansion of local authorities' spending. Since the beginning of the 1980s, the real growth of their spending, as of their average tax rate, has also declined sharply. However, this development seems to be more a result of slow economic growth than of the relatively weak fiscal pressure imposed on the local authorities by the central government to date.

If the local income tax were replaced by a poll tax, the tax burden of local services would be redistributed from high-to-middle income earners. A tax redistribution of this kind appears not to be reconcilable with either the ability-to-pay or the benefit principle. Nor has a poll tax ever been proposed as a genuine alternative in the political debate.

In combination with the tax equalization grant, the local income tax in Sweden seems generally not to have prompted any inefficient fiscal migration, at least not between 1975 and 1985. Nor, contrary to the previous situation, has the buoyancy of the income tax in this period been in manifest conflict with the principle of local accountability.

REFERENCES

Bailey, S.J. (1986)
'Rates Reform - Lessons from the Scottish Experience', Local Government Studies, May/June 1986, pp. 21-36

Barnett, R.R. and Topham, N. (1977)
'Evaluating the Distribution of Local Outputs in a Decentralized Structure of Government', Policy and Politics, vol. 6, pp. 51-70

Bennett, R. J. (1981)
'The Local Income Tax in Britain: A Critique of Recent Arguments against its Use', Public Administration, vol. 59, Autumn 1981, pp. 295-311

Bramley, G. (1986)
Horizontal Disparities and Resource Equalisation: A Critique of 'Paying for Local Government', School for Advanced Urban Studies, University of Bristol, Bristol

-- Evans, A., Leather, P. and Lambert, C. (1983)
'Grant Related Expenditure: A Review of the System', SAUS Working Paper 29, Bristol

Dawson, D.A. (1983)
'Financial Incentives for Change', in Young, K. (ed.), National Interests and Local Government, Joint Studies in Public Policy 7, Heineman, London

Foster, C.D., Jackman, R.A. and Perlman, M. (1980)
Local Government Finance in a Unitary State, George Allen & Unwin, London

Greenwood, R. (1981)
'Fiscal Pressure and Local Government in England and Wales', in Hood, C. and Wright, M. (eds), Big Government in Hard Times, Martin Robertson, Oxford

HMSO (1986) Paying for Local Government, Cmnd 9714

Jackman, R. (1986)
'Accountability, the Control of Expenditure and the Reform of Local Government Finance in he United Kingdom', unpublished paper, London School of Economics, London

Jones, G., Stewart, J. and Raine, J. (1981)

'Local Government is Worth Defending', in Raine, J. (ed.), In Defence of Local Government, Institute of Local Government Studies, University of Birmingham, Birmingham

Jonsson, E. (1972)
Local Government Finance (in Swedish), EFI, Stockholm School of Economics, Stockholm

--(1986) Effects of State Grants to Local Authorities (in Swedish), Ministry of Finance, DsFi 1986:7, Stockholm

King, D. (1984)
Fiscal Tiers. The Economics of Multi-level Government, George Allen & Unwin, London

Larsson, R. (1985)
From Directives to Objectives. A Review of Administrative Developments in Sweden 1975-1985, School of Public Administration, University of Stockholm, Stockholm

Le Grand, J. (1982)
The Strategy of Equality: Redistribution and the Social Services, George Allen & Unwin, London

Newton, K. (1980)
'Central Government Grants, Territorial Justice and Local Democracy in Post-war Britain', in Ashford, D.E. (ed.), Financing Urban Government in the Welfare State, Croom Helm, London

Ostlin, S. (1984)
Who makes use of public-sector services? (In Swedish), Ministry of Finance DsFi 1984: 2, Stockholm

Statistics Sweden (1986)
(SCB - formerly the National Central Bureau of Statistics), 1975, 1980, 1985, Statistical Yearbook of Administrative Districts of Sweden, Stockholm

--(1975, 1980, 1985) Local Government Finance (in

Swedish), Stockholm

--(1985) Local Government Finance - Prospects for 1986 (in Swedish), 0 13 SM 8501, Stockholm

--(1986) National Accounts 1970-1985 (in Swedish), SM N 1986:10

Swedish Employers' Confederation (SAF) (1985) Facts about Swedish taxes (in Swedish), Stockholm

--(1986) Facts about the Swedish economy (in Swedish), Stockholm

11 LOCAL GOVERNMENT FINANCE IN THE REPUBLIC OF IRELAND - THE AFTERMATH OF RATES ABOLITION

R. B. Haslam and Neil Collins

> The present arrangements for financing local authorities owe much to past expediency but little to reason. They are the product of a series of piecemeal and often ill-considered decisions. (The Financing of Local Authorities, National Economic and Social Council, Report No. 80, May 1985, C. Foster, R. Jackman, Q. Thompson, p.3),

Ireland is frequently quoted as an example of a country which abolished the domestic rates successfully. Many problems remain in the carrying out of this reform, however, and this chapter will outline some of these.

The Irish local government system is largely based on the pre-Independence single-tier and double-tier pattern of County, County Borough and Urban District Councils. The services it provides are broadly similar to its British equivalent without responsibility for education, police and many social services. (See Table 11.1). The chief Irish innovations have involved the establishment of a national agency for local government appointments (1926), a concentration of administrative powers in the office of City/County Manager (1940), and the 'abolition' of the domestic rating system (1978). The major Irish legislation is, in effect, nineteenth-century British statutes with a time lag, e.g. the 1834 (British) and 1838 (Irish) Poor Law Reforms, 1835 (British) and 1840 (Irish) Municipal Corporation Acts and 1888 (British) and 1898 (Irish) Local Government Acts.

Table 11.1: Major responsibilities of non-Metropolitan County Councils in England and County and County Borough Councils in Ireland

	England	Ireland
Consumer Protection	/	
Education	/	/ (a)
Fire Service	/	/
Police	/	
Housing		/
Libraries	/	/
Museums and art galleries	/	/
Parks and Recreation	/	/
Personal social services	/	
Refuse collection		/
Refuse disposal	/	/
Sewerage (local servicing)		/
Town and country planning	/	/
Roads	/	
Transport	/	
Youth employment	/	
Drainage		/
Water supply		/
Environmental protection		/

Note: a. Vocational education only through semi-autonomous Vocational Education Committees.

A financial crisis exists in local government in Ireland at present. The immediate cause is generally recognized as the failure of successive governments to grant full recoupment for domestic relief promised by the Fianna Fail Party before the General Election of June 1977.

> In government, Fianna Fail will remove rates from all private houses, will abolish the rates content from rent paid by local authority and other tenants, will remove rates from the residential portion of business premises, from

> secondary schools, from community halls being used for bona fide community purposes and from farm buildings (Policy statement on rates, January 1977),

Fianna Fail swept to victory in the election, gaining 84 seats, as against a combined opposition of 64 seats, the greatest majority ever. Their manifesto contained other promises but it is generally accepted that the rates reform attracted much of the increased Fianna Fail support at the polls.

On assuming office, the Fianna Fail government honoured its pledge in the Local Government (Financial Provisions) Act, 1978. This legislation was not only the result of short-term electoral pressures. The rating system had been criticized for several decades. The newspapers reflected the popular antipathy to this tax even before Independence in 1922.

The whole question of local government finance was the subject of an early report of the Economic Research Institute (Walker, 1962). The study was initiated by the then Taoiseach (Prime Minister) Sean Lemass. Some time later the problem was also addressed by an Inter-Departmental Committee on Local Finance and Taxation, which published three reports:

(i) Valuation for Rating Purposes, August 1965
(ii) Exemptions from and Remissions of Rates, October 1967
(iii) Rates and Other Sources of Revenue for Local Authorities, July 1968

These studies highlighted the pressure for change. The system appeared archaic, inequitable and urgently in need of reform.

In 1970, under the Local Government (Rates) Act, statutory provision was made for the adoption by local authorities of Waiver Schemes. This Act was a genuine effort to relieve hardship caused by payment of rates but it was limited in scope.

A further development was the publication in December 1972 of a White Paper (SO, 1972). The key sentence appeared to be:

> The Government have come to the conclusion that the real issue is not the abolition of the rating system (with all the consequences this would involve for local financial independence and, indeed, for the tax-payer) but the reform of the system so as to eliminate its undoubted defects (SO, 1972, p.10).

The 1972 White Paper proposed various ameliorative measures to counter the regressive elements in the domestic rating system and to update existing valuations. Domestic rates remained a widely unpopular tax although in contrast to the general increase in taxation, they were a fairly stable proportion of personal disposable income until the mid-1970s.

Local finance again came to the fore during the unexpected General Election in February 1973. The 'coalition' parties, Fine Gael and Labour, proposed a phased reduction of the domestic rate by transferring health and housing charges to the central exchequer. Fianna Fail responded to these proposals by promising the abolition of the domestic rates. The 'National Coalition', on assuming office, honoured its election promise by a phased transfer of charges between 1973 and 1977. The popularity of these moves was not lost on Fianna Fail in opposition and their rates pledge was made early in 1977 well ahead of the expected election. Fianna Fail offered immediate abolition of domestic rates while their opponents gave a further 25 per cent rates remission on domestic dwellings in the budget of January 1977. As already pointed out, Fianna Fail won a resounding victory in June 1977.

The Local Government (Financial Provisions) Act, 1978, undertook to reimburse local authorities by a grant equal to the rate income on domestic dwellings, secondary schools, community halls and farm buildings not previously exempted from rates. Crucially, the Act also gave the Minister for the Environment a power of limitation with regard to local authority finance. The Minister was able to set the maximum rate increase. The central government wished to prevent 'local authorities from increasing rates indiscriminately' (SO,1979). Councils retained the power to set the rate level but, with the Minister's control of the maximum, the financial independence of local government has been drastically curtailed. The rate level has become an instrument of central government economic management and consequently has been held well below inflation, as Table 11.2 shows.

Table 11.2: Rate level increase as compared to inflation. 1978 to 1982 in percentages

	1978	1979	1980	1981	1982
Rate limit	11	10	10	12	15
Average inflation	7.6	13.2	18.2	20.4	17.4

A circular from the Department of the Environment set out the 'guidelines' for the annual rate increase. Thus, in effect, the central government controlled each authority's gross rate income. No authority accepts the advice that they are 'free to determine rates lower than the upper limit' (Circular Letter Fin. 4/80). Central government control was thus further increased.

Between 1978 and 1981 local authorities adjusted to the new regime of high inflation and decreasing income by reducing the level of services. The shortfall was also met by running down reserves. The impact varied according to the levels of rates in 1977 and the reserves of each authority. There is no mechanism for rate equalization. Some authorities, especially in areas of urban and suburban growth, enjoyed some rate buoyancy from new developments. On the whole, however, the effect on local government was generally cutbacks, restrictions and retrenchment. The system suffered a corresponding decrease in morale, public image and effectiveness.

The 1982 circular on rates introduced a new element to local government finance. While notifying a 15 per cent increase in permitted maximum rate levels it also announced a shortfall in the grant. The government in effect was putting up only 92 per cent of the actual figure required. The gap was to be made up by each authority by charges, though the statute authorizing this was not in place. The Minister promised to introduce the appropriate legislation 'at an early date' aimed at (a) providing for a scale of fees for planning applications and (b) giving local authorities a general power to charge for local services. The idea of charges as a relief to local taxation had been mooted as far back as the 1960s but its introduction in 1982 was unexpected.

Before the promised bill could be introduced Fianna Fail lost office at a general election in November 1982. The position of local government charges was unclear until March 1983 when the coalition government's Minister for the Environment issued his annual rates circular. Essentially, the new provisions were a continuation of those of the previous government:

(a) a fixed domestic rate grant below 100 per cent recoupment;
(b) an encouragement to review the level of existing charges, mostly for water services;
(c) a promise of legislation to confer a general power to levy charges.

The Local Government (Financial Provisions) (No. 2) Act, 1983, gave force to the provisions in the Minister's circular. The Act was in part retrospective. The most important feature of the legislation is that the Minister is no longer obliged to make up all of the losses involved in granting rate relief. He can now simply announce a fixed grant to each local authority. The authorities in theory gained some discretion and autonomy. In fact, they merely took up the duty of collecting taxes on behalf of central government. Significantly, the power to fix the charges was given to the County/City Managers, rather than the Councillors themselves (Collins, 1987). The democratic implications of this legislation were deemed less pressing than the fiscal dangers of councillors refusing to raise revenue locally by new charges.

The popular resistance to charges was much greater than the government anticipated. The opposition was not confined to non-government parties but also found support among local councillors belonging to the coalition partners. The opposition was most noticeable in City (County Borough) and town (Urban Districts) as County Councils had charged for domestic water for many years although the amount in most cases was little more than nominal.

> The Minister for the Environment yesterday denied that the government was endeavouring to reintroduce rates by the back door. ... Mr Spring contends that the proposed legislation restores to the elected representatives a proper degree of financial independence, and a general discretionary power to charge for services they provide which they lack now ... but in the context of the time, the introduction of the bill will not be unanimously read this way. The most jaundiced view will be that it is merely a vehicle to relieve the Central Exchequer of the responsibility of financing local authorities in the manner of the past six years (Irish Times, 2 June 1983).

The returns made available to local authorities through charges have not met the shortfall in the government grant. This situation did not materially alter when the onus was transferred from the Manager to the Members by Ministerial order in October 1985. The charges for water, in particular, are unavoidable and do not vary with the quantity consumed. They are essentially a tax. The aim of the new burden on local residents is to make up the balance in the amount of money the state provides. There is no obvious improvement in services. Many opponents charge that there is an element of double taxation. Councillors understandably see little political advantage in being seen to move towards economic charges for local services.

Local elections in Ireland are relatively infrequent. In 1985, an election was held for the first time since 1979. A recurring campaign theme was the financing of local government and the level of water and other service charges. The result was a triumph for the major opposition party, Fianna Fail.

Table 11.3: Control of Councils in 1979 and 198!

Dominant party	Percentage of councils	
	1979	1985
Fianna Fail	10	55
Fine Gael	3	0
Fine Gael/Labour	45	6
No overall majority	42	39

(Based on Dublin County as one council)

They took control of a majority of Councils (see Table 11.3).

After the 1985 election, some councils voted to discontinue collection of water charges. In Dublin County, for example, nearly £5 million were outstanding in arrears and in Cork City the shortfall was over £2 million. Both councils were among those to have voted against levying water charges in future. Fianna Fail feel that their election success was helped by their hostile attitude to local charges, especially in the urban areas where many householders are withholding payment.

Despite their opposition, most local authorities have accepted some charges since the function of setting them was given to councillors. The story of charges is, however, littered with public protests, court battles and disruption of services. One authority, Naas UDC (pop. 8353), refused to accept an estimate which included charges and subsequently its members were removed from office by the Minister and a commissioner appointed. A special allocation of £5m for strengthening works on county roads was apportioned to County Councils on the basis of the domestic water charges in 1986 and the percentage collected in 1985. The manifesto for the Fianna Fail party for the local elections of 1985 opposed charges and promised to repeal the legislation. Recently, however, the new Fianna Fail Minister for the Environment stated that charges were a matter for individual authorities.

Finance in the Republic of Ireland

The difficulties of Irish local authorities in regard to finance are not confined to changes in the domestic rating system. Farmers had been given partial relief from rates for many years when in 1978, the last vestiges of rates on farm buildings were removed. In 1981 small farmers, i.e. those with land of rateable value £50 or less, were exempted from rates. The High Court continued the process in 1982 when it effectively ruled against the rating system as it applied to farms. The Supreme Court in 1984 upheld the contention that it was unconstitutional to levy a tax on the basis of grossly inequitable valuations. In effect, farmers are no longer liable to rates on agricultural land and many of them had stopped paying them as of 1982. The government now makes an ex-gratia grant to compensate partially for the loss of the agricultural rates but again there is a considerable shortfall in each authority's income.

Taxation levels in Ireland generally are very high. A particularly burdened group are the PAYE earners whose grievance is heightened by the widespread belief that farmers and self-employed avoid their 'fair share' of taxation. The PAYE sector's sense of injustice has led to large demonstrations in recent years. The reason is fairly clear. In the past decade, the proportion of taxpayers facing a marginal income tax rate of 45 per cent or above has risen from 1 to 40 per cent. At the same time, a single person on the average industrial earnings pays at a marginal rate of around 60 per cent. Taxes on capital and property, excluding stamp duties, are low and the base narrow. The major needs for Irish governments is to broaden the tax base and, for electoral as well as financial reasons, to reduce the burden on PAYE taxpayers.

It is in this context that the National Economic and Social Council (NESC) produced its proposal for the financing of local authorities in May 1985. The NESC report was prepared by a team of consultants from Coopers and Lybrand. It recommended that a local property tax be introduced. Obviously, the team were at pains to distance their proposals from the previous domestic rating system. The council, which represents various groups including employers, farmers and trade unions, endorsed the report in its introductory comments:

> A considerable degree of local discretion can be maintained in a grant financed system. ... However, the Council believes that local authorities should have greater discretion to determine their own overall spending levels; in effect, that they should have an independent source of revenue ... a property tax offers the best means of restoring a local revenue base. ... The Council agrees in principle with the introduction of a property tax and believes it would be practical, would ensure accountability and would provide local authorities with a predictable and variable source of finance (NESC, 1985).

The NESC reported that unless the existing system of allocation from central government was changed, local government's financial crisis would worsen. Charges for services are not realistically a major source of money. Under the NESC proposals, a comprehensive property tax would encompass dwellings, commercial and industrial property, farmland, public buildings and all other 'immovable structures'. A tax based on land acreage was not envisaged because the report states some farms are much more profitable per acre than others. The property tax as proposed was to be based initially on self-assessed capital values which would be subject to an audit by the local authority, with market values being used as they were made available. Provision for appeal would also be made. NESC suggested that the reduction in national taxation brought about by the new tax should be clearly demonstrated. But central government grants would be needed to compensate authorities with a low tax base or high spending needs, and to finance national services provided by local authorities on behalf of central government.

Reaction to the NESC report from the political parties was cool to hostile. Significantly, Fianna Fail rejected it as 'a continuation of the softening up process on the public mind to accept new rates'. The rates continue to be a contentious political issue though more people may now agree with Professor Brendan Walsh who said in 1982: 'The abolition of rates was socially and economically a mistake.' Walsh was not calling for rates in the pre-1978 form but claimed that their removal for householders had bestowed more benefits on the middle and upper income groups than the poor (Irish Press, 29 September 1982).

The Irish experience of the abolition of domestic rates has not been encouraging. Central government has been unable or unwilling to fulfil its promised support of local authorities in the face of fiscal pressures. The temptation to cast local government in the role of tax collector has been too great. The current system for financing local government in Ireland is far from satisfactory. There were problems up to 1977 of matching the burden of rates with the ability to pay, of equalizing services between authorities with divergent needs and resources, and, of antiquated valuation. There was also the pressure on the system of very large increases in rate bills (in money terms) in 1975 and 1976 as local authorities sought to restore their incomes in the face of inflation. The remedy for these difficulties, the virtual abolition of the rates, has not proved effective as yet. Twenty years later, Ireland is still seeking an acceptable way of financing locally provided and democratically accountable services. It may be that a property tax of some form or other is inescapable if local government is to recover its autonomy and independence.

Editors' note: Following the re-election of a Fianna Fail Government and the budget statement of 1987, the reintroduction of local rates was proposed.

REFERENCES

Collins, N. (1987)
Local Government Managers at Work, Institute of Public Administration, Dublin

National Economic and Social Council (1985)
The Financing of Local Authorities, NESC, Dublin

Finance in the Republic of Ireland

SO (1972)
Local Finance and Taxation, (P.L. 2745), S.O., Dublin

-- (1979) Local Government Authority Estimates, SO, Dublin

Walker, D. (1962)
Local Government Finance in Ireland, Economic Research Institute, Dublin

12 LOCAL GOVERNMENT FINANCE IN BRITAIN

Stephen J. Bailey

> Local government finance is at a crossroads. The Government needs to be able to influence the total of local authority expenditure, as part of its overall economic policies. Yet its attempts to do so are frustrated by a local tax and grant regime which depresses and distorts the cost of marginal increases in expenditure (Cmnd 9714, para 1.43).
> But neither structural reform nor increased central control offers an attractive way of fulfilling that responsibility. The alternative is to make local authorities more accountable to their electors within the present structure of local government (Cmnd 9714, para 1.51).
> This suggests that there should be three main elements in a new finance system based on improved local accountability - better arrangements for the taxation of non-domestic ratepayers; a more direct and fairer link between voting and paying; clearer grant arrangements (Cmnd 9714, para 1.54).

THE DEGREE OF LOCAL DISCRETION

Britain has a long history of central government subventions to local authorities concomitant with an undefined central-local relationship based on various legal requirements, conventions and voluntary co-operation. Hence the relationship between central and local government is in a state of continuous flux due to changing central and local perceptions of local autonomy, accountability, equity and the need for macroeconomic control.

Powers have been granted to local authorities by Parliament over a considerable period of time through innumerable separate Acts, both general and local. Such powers are accompanied by wide-ranging statutory duties concerning provision of specific services as well as general enabling powers. In most cases local authorities themselves determine the actual level and standard of service provision, having considerable discretion in this respect. Indeed past attempts to categorize local authority services into discretionary and mandatory components were notable by their failure to do so.

> The bulk of local government expenditure falls somewhere between the two extremes, being determined not by formal requirements alone nor by free local choice alone but by a complex mixture of pressures and influences. Informal advice and exhortation from government departments, inspection, nationally accepted standards, accumulated past practice, professional attitudes, political influences and actions by various pressure groups, national and local, all play a part in determining local government expenditure, along with the statutory provisions (Cmnd 6454 - Layfield Report, Annex 12, para 4).

Further attempts since 1976 to differentiate permissive and mandatory functions have likewise failed to make any progress (e.g. Cmnd 7643) and the Department of the Environment concluded that it would be impractical to define minimum statutory requirements for particular services.

> The statutory provisions thus provide only a loose framework within which local authorities are left with a very wide but largely undefined measured of discretion. The limits for central government intervention have thus become a matter for political determination ... reinforced by the provision of financial incentives through the grant scheme (NAO 1985,p.11,para.2.4 and p.18,paras 4.22 and 4.23).

The quote in the introduction to this chapter reflects the Government's desire further to reinforce the financial incentives towards more discerning use of local discretion, particularly through the proposed reforms of grants and local taxation.

EXCHEQUER GRANTS

Central government grants are paid to local authorities in furtherance of a number of objectives. These have varied in emphasis over time, reflecting the changing political complexion and economic policies of central government. They are also potentially conflicting. Firstly, Exchequer grants are paid in support of local ratepayers to lighten their fiscal burden (and hence the main grant is called the Rate Support Grant). Grant arrangements also attempt, secondly, to constrain the total current expenditure of local authorities consistent with central government's macroeconomic policy; thirdly, to bring the actual pattern of service expenditures more into line with central government's own priorities (particularly through payments of specific grants); fourthly, to equalize for differing per capita rateable resources and expenditure needs; fifthly, to maximize local discretion subject to points two and three above; and, finally, to be comprehensible to practitioners and voters so as to improve accountability for local service provision.

These are clearly rather daunting objectives for any grant system and, not surprisingly, the mechanism for grant determination and distribution has been subject to continual modification both as the balance between objectives has changed and as defects within successive grant regimes have become increasingly salient.

Specific grants predate general grants which were introduced in 1929 and made some attempt at equalization. In 1958 the new General Grant replaced a series of specific grants and was paid as a percentage of relevant expenditure agreed by central and local government. The Rate Support Grant (RSG) was introduced in 1966 and was determined as the residual of Aggregate Exchequer Grant (again a percentage of relevant expenditure) after deduction of specific grants. RSG was divided into three elements. The domestic element was paid as additional relief to domestic ratepayers as distinct from non-domestic ratepayers, mainly industry and commerce. It was (and still is) paid in the form of a reduction in domestic rate poundage (the tax rate) applied to domestic rateable value (the tax base). The residual of the RSG (after calculation of the domestic element) was split between the resources and needs elements. The former made partial compensation for lack of rateable resources per capita (i.e. below standard per capita property tax revenues); the latter compensated for differences in need to spend per head of population, 'need' being assessed by central government.

This grant structure still exists in Scotland. However, in England and Wales it was modified by the 1980 Local Government, Planning and Land Act which introduced the unitary grant. This has, itself, been subsequently modified (e.g. by the Local Government Finance Act, 1982) but basically it combines the former needs and resources elements into a single grant called the Block Grant. Hence the RSG now comprises the Domestic Rate Relief Grant (effectively the same as the former domestic element) and the Block Grant which simultaneously equalizes for per capita needs and rating resources (see Table 12.1).

The former RSG structure in England and Wales had been criticized as providing an incentive for high-spending authorities to increase their expenditure further so as to gain more grant (Rhodes and Bailey, 1979). The new Block Grant (applied separately in England and Wales) was designed so as to increase the pressures on local authorities to conform with the expenditure levels deemed appropriate by the Government. Central government assesses each authority's need to spend taking account of various demographic, geographical, social environmental and other factors which are thought to affect spending need. This assessment is made for individual services and then aggregated to derive the Grant Related Expenditure Assessment (GREA) for each authority. An authority is not obliged to conform

Table 12.1: The Government's contribution to the financing of local authority relevant expenditure (£ million)

1987-88	England	Scot-land	Wales	Great Britain
Relevant current expenditure	25,671	3,339	1,526	30,536
Rate fund contributions to Housing Revenue Accounts	437	-	2	440
Public expenditure relevant for AEG	26,108	3,339	1,529	30,976
Revenue contributions from rate funds to special funds and capital expenditure	19	17	34	70
Loan charges	2,560	603	221	3,384
Interest receipts	-521	-10	-20	-551
Relevant expenditure	28,166	3,949	1,764	33,879
financed by:				
Aggregate Exchequer Grant	13,025	2,190	1,174	16,389
of which				
Block Grants (a)	9,015	1,803	919	11,737
Domestic rate relief grant	717	91	26	834
Supplementary grants (b)	187	-	24	211
Specific grants	3,106	296	205	3,607

a. Block Grant does not exist in Scotland: its place is taken by the needs and resources elements of rate support grant.

b. Supplementary grants in England and Wales for Transport and National Parks.

Source: The Government's Expenditure Plans 1987/88 to 1989/90, vol.2, CM56-II, p.363, HM Treasury, January 1987.

with either the distribution or the total of spending over services. However, expenditure in excess of the GREA attracts extra Block Grant at a diminishing rate (the marginal grant rate), sometimes even becoming negative. This system therefore increases the cost to local ratepayers of marginal increments in expenditure in excess of an authority's own GREA.

The mechanism used to achieve this is the schedule of Grant Related Poundages (GRP) appropriate to each level of spending relative to GREA. The higher the relative level of expenditure the higher the GRP. Each authority receives an amount of Block Grant equal to the difference between its actual total expenditure relevant for Block Grant (largely relevant expenditure minus specific grants) and the rate income it would receive by levying the GRP appropriate to that relative level of expenditure. Hence the authorities providing similar standards of services are able to finance them by setting similar rate poundages. This therefore promotes several of the objectives listed above, namely equity or equalization between authorities, leaving authorities free to determine distribution of the Block Grant over services, and at the same time constraining total expenditure so as to reflect the Government's macroeconomic policy.

As originally envisaged, this system was to rely solely on the steepening cost in rate poundage terms of spending in excess of an authority's GREA so as to restrain local expenditure. However, the introduction of the Block Grant system in 1981/2 was accompanied by a separate and supplementary system of expenditure restraint whereby each local authority was notified of an expenditure guidance target, usually below its previous year's level of spending and consistent with the Government's overall expenditure plans. Authorities exceeding their targets were generally penalized by reductions being made in their Block Grant allocations on a sliding scale related to the level of overspend against target.

The target system was abandoned in 1986/7 in England and Wales due to increasingly anomalous effects (e.g. authorities overspending against target but underspending against GREA still lost Block

Grant) with the result that the equalizing objective of Block Grant was compromised. Expenditure restraint is now to be achieved through progressively severe reductions in marginal grant rates within the GREA mechanism. This is a grossly simplified explanation of the grant mechanisms and a more detailed exposition is available elsewhere (Bailey, 1985a). There are some subtle differences in the separate Welsh Block Grant system (Bailey, 1985b). Expenditure guidance and grant penalties for spending above guidelines are still in operation in Scotland as part of a completely different grant system.

Simultaneous with these measures to increase cost to ratepayers at the margin of increased expenditures, the Government implemented further expenditure restraints between 1981 and 1986. First, the proportion of total relevant expenditure funded by central government grants was reduced year by year to increase the average rate bill and so encourage expenditure restraint. Second, the accounts of local authorities became subject to increasing scrutiny under the auspices of the Audit Commission for England and Wales and the Accounts Commission for Scotland. Third, the powers of local authorities to levy supplementary rates were abolished. Fourth, the Government took powers directly to limit the level of rates levied by individual authorities ('rate-capping') and so directly controlled net expenditure of capped authorities. Fifth, the Greater London Council and the Metropolitan County Councils in England were abolished, so removing what the Government considered to be an unnecessary and profligate tier of local government. (Their duties were transferred elsewhere.) Such actions will clearly have had implications for local autonomy, local accountability, equity and macroeconomic control and they will now be examined separately although, in practice, these issues are clearly intertwined.

LOCAL AUTONOMY

As noted earlier it is not possible clearly to delineate the mandatory and discretionary functions of local authorities. Similarly authorities provide services for national as well as local purposes but precise standards of service are not usually prescribed. However, it is clear that the Government is progressively increasing its own controls and hence is constraining the exercise of local autonomy to an increasing degree. This is achieved through the increasing proportion of total grants paid in respect of specific services, through the operation of the Block Grant system and through controls over property tax rates.

Specific grants are still a relatively small proportion of expenditure relevant for grant calculation at about 10 per cent but they have been increasing as a proportion of total Aggregate Exchequer Grant (AEG) throughout Britain. In England, for example, specific grants accounted for 14 per cent of AEG in 1977/8, 17 per cent in 1981/2, 20 per cent in 1983/4, 22 per cent in 1985/6, and 24 er cent in 1987/8 (see Table 12.1). This trend reflects the rising cost of police services (the main specific grant), newly perceived needs for specific grants and a decline in the real value of AEG. Whatever the reason, this trend reduces the degree of local discretion over the distribution of expenditure between services.

Such distribution may also be influenced through the operation of the Block Grant system. As noted earlier local authorities in each of England, Scotland and Wales have their need to spend assessed by central government. This is done on a service by service basis and expenditure needs are then aggregated into a total expenditure need figure against which budgeted and actual expenditure is compared for the purpose of administering grant payments (positive or negative at the margin). The annual Rate Support Grant reports invariably point out that local authorities are free to decide their own priorities and are not required to follow the government's expenditure assessments for individual services.

The same disclaimer is made for the expenditure plans for individual services published in the Government's annual Public Expenditure White Papers (Table 12.2). In both cases the Government's figures

Table 12.2: Local authority public expenditure in England by function (£ million) (a)

	1981-82 outturn	1982-83 outturn	1983-84 outturn	1984-85 outturn	1985-86 outturn	1986-87 estimated outturn	1987-88 plans	1988-89 plans	1989-90 plans
Current expenditure in England									
Agriculture, fisheries, food and forestry	95	97	109	117	128	149	143	150	150
Industry, trade and employment	115	128	141	152	159	174	178	180	190
Arts and libraries	308	339	362	383	408	434	453	470	480
Roads and transport	1,543	1,751	1,837	1,918	1,785	1,876	1,950	2,010	2,060
Housing	525	547	647	584	623	608	593	610	630
Other environmental services	2,050	2,218	2,380	2,478	2,683	2,761	2,850	2,940	3,010
Law, order and protective services	2,595	2,875	3,134	3,557	3,571	3,964	4,134	4,260	4,370
Education and science	9,619	10,227	10,792	11,224	11,655	12,964	13,547	14,220	14,610
Health and personal social services	1,795	1,970	2,135	2,274	2,406	2,676	2,847	2,940	3,010
Social security	495	883	2,203	2,481	2,736	3,021	3,070	3,000	3,200
Total current expenditure	**19,140**	**21,035**	**23,739**	**25,168**	**26,154**	**28,627**	**29,766**	**30,800**	**31,700**

Capital expenditure in England									
Agriculture, fisheries, food and forestry	114	113	69	46	35	39	28		
Industry, trade and employment	4	5	4	6	5	6	6		
Arts and libraries	20	28	40	48	40	49	16		
Roads and transport	621	728	797	853	660	598	767		
Housing	768	596	1,287	1,425	949	895	1,208		
Other environmental services	501	734	670	743	599	796	474		
Law, order and protective services	92	114	109	114	99	164	156		
Education and science	362	413	424	423	411	471	364		
Health and personal social services	70	67	73	78	76	86	81		
Total capital expenditure	**2,552**	**2,799**	**3,473**	**3,736**	**2,872**	**3,104**	**3,099**	**2,840**	**2,920**
Total local authority expenditure	**21,693**	**23,834**	**27,212**	**28,904**	**29,026**	**31,731**	**32,865**	**33,600**	**34,600**

Note: a. The picture represented by the data is similar for Scotland and Wales, although England accounts for the bulk of local authority public expenditure in Britain.

Source: The Government's Expenditure Plans 1987/88 to 1989/0, vol. 2, CM 56-II, p.365, H M Treasury, January 1987.

are meant only to be indicative both for individual authorities and for local government as a whole. Nonetheless, in times of fiscal restraint, such service-specific assessed expenditure figures may have influence over the budgetary decisions of individual authorities and hence limit the exercise of local autonomy.

As noted earlier, central government also has powers to cap the rates of local property tax levied by individual authorities. These rate-capping powers have been used for several years in England and Scotland to constrain the expenditure of 'profligate' authorities. Whilst they have been applied to only a minority of authorities, the existence of such powers will serve to constrain the total expenditure decision of many authorities who fear the possibility of being rate-capped. Clearly if central government has control over both grant and rate income then an individual authority is left with almost no discretion over the total of its expenditure, income from fees and charges being a relatively small source of funds. In such a case discretion becomes confined to the distribution of a fixed sum of spending over services.

LOCAL ACCOUNTABILITY

A declared objective of the new RSG system (introduced in 1981/2 in England and Wales) was to improve local accountability by making the costs of local services more apparent to local electors (Cmnd 9008, paras 1.15 to 1.16). This was to be achieved on both an average and marginal basis. The percentage of relevant expenditure funded by AEG was progressively reduced,

> so that all authorities had to consider more carefully whether the cost of extra spending, with a lower contribution from central Government, was justified. In England grant fell in stages from 60% of planned expenditure in 1980/81 to 49% in 1985/86. Over the same period it fell from 74% to 67% in Wales and from 68.5% to 57.7% in Scotland (Cmnd 9714, p.3).

Hence the average rate burden rose as the grant percentage was reduced. The new systems for distributing grant (outlined above) also sought to increase the cost to the ratepayers at the margin of increased service provision. This was meant to discourage higher levels of expenditure by ensuring that a greater proportion of incremental costs falls on local ratepayers so improving accountability.

However, the Audit Commission (1984, p.47) argued that local accountability had been blurred (rather than strengthened) by the new grant system. There are two main problems perceived by the Audit Commission. First, the confusion about the division of responsibility between central and local government caused by the separation in practice between the Public Expenditure White Papers' plans, assessed expenditure needs, and what local authorities actually spend on services. Second, there is no clear relationship between the increase in an authority's spending and the resultant increase in local rates. For example, the reduction in the English grant percentage between 1980/1 and 1984/5 increased the proportion of relevant expenditure to be borne by ratepayers by almost a third or about £3 billion in 1984/5 alone and this was in addition to the ratepayer costs of any expenditure increases. This confusion between the rate impact of grant reductions and expenditure increases was further exacerbated by the use of expenditure targets superimposed on the RSG system (described above). Similar effects occurred in Scotland and in Wales (Cmnd 9714, Chapters 8 and 9).

Notwithstanding the increasing burdens on local ratepayers the Government came to the conclusion that fundamental reform of the financing of local government is necessary to improve local accountability. Reform is proposed at two levels: first the system of local taxation and, second, the system of central government grants to local authorities.

> Local accountability depends crucially on the relationship between paying for local services and voting in local elections. At the moment

> there are worrying gaps. 60% of net rate income in England comes from non-domestic ratepayers with no vote. Of the 35 million local electors in England only about 18 million are liable to pay rates and about a third of those receive full or partial rebates (Cmnd 9714, para 1.52).

Hence the Government proposes that all domestic ratepayers should be required to pay at least 20 per cent of their rate bill to establish a financial link with local authority service levels. In the longer term, however, the Government proposes to replace the local property tax by a local poll tax (called the 'Community Charge'). With only very limited exceptions, this will be payable by all adult residents (effectively all local electors plus foreign residents). The implications of a poll tax for equity is discussed further in the next section.

> In addition to bringing the tax base more closely into line with the electorate, however, the new arrangements must also ensure that taxpayers can see a clear link between changes in their authority's expenditure and the corresponding changes in local tax bills. The grant system must operate in a way that enables local residents to see the extent of the support that is being provided. In addition, it must not obscure the spending behaviour of their authority by distorting the relationship between expenditure and taxes at the margin. And it must be stable; otherwise changes in grant entitlements within and between years will prevent local residents from seeing the link between their authority's spending and their local tax bills (Cmnd 9714, para 4.3).

Hence the Government proposes a new system of local government finance based on four elements. First, the pooling of non-domestic rate income and its redistribution as an equal amount per adult head of population. Second, payment of a standard grant again as an equal amount per adult. Third, payment of a needs grant which would vary between authorities depending on their respective assessed expenditure needs. Fourth, the poll tax (Community Charge). The first three sources of income would be fixed at the beginning of the grant year irrespective of what an authority spent. The Community Charge would therefore act as the residual source of finance carrying the full burden of any excess of an authority's expenditure over its centrally-assessed need to spend. Hence local taxpayers will bear the full cost of any 'excess' spending so improving local accountability in the eyes of the Government. The likely success and further implications of these proposed reforms have been analysed in detail elsewhere (Bailey and Paddison, 1988; Midwinter and Mair, 1987). In terms of local accountability a synopsis of the Government's view is that:

> The present local domestic taxation arrangements leave too great a gap between those who use, those who vote for, and those who pay for local services. Although domestic rates are perceptible to those who actually pay them, they provide a poor basis for local accountability (Cmnd 9714, para 3.47).

EQUITY

The concept of equity is applied at two levels: that of the local authority and that of the local ratepayer. As noted above, the present Block Grant is designed to enable local authorities to provide similar levels of service for similar rate poundages. Authorities differ in terms of rateable resources per capita (reflecting the uneven distribution of industrial and commercial activity) and in terms of need to spend per capita (reflecting differences in the demographic and socio-economic mix of their populations). Hence local authorities receive grant payments to offset deficiencies in per capita rateable resources and differences in per capita expenditure need. With only a few exceptions, complete equalization of resources and needs is achieved for local authorities. However, the grant system equalizes rate poundages rather than rate bills. The latter depends upon the rateable value of the property occupied by the local ratepayer so that individual ratepayers in receipt of similar standards of services may still face radically different rate bills.

Furthermore, equalization of rate poundages for similar standards of service has itself been distorted by a number of factors. First, 'safety nets' are used to limit changes in grant from year to year. Second, the effects on ratepayers of the high rateable values of properties within Greater London are mitigated within the English grant system. Third, penalties are imposed for spending above target expenditure levels. In all three cases the distribution of grant is adjusted by 'multipliers' which are an additional factor introduced into the Block Grant calculation to increase or reduce an individual local authority's entitlement. The multipliers used to implement the system of targets and penalties had the greatest impact in terms of destroying the equalizing nature of the grant system. For example the 1984/5 targets for the major spending authorities in England varied from nearly 10 per cent below the Grant Related Expenditure Assessment to over 50 per cent above. An authority losing grant as a penalty for exceeding target had to levy a higher rate poundage than another authority not exceeding target even if both were spending the same in relation to their GREAs.

> The scale of variation ... appears to be the result of a series of ad hoc decisions rather than a considered judgment about the degree of inequality which is acceptable for the sake of other policy objectives. It seems to me that the consequence has been the virtual abandonment for many large authorities of the equalisation that had been the primary purpose of the Block Grant distribution system (NAO, 1985, para 24).

Furthermore, the reliability of GREAs is crucial for the operation of the Block Grant system. They are meant to be an objective assessment of the cost of providing services to a given standard and hence determine the rate of grant payable on expenditure. However, the Audit Commission (1984, p.1) concluded that:

> Because some information on local needs is often inadequate and that on local resources is out of date, serious distortions result. Some authorities are receiving less grant than their circumstances might warrant; and, by the same token, some are receiving more. The difference for a large city could easily amount to plus or minus £15 million in grant every year.

Even data on resident populations in authorities are often in error by as much as 10 per cent which, given that about a third of Grant Related Expenditures are population based, causes significant inequities in the distribution of grant. Furthermore, data by authority on the numbers of elderly people living alone, of single-parent families and so on is often even more inaccurate, with the result that it is not possible accurately to determine local needs for personal social services.

Similarly an authority's entitlement to Block Grant is also dependent upon the rateable value of its area. Low rateable values attract more grant as expenditure increases than high rateable values. However, in England and Wales there has been no revaluation of rateable values since 1973 with the result that they are seriously misrepresentative of current resources. In particular, rate burdens are thought to be too high for larger, older, labour-intensive factories in the Midlands and North of England and for older steelworks (Cmnd 8449, p.51) whose relative profitability has declined since 1973. Modern industrial estates are thought to be relatively undervalued for rating purposes. The uneven distribution of such classes of economic activity results in inequity between authorities. 'The continued use of inadequate information about local property values inevitably introduces serious distortions to the grant distribution process' (Audit Commission, 1984, para 69). Scotland has had two revaluations since 1973 (1978 and 1985) with the result that such distortions have been largely ameliorated.

Even if such inequities were completely overcome

at the local authority level there could still exist inequities at the local taxpayer level since, as noted earlier, for given standards of service provision the grant system equalizes rate poundage rather than rate bills. One of the criticisms of the local property tax is that a householder living in the same house type and receiving a given standard of services would face radically different rate bills in different parts of the country. This is because rental values, from which rateable values are derived, vary geographically.

Similarly, within a given locality, two householders occupying the same house type and being outwith the rate rebate scheme, will face the same rate bill irrespective of income and therefore of ability to pay the rate bill. Hence horizontal inequity occurs at the ratepayer level simply because rate bills are a function of rateable values (and associated rate poundages); they are not directly related to income.

Such inequity is partially ameliorated by the rate rebate scheme for low-income householders. It could be completely removed by a local income tax but many arguments have been advanced against such a tax (Bennett, 1981). In the 1986 Green Paper the Conservative Government argues that it is committed to reducing taxation of incomes, that a local income tax would not underpin local accountability and that it would not be appropriate to rely too heavily on a redistributive tax to fund local authority services (Cmnd 9714, p.23) because it breaks the link between those who vote for, those who pay for and those who use local authority services.

It is clear that the concepts of equity and accountability have now changed. It is seen as inequitable and bad for accountability that there is no direct link between voting, paying local taxes and using services. Those who make no contribution through local rate payments can vote for higher levels of service provision with no fear of the financial consequences. This does not promote accountability and makes largely irrelevant the sophisticated attempts to reduce the marginal grant rate on expenditures in excess of the GREA.

Furthermore, it is now seen to be inequitable

that only ratepayers should bear the costs rather than all voters or residents and, moreover, that non-domestic ratepayers in particular, with no vote, should have to contribute more than half of rates income. Hence, as noted earlier, the 1986 Green Paper proposes replacement of domestic rates by a 'Community Charge', the central control of non-domestic rates and a reformed grant system.

This proposed system would dispense with the need for a resources-equalizing grant since the local tax resource is now to be per adult rather than rateable value. There would be some relief to low-income Community Charge payers but this would be limited to at most 80 per cent of the national average local tax for very low incomes. The vast majority of adult residents would pay the full Community Charge. Therefore the proposed system is seen by the Government as achieving greater equity both between local authorities (in terms of equalizing the resource base) and between adults resident in the community (in that all make some contribution to the cost of local services).

MACROECONOMIC CONTROL

The Government's Medium Term Financial Strategy (MTFS) requires the control of the Public Sector Borrowing Requirement (PSBR). However, local authority expenditure financed from the rates does not add to the PSBR. Indeed, in the past, if local authorities spent above target the PSBR could be reduced since the Exchequer paid out less Rate Support Grant in administering grant penalties. Even after the abolition of targets in England and Wales a similar result is achieved with the ending of 'flowback'. Any Block Grant lost by authorities spending in excess of GREAs (i.e. those which are incurring negative marginal grant rates) no longer flows back into the Block Grant pool for redistribution to other authorities. It is now simply returned to the Exchequer. Hence the Exchequer again pays out less grant in such cases. This point was picked up by the Committee of Public Accounts which therefore asked the Department of the

Environment what precise objectives the constraint on total local authority spending was intended to serve.

> We were told that the MTFS also involved reducing the rate of inflation and the burden of taxation, which included local rates. The Government was therefore concerned with the level of public spending by local authorities and its effect on the burden of taxation. We recognise that the Government would prefer an arrangement whereby central grant was reduced and local rates were either restrained or actually fell, following local economies. But that is not how it has worked in practice, as the overspending figures show. We observe that while the indirect effect of some of the instruments of constraint used by the Government, including the proportionate reductions in central government funding and the holdback of grant penalties in the Exchequer, may be to stimulate ratepayer pressure against spending, their direct effect has been to shift the burden from central taxation to rates rather than to reduce it in total (CPA, 1985, para21).

Furthermore, the reaction of local authorities to such financial restraints was not as straightforward as may at first be expected. Certainly, English authorities were increasingly taking steps to maximize their grant income by avoiding penalties, etc. However, they were also increasingly protecting themselves

> against harsher penalties in future years, by maintaining estimated and reported outturn spending levels above that which is strictly necessary to meet current service standards, and by creating reserves as a cushion against future increases in penalties and changes in GRE and expenditure targets (Audit Commission, 1984, p.21).

Hence higher rates were caused by local authorities' responses to uncertainty within the grant system. This is an understandable response to uncertainty. Furthermore, some authorities began budgeting to spend in excess of target in order to protect their base spending levels for future financial years. There was therefore an incentive for all authorities to spend up to target, whilst those in excess of target increasingly avoided grant penalties by financing expenditure from special funds, by capitalizing expenditures previously funded from the revenue account and by rescheduling debt. These practices came to be known as 'creative accounting', whereby expenditure would be reclassified or rescheduled to reduce spending defined as relevant expenditure (for grant purposes), avoid grant reductions, yet maintain overall levels of service provision. In doing so they acted within the law.

The Government also adjusted its targets for authorities' expenditures from year to year which in turn frustrated the original objectives. Targets were meant to be realistically attainable levels of expenditure that local authorities could achieve. However, as it became increasingly clear that they were not going to be adhered to, the Government reduced the severity of expenditure reductions required to meet the target from year to year.

> When it became apparent each year that these targets were not going to be met the Government progressively increased its previously planned levels of local authority spending for subsequent years (by £1.3 billion for 1982/83, £1.3 billion for 1983/84, £0.6 billion for 1984/85 and £0.9 billion for 1985/86 for Great Britain as a whole) to allow the overspending authorities more time to moderate their expenditure. Taking into account the involuntary adjustment each year of the Expenditure Plans on which the targets were based, the system of targets and penalties has clearly fallen some way short of producing the results intended by the Government (NAO, 1985, para 4.6).

Whilst the Government believes that local authority spending was reduced below what it otherwise would have been without targets and penalties, the use of creative accounting and adjustments to the base for targets make such conclusions of dubious validity.

Indeed, it could be argued that expenditure would actually increase as 'underspenders' spent up to targets and it proved difficult in practice to bring 'overspenders' down to targets. It is not without reason that the Government took powers under the 1984 Rates Act directly to limit rates set by local authorities and therefore control total spending. Rate-capping has also been used on several Scottish authorities. Admittedly they have only been used on a minority of authorities so far (18 in 1985/6 and 12 in 1986/7) and have little impact on the aggregate of overspending, but the adoption of such powers does serve to illustrate the Government's increasing frustration over its failure to control local authority expenditure. As noted earlier, the Government also abolished the Greater London Council and the Metropolitan County Councils which it regarded as an unnecessary and expensive tier of local government.

CONCLUSIONS

The original objectives of the RSG system introduced into England and Wales in 1981/2 'were to provide a fairer and more objective method of grant distribution and to eliminate previous incentives to high spending' (NAO, 1985, para 37). The underlying structure of the Block Grant system was conducive to the achievement of these objectives but its detailed provision, together with the overlying system of targets and penalties, increasingly compromised them. The overriding aim of restraining total spending caused the grant system to increasingly deviate from its original purpose. 'We consider that the system as now operated is seriously defective in a number of respects' (CPA, 1985, para 54). The Comptroller and Auditor General concluded that 'The addition of a regime of targets and penalties unrelated to objectively assessed spending needs, but designed to restrain spending, has detracted still further from the original purposes of the system, to the point of making its sophistication worthless' (NAO, 1985, para 38).

The Committee of Public Accounts made a number of

detailed recommendations to improve the RSG system (CPA, 1985, para 55). For grants it recommended the avoidance of unnecessary complexity, highlighting the general principles governing the distribution of RSG. For authorities' local accountability it recommended a clear definition of the responsibilities of local authorities, an obvious relationship between spending and rate levels and provision of more information about service standards and efficiency. However, the measures outlined above were based on the assumption that when faced with the increased rating cost of growing expenditures, local ratepayers would vote for lower expenditure levels. This was largely unsuccessful and for some authorities the Government resorted to rate-capping to reduce expenditure.

The 1986 Green Paper '<u>Paying for Local Government</u>' argued that more fundamental reform of both the grant system and the system of local taxation is required. The grant system is seen as being handicapped in achieving its objectives by its over-sophistication. Similarly it is believed that too few electors have a direct financial commitment to covering the costs of local service provision. The Government hopes that the proposed reforms will temper the use of local discretion with its financial consequences. However, although the introduction of a poll tax into Britain could be regarded as a radical measure, local authorities will continue to receive substantial financial support from central government. Indeed, that support may be much greater than in the past.

Whilst local government finance may be at a 'crossroads', central government is not purposively directing it down any particular highway, i.e. neither towards complete central control nor towards complete local discretion. The relationship between central and local government in Britain will remain in a state of continuous flux for the foreseeable future.

REFERENCES

Audit Commission (1984)
The Impact on Local Authorities' Economy, Efficiency and Effectiveness of the Block Grant Distribution System, HMSO, London

Bailey, S.J. (1985a)
'The Relationship Between Housing Rents and Block Grant', Urban Studies, vol. 23, no. 3, pp.237-48

-- (1985b)
'The Relationship Between Welsh Council Rents and Block Grant', Centre for Urban and Regional Research, Discussion Paper No. 21, University of Glasgow

-- and Paddison, R. (1988)
The Reform of Local Government Finance in Britain, Croom Helm, Beckenham

Bennett, R.J. (1981)
'The Local Income Tax in Britain: A Critique of Recent Arguments Against its Use', Public Administration, vol. 59, Autumn, pp.295-311

Cmnd 6454 (1976)
Local Government Finance Report of the Committee of Enquiry (Layfield Report), HMSO, London

Cmnd 7643 (1979)
Central Controls over Local Authorities, HMSO, London

Cmnd 8849 (1981)
Alternatives to Domestic Rates, HMSO, London

Cmnd 9008 (1983)
Rates: Proposals for Rate Limitation and Reform of the Rating System, HMSO, London

Cmnd 9714 (1986)
Paying for Local Government, HMSO, London

CPA (1985)
Operation of the Rate Support Grant System: Department of the Environment, Seventh Report from the Committee of Public Accounts, HMSO, London

Midwinter, A. and Mair, C. (1987)
Rates Reform: Issues Arguments and Evidence, Strathclyde Business School, Glasgow

NAO (1985)
Department of the Environment: Operation of the Rate Support Grant System, Report by the Comptroller and Auditor General, National Audit Office, HMSO, London

Rhodes, T. and Bailey, S. J. (1979)
'Equity, Statistics and the Distribution of the Rate Support Grant', Policy and Politics, vol. 7, no. 1, pp.83-97.

13 CONCLUSIONS

INTRODUCTION

As we argued in the introductory chapter the comparative analysis of local government finance on a cross-national basis is fraught with difficulties. One of the few generalisations which can be made, and which does approach being a universal truth, however, is that the structuring and restructuring of the system of local government finance is a continuing concern of national politicians. Whether it is on the scale of modifying the system of grants paid by the centre to the localities, or the installation of a new tax option, local finance is never far from the political agenda.

There are several reasons why this should be so. In mature capitalist states local government has become an essential part of the state apparatus and one which, broadly, is differentiated from the centre. Thus while the centre is more concerned with broader issues of economic production, the locality is more concerned with basic services of immediate relevance to reproduction of the labour force. Second, to the extent that local government is a mechanism of service delivery, its fiscal ability to meet commitments is invariably a weak point, emphasising its dependence on the centre for the transfer of new tax options or, as is more common, the payment of grant. Third, local government is based on a democratic footing so that the demand for services to be provided in accordance with local preferences, and its ability to underwrite these financially, is a legitimate principle. Each of these arguments emphasises the important functional role local government has within the state and, accepting this, it is only logical that local finance should pre-occupy national as well as local politicians.

Between countries, of course, these arguments carry different weight, as do the implications to which local finance gives rise. The essays in this volume illustrate the variety inherent in different national systems of local finance. Such variety, set against the constitutional, political and economic environments in which local finance systems develop, precludes the feasibility of a comparative approach in the strict sense of the term. Rather, the aim of this volume has been to develop within different national frameworks, current approaches to financing local government and its restructuring. David King's chapter on Fiscal Federalism developed some of the key theoretical arguments, focusing on four key dimensions, autonomy, equity, accountability and macroeconomic control. In developing their case studies contributors were to use the four factors as a backdrop for discussion purposes but without necessarily structuring their paper formally around these. In this final chapter some basic issues are used to draw general conclusions and suggest possible areas for further research.

SOME BASIC ISSUES RAISED BY LOCAL FINANCE

1. The Role of Local Government and the Ambivalence of the Local Finance Issue

Central to the whole debate of the structure of local finance is the role of local government, and the part it should play within the overall administration of the state. There is basic agreement as to what local government is - a democratically elected, accountable, local body, providing services according to local preferences, which is subordinate to some higher level of government. This says little, however, as to what sort of services it should provide and, as Karran shows, there is considerable variety on this score between countries, just as there is in terms of the structure of local councils.

The point to be made here is that the broad role(s) given to local government rarely make mention of how local government is to be financed. Thus the Irish White Paper 'Local Government Reorganisation' argued that 'a system of local government is one of the essential elements of democracy. Under such a system, local affairs can be settled by the local citizens themselves or their representatives, local services can be locally controlled and local communities can participate in the process and responsibilities of government' (Eire, 1971, para. 2.1.1). Admittedly it was a review of the structure and functions of local government, rather than its finance. But the fact that the financing of local government was considered a separate issue is important in itself, and the Irish case is by no means alone in this respect.

What is needed here is research linking the ways in which central governments view the role of local government, its structure and functions, and its financing. In Chapter 2 King argues with some logic that local government should be able to meet the bulk of its expenditures through its own taxing effort. In fact, though a difficult argument to evaluate, countries which meet the test are the exception. In other words, there is a credibility gap between the rhetoric as to the purpose of local government and its fiscal ability to meet these from its own resources. At least part of the answer lies in the vexed question of local autonomy.

2. Local Autonomy and Local Fiscal Autonomy

At the heart of the problem of local government finance lies the issue of local autonomy. The operational basis of local government is that it is a system of administration devolved to bodies which are democratically constituted and to which specific, or in some countries general, powers are allocated. Such a system, according to the fiscal federalism literature, will cater for local preferences which, notwithstanding the equity implications, may be the more politically acceptable, besides being more efficient than imposing national levels of service output. In practice the types of service responsibilities devolved differs sharply between countries. Even within King's basic point that local government is primarily concerned with resource allocation (p.145) there are clear differences cross-nationally, the reasons for which need to be more fully explored.

Varying patterns of service responsibility should not lead to the expectation that they will match with different levels of autonomy enjoyed by local government. To argue in this vein would be to over-simplify the nature of inter-governmental relationships. As is implicit in a number of the country case-studies these relationships emphasise the interdependencies between the different levels of government. As such these greatly complicate the issue of local autonomy.

At the very least it becomes necessary to 'unpack' the characteristics of a service to scrutinise the different mix of local and non-local responsibilities (as Keating shows in the case of France).

In spite of these interdependencies the basic premise on which local government is at least partly founded - that it can provide services in accordance with local preferences - should not be lost sight of. Through the process of devolution the centre provides the statutory framework within which local government operates: thus the concern of central government as to how services are delivered. Yet to devolve power is to accede to the value of establishing some measure of local autonomy.

The political acceptance of the need for a system of local government automatically raises the question of how it is to be financed. An acceptance of the argument for local political autonomy should be matched by one of local fiscal autonomy, though in neither case could this be sustained as an absolute. However, while accepting the general argument that at the very least some type of equalisation grant will be necessary to offset horizontal fiscal imbalances, local government should certainly avoid being over-dependent on externally-generated revenues because of the loss of political autonomy which would probably follow.

As the essays in this volume show, local fiscal autonomy varies between countries. In the United States autonomy over the types and levels of local internal revenues has generally been high. In Sweden, too, local government enjoys considerable fiscal autonomy. Localities are able to set the levels of local income tax (itself a much more elastic tax than those based on property rating tend to be) and are entitled to levy fees and charges, both with relatively little central supervision. In Britain, local fiscal autonomy has been reduced as a result of a succession of attempts to control local expenditure. With the implementation of the poll tax reform, local fiscal autonomy in numerical terms will be virtually the mirror image of the position in Sweden. Whereas in Britain local government will have the majority say (but by no means exclusive say, given the intention to retain rate-capping) over only 20-25% of its income, in Sweden only approximately 25% of local government income is 'determined' by the centre through the distribution of grant.

The classification developed by King (Chapter 5) enables these differences to be put into a basic perspective. King argues that it is possible to classify the fiscal autonomy of local government as being either high or low measured both for revenues which are internally generated and those which are externally derived. Measurement is subjective and strongly relativistic. Countries in which local government enjoys high autonomy on both sources are the exception. In Sweden where local government, as we have seen, has considerable autonomy over its own resources, the bulk of transfer revenues from the centre are in the form of specific grants. In the United States federal cutbacks have had the effect of municipalities diversifying their tax base, through invoking new tax options, thus 'increasing' local autonomy.

The argument for local fiscal autonomy does not stretch to one for local fiscal independence. Indeed, there are strong arguments against the latter. One has already been mentioned, the inconsistency of absolute financial independence with the need to meet equity in the provision of public services. To rely solely on the local tax base as the basis of service provision would lead to considerable spatial inequalities in their delivery. Were functions to be allocated to sub-national governments on the basis of the benefit area principle, then another problem is that meeting the need for financial independence would create far wider tax powers than local/regional governments currently have. This might conflict with the requirements of economic stabilisation and income redistribution policies.

Quite apart from the economic rationale which can be used to support local fiscal autonomy as opposed to independence, the central question remains as to why local government in the industrial nations should differ so much in this respect. Quite possibly the explanation is to be sought in terms of political factors rather than in terms of purely economic rationale.

3. The Influence of Political Culture and Ideology

It is difficult to escape from the argument that the ways in which local finance issues are resolved in different countries is rooted in differences of political culture and ideology. In terms of political culture, countries are distinguishable by the value which they set on at least two of the factors identified by David King in Chapter 2, autonomy and equity.

Some of the countries surveyed in this volume have a strong tradition of decentralisation, of which the prime example is perhaps the United States. (Some federation scholars have shunned the term decentralisation as applied to the United States, preferring the term 'non-centralisation' to indicate the nature of how formal powers are distributed). A commitment to decentralisation, whether political rhetoric or not, tends to run counter to the requirements for equity of service provision. King argues that this is appearing to be one of the outcomes of Reagan's policies. New Federalism has been interpreted to mean that states and local government should have more administrative responsibility for running their own affairs, playing to the traditions of the decentralised society. However, the ideology has meant reduced federal funding of sub-national governments and a reversal of the Great Society programme.

The Norwegian case, as Tore Hansen vividly shows, presents an altogether different picture. His survey showed that equity was weighted more significantly than local autonomy; i.e. 73% of local councillors and 70% of local administrators thought that local autonomy should be subordinated to equity of service provision.

What President Reagan's policies also attest to is the influence of political ideology on questions of local financial provision. In effect, the continuing forces of political culture are overlain (and sometimes contradicted) by the changing influences of partisan ideology.

Australia, particularly during the short-lived Whitlam administration, provides a case in point. The federal nature of the country attests to the basic trait of anti-centralism, particularly by State governments. The introduction of direct financial assistance to local government (in accordance with the direct aims of the Commonwealth Labour government to meet greater inter-regional equality of service provision) provoked the understandable wrath of the States.

Perhaps no better example of the influence of ideology is to be found than in Britain in the 1980s. Successive attempts at restricting the level of local tax burdens have had the outcome of reducing local fiscal autonomy. The justification was based largely on the need to control public spending. Local reaction has been predictable, but all the more vocal because central government itself was not restricting its own spending to a similar degree. Ideologically, both the need to control local spending and the introduction of the community charge reform can be traced to a basic commitment to market principles, the first with 'rolling back the state', the second with a somewhat tenuous appreciation of public choice ideas.

As Kieron Walsh argues of Thatcher's Britain, the

force of ideology (in attempting to redefine the relationships between the state, the economy and civil society) has had profound repercussions not only on the financing of local government, but also, more fundamentally, on its very existence. Controlling the fiscal resources available to local government is one way of weakening opposition, but it is also seen as an important means of pruning overall state expenditure. The crisis of local finance is being used as the means by which to achieve the wider aims of the New Right, to recast the role of the state. Most commentators have argued that one of the effects has been the growth of a more centralised state, and that, in this respect, within a West European perspective at least, Britain is at odds with its neighbours.

4. Laudable Characteristics of a Local Government Finance System

Bearing in mind the foregoing caveats concerning problems of comparability and of differing historical, institutional, political and other situations, what are the ideal characteristics of a system of finance for effective and efficient autonomous local government? Britain is an example of a sophisticated local finance system becoming lost in its own complexity and overridden by other factors, particularly the need (as perceived by central government) to achieve expenditure restraint. The ensuing ad hoc decisions have resulted in the virtual abandonment of equalisation which had been the primary purpose of the inter-governmental grant system. The lesson is that, at best, equalisation can only be rough and ready; full equalisation is an unrealistic objective and tends to lead to an over-dependence on inter-governmental grants.

Such over-dependence has to be tempered by a plurality of fiscs at the local level. Reliance on the property tax is fairly common (e.g. Britain, Canada, Australia and, formerly, the Republic of Ireland). The case studies have clearly demonstrated the increasing vilification of the local property tax and the proliferation of Government enquiries, Royal

Commissions, etc., which have sought to remedy the salient criticisms. Ireland could only abolish the property tax and increase central funding but this is now regarded as unlikely to be tenable for much longer. The Canadian and Australian case studies reveal a widespread reluctance to adopt other local taxes and consequently their local government systems suffer from a weak local tax base.

Britain's solution is regarded as eccentric. Sole reliance on the local property tax is unusual but replacing that tax with a poll tax and assigned revenues is even more extreme. A local income tax is regarded as the foundation of the high level of autonomy enjoyed by both Norwegian and Swedish local government, even at a time of increasing dependence on inter-governmental grants. Many countries (and their States) have briefly considered, but then rejected, a local poll tax - even where it was only to be a possible supplementary local tax and where its rejection left a narrow local tax base (e.g. Australia and Canada).

By way of contrast, David King argues that any new local British tax should replace central government grants rather than replace the property tax. Des King's analysis of the American situation supports this suggestion by pointing to the autonomy over the types and rates of local taxes.

Hence, accepting that increased equalisation and increased autonomy are inherently contradictory, the policy problem is resolved to one of the desired level of trade off between centralisation and localism. The former is inevitable when there is a narrow and weak local tax system. The latter is encouraged (but not guaranteed) by the diversification of the local tax base so that it includes taxes which maintain their real (rather than nominal) income levels. This requires a primary dependence on local income and/or sales taxes, supplemented by property (and possibly poll) taxes as well as local business taxes etc.

Over-riding this emphasis on institutional arrangements, is the need to avoid the extremely damaging, deep division between central and local government that has occurred in Britain. The French case study suggested that negotiation across the territorial divide makes for better policy outcomes than the British system of rigid functional divisions and dogmatic attitudes. Institutional mechanisms in themselves are insufficient. Stronger political links must also be fostered. The territorial divide has allowed central government to create fiscal crisis at the local government level. For Walsh, the solution is a reappraisal and reaffirmation of the nature of citizenship and local democracy. A diversified and buoyant local tax base is probably a necessary but not sufficient condition for this to be achieved.

CONCLUSIONS TOWARDS COMPARATIVE STUDIES OF LOCAL GOVERNMENT FINANCE

The previous discussion has suggested some of the key issues underlying local government finance. These do not exhaust the broad headings under which future research could be considered. Others include the derivation of more accurate methods of measurement by which to assess local fiscal autonomy, tax types and levels, expenditure efforts and the distribution of grant. Second, at the international level there is a wealth of experience of different types of local tax, analysis of which will give points to their transferability potential. Third, are the more specific issues such as service charging. Though charging policies are normally at the margins of local finance in terms of their contribution to the local fisc, their advantages as a means of supplementation are real. Analysis of different service charging policies and their implications is a further area for research effort. One such example is Bailey (1988). A continuing problem to the analysis of these questions at the international level is the adoption of the comparative framework. The advantages of the comparative approach are real enough, particularly in the insights it gives to one's own country. Probably there is more to be gained from the 'limited comparison', restricting research to pairs or small groups of countries, chosen either on the basis of regional groupings or on the similarity of their political structures, as in the case of the federal state. The precedents for the limited comparison have already been established, through work comparing Britain and France, (Ashford, 1982), Western Europe (Newton, 1980) and, in the case of federal countries, Canada and Australia (McMillan, 1981). Their success lies in their indepth examination of relevant issues which broad overviews, using aggregate data, are less likely to achieve.

REFERENCES

ACIR (1981)
Responsibilities and Resources of Australian Local Government, Advisory Council for Inter-government Relations, AGPS, Canberra

Ashford, D. (1982)
British Dogmatism and French Pragmatism, Allen and Unwin, London

Bailey, S.J. (1988)
Practical Charging Policies for Local Government, Public Finance Foundation, London

Eire (1971)
Local Government Reorganisation, Dublin

Newton, K. (1980)
Balancing the Books, Sage, London

McMillan, M.L. (1981)
'Local Intergovernmental Fiscal Relations in Australia and Canada', Centre for Research on Federal Financial Relations, Occasional Paper 23, The Australian National University, Canberra

INDEX

Index

For Product Safety Concerns and Information please contact our EU representative GPSR@taylorandfrancis.com Taylor & Francis Verlag GmbH, Kaufingerstraße 24, 80331 München, Germany

Printed and bound by CPI Group (UK) Ltd, Croydon, CR0 4YY

08/05/2025

01864457-0002